Milledgeville's Sesquicentennial Murders

PRAISE FOR MILLEDGEVILLE'S SESQUICENTENNIAL MURDERS

As a member of the Stembridge family, born shortly after these events of 1953, I am happy to have more information regarding Marion Stembridge. I was not even aware of him or his actions until in my mid-20s, when my first job as a lawyer took me to the Baldwin County Courthouse record room. When the local bar learned I was a Stembridge, they took delight in "explaining my family." Many years later, I heard Kelly Kidd's story of the funeral he attended as a child which gave a different view of the man and his death. This tragedy was born in the mental illness of a brilliant man who reacted in a violent way to the persecutions in his mind. This book contains the facts from public records and private memories, coming as close as possible to what really happened. -- **EVELYN STEMBRIDGE HUBBARD**

Small town murders are always unique, but rarely do they have such a flavorful Americana setting like the one in 1953 Milledgeville, Georgia. Lindsley has brought her talent for writing about Southern subjects to the topic of the Stembridge murders that occurred on May 3, 1953. The deed played out literally right on the streets of a bustling town in the middle of its founding celebration. Lindsley's use of exceptional personal and eye-witness accounts, within her wonderful writing style, presents the background on villain, victims, and those involved in the lives of them for years preceding that day. Her book is a comprehensive study of one topic that has inspired fictional films and stories since it occurred. The old adage, "truth is stranger than fiction" still wins out. A riveting read. -- **MAURIEL PHILLIPS JOSLYN, AUTHOR AND SPECIAL COLLECTIONS LIBRARIAN AT GEORGIA MILITARY COLLEGE**.

In 1953 Milledgeville, Georgia, was traumatized when two respected lawyers were shot to death, just as the town, once the state capital, began to celebrate its sesquicentennial. Marion Stembridge, the killer, cast a dark shadow over the close-knit community that lingers to this day. Stembridge, who operated a grocery/dry goods store and a more private loan-sharking operation, was brilliant but deeply paranoid. He was convicted of manslaughter in the 1949 killing of a young black woman, yet never served a day in prison. He frightened many in the community and tormented his wife. Before he could be arrested for killing the lawyers, he took his own life.

These murders formed the basis for a short story by Flannery O'Connor and a 1988 novel by Pete Dexter. Lindsley provides an excellent new addition to the Stembridge corpus.

Ms. Lindsley was born and raised on a former plantation a few miles outside of Milledgeville. She knows the local countryside thoroughly and has written about her experiences in several books that capture life in the region in a completely captivating style. In this book she brings Marion Stembridge out of the shadows of fiction and rumor into reality.

This book is a fine example of historical detection leavened with her distinctive Southern writing style. Lindsley researched court records, transcripts, newspapers, and magazines. She interviewed eye witnesses such as the pioneering female lawyer Eva Sloan to tell this grisly tale. We learn what Lindsley calls "old-fashioned Southern justice." She illuminates the local terrain and separates fact from fiction in the life of this deeply troubled man.

This work of historical detection brings Stembridge and his time out of the shadows. She reinforces the events with photographs, some rarely or never seen, including one of Marion Stembridge, sought for 70 years and believed to not exist. -- **ROBERT J. WILSON III, PH.D., PROFESSOR EMERITUS OF HISTORY, GEORGIA COLLEGE & STATE UNIVERSITY**

Milledgeville's Sesquicentennial Murders

Susan Lindsley

ThomasMax

Your Publisher
For The 21st Century

ISBN-13 978-1-7377620-5-8

ISBN-10: 1-7377620-5-6

First printing, April 2023
Second printing, May 2023

Back cover photo of Ms. Lindsley by Roy Davis, Milledgeville.

Published by:

ThomasMax Publishing
P.O. Box 250054
Atlanta, GA 30325

ACKNOWLEDGMENTS

For seventy years, Milledgeville historians and state-wide journalists have sought a photograph of Marion Stembridge. No one could find one. But in January 2023, Mauriel Joslyn did not give up when I asked her to hunt for one in the GMC Archives. She located the cover picture after hours of searching, in a 1910 GMC Announcement. Her life-long interest in our history, and her professional persistence paid off for us all. I, my readers, and our history buffs owe her a great debt. GMC Archives also provided other pictures and information.

This book would never have been finished if not for Patricia Ruth Blanks, a buddy from school days who began encouraging me by transcribing many of the legal documents and then asking me through the years, "When are you going to do the Stembridge book?" Seventy years after the events of May 2, 1953, the "Web" has been a source of information (as well as misinformation), which has allowed me to research and gain insight into and some understanding of the man called "Milledgeville's mad man."

Nancy Davis Bray of Special Collections and her staff at Georgia College and State University have given me step-by-step support and help beyond measure for this project. They have been available from the start and only a phone call away. Nancy has also referred me to other sources.

James Owens, former researcher at GCSU and Special Collections, posted his research online and I am grateful for his legwork to be used here.

Many Milledgeville people have provided photographs and their memories. Sara S. Brantley provided information and directed me to other sources, and welcomed my requests for help through the private *Milledgeville Memories* website. Thanks also to Ann Overstreet Walden for the photograph of Pete Dexter; Derek Ennis Veal for information and the pictures of Marion Ennis; Tony Sloan Brown for the pictures of her mother and new information about her parents; Jane Morrison Sheppard for the *Hills of Home* program; Scott Little for pictures and information about Shep Baldwin; The Allen family for photographs; David Stembridge for access to the Stembridge family website and family information, and his constant support for this project; Randy Ellis and Donna Ellis Turner for photographs of their father.

Baldwin County Clerk of Court Mitch Longino and staff member Barbara Boyer searched records. She found and copied files in deed books too heavy for me to handle and made the copies I needed. He searched the archives in the basement, off limits because of renovation, and determined files for cases 3839 and 3840, relating to the July 1949 term of court, the State vs. Marion Stembridge, were not bound and stored in the packet containing cases before and after those numbers and therefore never filed in storage. Fortunately the 3839 file was part of the Johnson County legalities and available through their Clerk of Court, Patricia Glover. These files revealed the legal maneuvers used by Judge Roy Rowland to free Stembridge. Thank you, Patricia Glover.

The staff of our Probate Court searched for documents relating to Stembridge's will but apparently any such papers became part of the court case to break the will and were no long available at the county level.

David Stembridge provided access to the Stembridge family website and family information, and referred me to his Stembridge relative Evelyn Stembridge Hubbard. My thanks to both members of the Stembridge family for their interest in this book and for their encouragement.

Cornell University, college home for Pete Bivins, turned out a team of research personnel: Michael Cook, Alex Bond, Josh Waldorf, Eisha Neely, Zoe Russell, Frankie Foyle and Chelsea Benson,

Other sources of information include: David H. Israel for information on Roger Stembridge; The *Union-Reorder* and *The Macon Telegraph and News* (copies saved from the 1950s); Keith Barlow of the present-day *Union-Recorder*; transcripts of trials obtained from court records; conversations with Eva Sloan; and personal memories written down at those times. Mercer University and the University of Georgia researchers also helped with information.

Twiggs County Clerk of Court Rhonda Green provided the copy of the certificate of Stembridge's marriage to Lois D. Marchant.

Jim Chueh of Sprint Print was able to improve the layout of the book by cropping and straightening many of the news items and other materials scanned for the book from the 70-year-old Xerox copies.

Ms. Jamie Treadwell, UGA, and Jennifer Baker and Ani Karagianis of Duke University provided help in my research.

Someone, I cannot remember who, from the 1950s Xeroxed numerous newspaper articles and other material, which I have kept with high hopes of eventually writing this book. These copies provided information apparently missed by lawyers in the past, and answered the question everyone has asked for seventy years: How was Stembridge free to kill again?

Most of all, I thank Lee Clevenger, my publisher, for his patience and perseverance in producing this book.

-

For Patricia Ruth Blanks

Without her support and help
from before start until after finish,
this book would not be.

LIST OF TOPICS

"The evil that men do lives after them,
the good is oft interred with their bones."

Shakespeare, *Julius Caesar*, Act III, Scene ii,
Lines 76-77, Marc Anthony at Caesar's funeral.

INTRODUCTION

The year 1949 was not the best of times, but everyone in Milledgeville believed the worst of times lay behind. The Second Great War had come and gone, taking with it the Great Depression. Even the Ku Klux Klan seemed to have toned down since the horrors of the massacre at Moore's Ford Bridge brought Federal investigators into Georgia. Everyone in town knew the KKK would as soon take the whip to a white man who stepped out on his wife as to a black man who failed to step aside at the approach of a white woman. The group even took holiday baskets of food to local poor—black and white—and of course kept their faces hidden.

Milledgeville was Georgia's one-time capitol; it lay in the middle of the state. Almost a century and a half after its founding, it remained a small town. Nowhere else in the States did a train run down the main street and stop at traffic lights. Farmers still came to town on Saturday, some by wagon, some on their own feet.

Although prohibition was long over, moonshine was the drink of choice at many social events, even political victory celebrations held in the county courthouse. Family history still determined social levels. Race relations were on the road to improvement, but some still took advantage of the blacks while others went to court to support the suppressed.

Life remained segregated in town. In the county, some farms were operated by tenants; a few were owned by black families. Farm owners hired both black and white to work the fields, feed livestock, cut and haul hay to the barns. Farmers thereby began racial integration in the workplace.

White folks didn't talk about the cousin or uncle who lived "down the road" and had a black mistress.

The main businesses in the community were a hospital and two colleges: the boys-only Georgia Military College and the girls-only Georgia State College for Women. The Central State Hospital, called mostly by the name Milledgeville State Hospital or the Insane Asylum, fed 12,000 meals daily. Patients ranged from recovering drunks to malformed babies who would never leave a bed. Staff increased at the end of the Second World War with an influx of medical experts who fled the Nazis.

The newcomers settled mostly in Hardwick, the community that housed the State Hospital and also the private Allen's Institute, which also treated the mentally ill. Hardwick is also the location of the Rockwell Mansion, which was a governor's residence when Milledgeville was the capitol and the official Mansion was yet to be finished.

Downtown was basically a crossroads, Wayne and Hancock Streets meeting and stretching a couple of blocks each way. Most of the town's stores—dry goods, hardware, pharmacies, dime stores—lay in that small area. On the western edge stood the courthouse and the women's college. The house built exclusively to serve as the Governor's Mansion loomed over Clark Street on its western front, and to the east, the Cline House, home of Flannery O'Connor's family.

On the southeastern edge, Georgia's old capitol building dominated a four-square block area. The building became headquarters for Georgia Military College (GMC), a junior college and its associated high school and grammar school.

The Oconee River lies to the east as it glides on its journey to meet the Ocmulgee and become the Altamaha. Beside the river in 1949 lay Hank Brown Bottom, often referred to as the Bourbon Street of Milledgeville; it was home to the social life of the black residents.

Also in 1949, gossip centered around Marion Stembridge, who ran a downtown grocery/dry goods store and a private, loan-shark bank. He made high-interest loans to customers who were borderline illiterate and simply signed the agreements with an "X" or a semblance of their names. The town's only female attorney represented a black man and won a case against the loan shark.

She had also won when he filed a suit against her years before.

Anger was known to simmer.

Stembridge was said to be saving his urine in bottles in the store's refrigerator; he wanted to find a chemist to analyze it for the poison someone was feeding him somehow, to kill him.

When he went out to collect overdue payments, he went armed—but then, most folks said he was always armed. His assistant, Sam Terry, was brother of the recent sheriff.

I have included Stembridge's actions in a novel *(When Darkness Fell)*; my neighbor/friend Flannery O'Connor included him in a short story; Pete Dexter made him the subject of a novel *(Paris Trout)*. I won an award with a short story based on some of these events in which I jumbled up the time line.

This book is not fiction. I report the written words of the court records for his trial for murder in 1949 and his later trial for income tax evasion and attempts to bribe IRS agents. Just hours before Milledgeville's sesquicentennial celebrations were to begin Stembridge went on a killing spree. This attack on Marion Ennis and Stephen (Pete) Bivins, two Milledgeville attorneys, led to various articles in magazines, books and online sites. For those events, I rely on conversations with my dear friend Eva Sloan, who was in the building when Stembridge killed his first victim, her boss, who held her hand as he died on the hallway floor just outside his office.

I have studied many online posts, newspaper articles, various magazine articles, and legal documents; unfortunately, many "facts" vary from source to source.

Defining the truth has not been easy, but I am sure this book will clear up many rumors and mistakes that have hovered around Milledgeville for seventy years.

To avoid any confusion between names of Marion Ennis and Marion Stembridge, I use only the last names of these two. Omitting "Mr." is not meant to be disrespectful of either.

Shakespeare said, "The evil that men do lives after them, the good is oft interred with their bones." I have found much evil that still lives but some good that was not laid to rest with him.

THE VILLIAN

MARION WESLEY STEMBRIDGE

Stembridge was a son, a brother, a soldier, a storekeeper, a husband again, a mental patient, a brilliant man, a loan shark, a landlord, an excellent business man, a resident of a small middle-Georgia town, and a killer. A man to be remembered, talked about and disliked for almost a century.

His killing a black girl in 1949 created a tremor of forewarning of the earthquake to come. Only two attorneys in a distant county knew why he never served time for that manslaughter conviction when the trial verdict was upheld by the Georgia Court of Appeals and the U. S. Supreme Court.

The Stembridge earthquake shook the foundations of Milledgeville, Georgia, on Saturday morning, May 2, 1953, a few minutes after 10:00 a.m. when he shot two attorneys and then himself. Tremors of hate still rumble in his community, and he is no longer mourned by his family.

Anyone remembering Stembridge still wonders how come he never served a night in jail after being convicted of voluntary manslaughter. Was he free because he managed to wrangle some good ole Southern hanky-panky justice?

Whatever other category Stembridge fits, in Milledgeville he still fits the category: Insane killer. Or in today's gentler and understanding terms, *mentally ill*.

A teenager at the time, I still remember the stories and rumors that ran rampant over Milledgeville then, and many that still do. I have sought the truth through notes I made at the time and from documents I saved in the 1950s and ones I have found in the 2020s.

I hope for the quakes to subside into memories.

IN THE SOUTH,
WE WANT TO KNOW ALL ABOUT THE FAMILY.

From: Mrs. Anna Maria Green Cook, History *of Baldwin County Georgia*, The Reprint Company, 1978, pp. 396-397.

Marion Stembridge's family came to Baldwin County from Washington County. F. M. Leverette, his grandfather, married Hannah Whitaker, daughter of Willis and Rebecca Whitaker. The Leverettes moved to Baldwin County and reared two daughters, Mary and Mattie. Mary married John Stembridge, and Mattie lived with them.

John and Mary Stembridge had two sons: Roger and Marion Stembridge, who both served during World War I.

They also reared four daughters. Interesting that Thelma, the youngest girl, was unmarried at Marion's death, and she inherited the "balance of Marion's estate"; Gladys died unmarried in 1938, which explains why she was not listed in the will.

When Marion Wesley Stembridge was born on August 28, 1892, his father, John Wesley Stembridge, was 35 and his mother, Mary Leverett, was 25.

Census records dated 22 April 1910 list his siblings. Life dates are given when known; otherwise, age at the time of the census is given.

Marion's father: John W. Stembridge: farmer, employee

Marion's mother: Mary 42

Marion W. our villain (1892-1953)

William M. (17 years old)

Roger Walton (1893-1960)

Mildred Whitaker (1895-1991) m. Edward Beman

Martha Claire (1897-1969) m. Leon Callaway

Ellen Gladys (1902-1938)

Thelma (1904-1972) (unmarried at Marion's death)

Virginia (1 year old)

WHO WAS STEMBRIDGE TO HIS FAMILY AND FRIENDS?

We have no information on Marion's youth other than he attended the local grammar school and high school associated with the Georgia Military College, and the junior military college itself where we know he reached the rank of second lieutenant of Company A. This picture is dated 1910.

4. MARION W. STEMBRIDGE,
Second Lieutenant Co. A.

Photo discovered by Mauriel Joslyn in GMC Archives

In 1917, a column in the local paper reports Marion Stembridge serving as "guardian" for the Woodman Circle, auxiliary to the Woodmen of the World's local chapter, Elm Grove 108.

WOODMAN CIRCLE
By Mrs. Ella J. Gholson

On March 19, 1913 in the K. P. Hall as State Deputy I organized the Woodmen Circle, auxiliary to the Woodmen of the World with ten charter members. From this little bunch we have grown slowly to twenty-five in number. This order which is for Woodmen, as well as ladies, is one of the finest fraternal orders for insurance I know. It's features in a social and fraternal way are beautiful, each sovereign loves the other, and we are drawn together by the sweet ties of our order in Love, Wisdom, Power and Rememberance.

Elm Grove 108, Woodmen Circle is steadily growing under the leadership of the following officers: Past Guardian—Pearl R. Chapman; Guardian—Marion Stembridge; Adviser—Lillie Gholson; Clerk—Ella J. Gholson; Banker—Agnes Davis; Chaplain —Carrie G. Banks; Attendant—Cleo T. Collins; Outside Sentinel—Dumpie Monace; Inside Sentinel—Ada B. Johnson.

Today people remember only the evil, but family members who knew the other side of him remember him with love that only a family member can explain or express. I found this online:

FAMILY MEMORIES
Salem Community: 1892

Late August 1892 on a summer day in Georgia on the Lower River Road across the Oconee River from Milledgeville, twenty-five-year-old Mary L. Stembridge delivers a son into the world. It was, most likely, typical August heat. Mary saw her baby boy's face for the first time wiped with blood and crying. Mary's skin must've beaded with sweat after childbirth. Mary's husband, John Wesley Stembridge, was no doubt a proud father that day as a gentle breeze might've gifted itself through open windows. As the day became night in a time before air conditioners and electric fans, Mary and John Wesley Stembridge will say the baby boy's name: Marion Wesley.

By June of 1917, Mary's baby, Marion Wesley Stembridge, has grown up to be a young man. Civilization is modernizing, and the Stembridge family farm has endured for generations in the Salem Community just across the river from Milledgeville. In the nights for perhaps generations, they might've dreamed of becoming merchants and growing a business in downtown, leaving the farm.

In the year America enters its first World War with America's first transatlantic offensive soon to occur in Saint-Miles, France, Marion is described as "a natural born citizen" with "blue" eyes and "brown" hair. Marion is "tall" either describing himself or is being described by the United States Army registrar who is officially enlisting the "slender," "single," and "Caucasian" Marion into the military. By 1917, Marion is near his mother Mary's age when she birthed him, sweating and bloody. But, by the summer of 1917, Mary's baby boy may go to war dressed as a soldier in the classic tan uniform of the United States of America's doughboys.

Almost summer, the Georgia sun must have beat down on Marion as he signs his life over to the Army, knowing he'd be going to Georgia's newly established Fort Gordon.

Only a few months after America declares war on Germany, Marion Wesley Stembridge is called to serve.

Extensive research has not resulted in any information about Stembridge's service other than his sister Mildred stated he received a medical discharge. Without a service number or social security number (which did not exist in 1917), the National Archives has been unable to locate his military records. If, as she also implied, his problems began while in the military, his discharge might have been related to his emotional/psychiatric condition.

Form 46   REGISTRATION CARD   No. 1

1. Name in full: **Marion Stembridge** 25

2. Home address: RFD 17 Milledgeville, Ga

3. Date of birth: **Aug 26 1893**

4. Are you (1) a natural born citizen, (2) a naturalized citizen, (3) an alien, (4) or have you declared... **A natural born citizen**

5. Where were you born: Baldwin Co. Ga.   **U S A**

6. If not a citizen, of what country are you a citizen or subject?

7. What is your present trade, occupation, or office? **Farming**

8. By whom employed? **Myself**   Where employed? **Baldwin County**

9. Have you a father, mother, wife, child under 12, or a sister or brother under 12, solely dependent on you for support (specify which)? **No**

10. Married or single (which)? **Single**   Race (specify which)? **Caucasian**

11. What military service have you had? Rank ____ branch ____ **None**   years ____ Nation or State ____   56

12. Do you claim exemption from draft (specify grounds)? **Yes**

I affirm that I have verified above answers and that they are true.

Marion Stembridge

10-3-3-A

REGISTRAR'S REPORT

1	Tall, medium, or short (specify which)?	**Tall**	Slender, medium, or stout (which)? **Slender**
2	Color of eyes? **Blue**	Color of hair? **Brown**	Bald? **No**
3	Has person lost arm, leg, hand, foot, or both eyes, or is he otherwise disabled (specify)? **No**		

I certify that my answers are true, that the person registered has read his own answers, that I have witnessed his signature, and that all of his answers of which I have knowledge are true, except as follows:

Marion O Stucki
(Signature of Registrar)

Precinct ___ **115**

City or County ___ **Baldwin**

State ___ **Georgia**

June 5 1917
(Date of registration)

Roger Stembridge   **Marion Stembridge**

Roger's military information was posted on "Find A Grave" and is shared by David H. Israel.

The President of the United States of America, authorized by Act of Congress, July 9, 1918, takes pleasure in presenting the Distinguished Service Cross to First Lieutenant (Infantry) Roger Walton Stembridge, United States Army, for extraordinary heroism in action while serving with 21st Machine-Gun Battalion, 7th Division, A.E.F., near Vieville-en-Haye, France, 31 October 1918 to 1 November 1918. Although wounded by a shell fragment and suffering from the effects of an anti-tetanic serum, Lieutenant Stembridge continued to lead his platoon through the night of October 31 and the offensive operation of 1 November under heavy enemy shell fire, encouraging his men by his gallant conduct.

After his discharge, Marion Stembridge attended the Georgia State College of Agriculture. The GSCA was eventually absorbed by the University of Georgia and their archives/special collections no longer have any GSCA records.

Personal comment: In researching for this book, I found numerous online references to Marion Wesley Stembridge's marriage to Miss Lois D. Marchant. Dates varied: Some said 1921; others 1927. Location was Tift County, Georgia. Many listed their five children, with birth dates for all and death dates for some. A request to Tift County Probate Court yielded the marriage certificate for Marion (no middle name) Stembridge and Lois Marchant.

The first edition of this book carried this misinformation. A question from the sponsor of the **Milledgeville Memories web site***, Sara Smith Brantley, resulted in a week's worth of online digging. The 1950 census settled the matter. The Marion Stembridge who married Lois D. Marchant was not Milledgeville's Marion Wesley Stembridge; he was a carpenter in Chatham County.*

Marion Wesley Stembridge's only wife was Sara Hunter Jordan Terry.

In Milledgeville he opened a store, located on South Wayne Street, at the location of what later became a bakery, 135 South Wayne Street. He was next door to the Merchants and Farmers Bank; now the Century Bank occupies the old M & F Bank site. (Photo by author, March 2013)

At some point, life began to change drastically for Marion Stembridge.

The family's first acknowledgement that Marion had emotional problems came in November 1933 when he voluntarily admitted himself into Allen's Institution, the private mental hospital alternative to the State Mental Hospital (labeled the State Lunatic Asylum). He remained at Allen's for two weeks. He acknowledged he suffered delusions and hallucinations that people were trying to kill him with poison and/or X-rays. These problems remained with him for life.

In 1942 he was jailed on a peace warrant and a lunacy warrant and brought to Allen's Institution by the sheriff. No other information is available on that hospitalization. Nor have I found any confirmation that he was ever in the State Hospital or admitted to either institution by his mother.

In 1948 he demanded that his wife Sara not associate with his relatives because his sister Mrs. Callaway (Martha) and brother Roger were trying to poison him.

In 1949, he shot Emma Johnekin to death at point blank range, over a car debt owed by someone else. He was found guilty of voluntary manslaughter, and his court problems continued until his death. But his fractured mind was clever and he finagled his freedom and stayed out of prison.

THE VICTIMS IN 1953

Marion Ennis was a Milledgeville attorney, politician, Stembridge murder victim. His law partner, Eva Sloan, had been sued by Stembridge and Ennis had represented her. He also represented Stembridge in the 1949 murder trial.

From the Georgia Official Register, 1939-1943:

O. M. Ennis was born in Washington County (adjacent to Baldwin County) on May 10, 1907. He was the son of Oscar Marcellus and Marie Manning (Gilmore) Ennis, and the grandson of Pleasant Theodosheus and Elizabeth (Haygood) Ennis, and of Stephen Mathis and Mary Frances (Jordon) Gilmore.

He attended the high school associated with Georgia Military College as well as the junior college itself, and obtained his bachelor's and law degree from Mercer University. He opened his law office on June 2, 1931.

On October 16, 1936, Ennis married Antoinette Bonner, born August 11, 1909, in Madison, Georgia.

Ennis was a member of Pi Kappa Alpha (a pre-law fraternity), a Mason, president of the GMC Alumni Association, clerk and attorney for the Baldwin County Commissioners. He served four terms as representative in the Georgia House and one term in the Georgia Senate.

While in the state legislature, he was responsible for updating the technology at the Central State Hospital and also for building the Boys Training School. The Boys Training School was a semi-prison for delinquents, with shared barracks.

He is also credited with many improvements in the county: The District Forestry Office, a new public works camp, a new armory site, and arranging for the building of a modern health clinic. He served on the Sesquicentennial Committee, and as judge of its Kangaroo Court. One newspaper article stated, "He loved practical jokes. When the Brothers of the Brush sponsored the trip to Atlanta just a week before his death, he was the life of the party."

While at GMC he was a member of the ROTC; he played in the band and was its librarian. He was a second lieutenant in Company B.

Photo of Marion Ennis provided by GMC Archives.

Photos provided by Derek Ennis Veal.

Stephen Thomas (Pete) Bivins was an attorney and represented Sara J. T. Stembridge in her divorce; said to also serve as attorney for Stembridge in one of his appeals. Pete was one of two attorneys killed by Stembridge on May 2, 1953.

Pete was only 27 when he was killed. His life has been spent in being first: First Boy Scout to attain the rank of Eagle Scout in Baldwin County; first honor graduate of the local Georgia Military College (GMC) high school, youngest student to become president of Student Government at Cornell, as a sophomore at age 17.

Pete was active in student government from his freshman year at Cornell University, which began when he was sixteen. He was not shy and made the news in the *Cornell Daily Sun*; these few clippings reflect some of his activities on campus.

He ran this ad in the *Cornell Daily Sun* on December 1, 1942. It was effective; I am sure he also knew enough to get out and about, meet his fellow students, and shake a lot of hands.

TOM "GEORGIA" BIVINS

For Freshman Office

We stand for:

1. More freshmen as leaders in campus activities.
2. A better intramural sports program culminating in a '46 class championship.
3. More extensive social program including at least one open house a month for freshmen exclusively and a major freshman dance compatible with war times.
4. Better representation to the faculty promoting a clearer student-administrative understanding.

Cornell Daily Sun, **December 1, 1942**

FRESHMAN VOTERS December elected as their Class Governing Board S. Thomas Bivins of Milledgeville, Ga., Stewart A. Sailor of Hinsdale, Ill., and David Summerville of Scarsdale. Fifteen candidates, approved by the Student Council, outlined their platforms at a Class meeting in Willard Straight Memorial Room November 30, and an ad for Bivins in the Sun *election day morning gave his four planks.*

February 19, 1943

"46 Day' Dance News Leaks Out

'Tell me, Mr. Anthony, where can I get a date for the freshman '46-Day Dance that is to be held in the seasonally decorated Memorial Room of Willard Straight on March 8."

Somewhere someone had talked — the news was out, and already requests for assistance were on their ways. The letter itself, evidence that the news of the coming freshman class dance had leaked out, accidentally fell into the hands of the Freshman Dance Committee after a well-bludgeoned letter-carrier was invited to attend one of their meetings.

Rising to meet the critical situation, an emergency meeting of committee chairmen was called by S. Thomas Bivins, and he was joined by Dance Committee head, Ansley Sawyer, publicity boss David Gler, and banquet charge d'affairs Frank Wright in a discussion of the problem.

From this meeting stemmed two official announcements; first, that a formal announcement of the freshman class dance on March 6 would be forthcoming; and second, that a date bureau would be organized to lighten Mr. Anthony's load.

August 10, 1943

Bivins Succeeds Eddy as Acting Head of Council

Meeting in Willard Straight North Room last night, the Student Council appointed as Acting President S. Thomas Bivins '46, and discussed plans for future activities.

Bivins succeeds Acting President Edward D. Eddy '44 who resigned due to other commitments. The Council approved the appointments of Edward H. Lannon Jr. '45 and Olin G. Shivers '46 to the Committee on Freshman Elections. Petitions for freshman nominations are due at 12 noon tomorrow at the Willard Straight Main Desk.

William W. Ward '44, treasurer of the Council, reported that the organization would receive again this year the annual appropriation of $1,000 from the University Board of Trustees given to finance Council activities.

The Council will meet again at 8 p.m. Monday, August 23.

October 5, 1943

Pershing Rifles to Act as Officers At President's Regimental Review

Officers, from regimental commander to platoon leaders, at the presidential regimental review to be staged by all ROTC units in the University quadrangle at 5 p.m. tomorrow have been selected from Company E-5, the Cornell division of the National Society of Pershing Rifles.

Captain S. Thomas Bivins '46, who is in charge of the training of the Riflemen for this review, has announced that all officers will be armed with sabres, and that the color guard of Pershing Rifles will also assist at the parade.

Active at Cornell since 1936, the society serves the purpose of furthering the ability of basic course students in military service and science. Its primary aim at present is to enable ROTC students to enter the armed forces with a better chance of becoming officer candidates.

After three years at Cornell, his education took second place to his country and he went on active duty in 1943. Cornell University provided this summary of Pete's service:

Full Name: Stephen T Bivins

Army Serial Number: 12214861

Enlistment Place: Ft Dix New Jersey

Enlistment Date: 9 Nov 1943

Army Branch: Detached Enlisted Men's List

Service Branch: Army

Race or Ethnicity: White

Residence: Baldwin County, Georgia

Enlistment Term: Enlistment for the duration of the War or other emergency, plus six months, subject to the discretion of the President or otherwise according to law

Source of Army Personnel: Enlisted Reserve or Medical Administrative Corps (MAC) Officer

Army Component: Reserves - exclusive of Regular Army Reserve and Officers of the Officers Reserve Corps on active duty under the Thomason Act (Officers and Enlisted Men -- O.R.C. and E.R.C., and Nurses-Reserve Status)

Level of Education: 1 year of college

Marital Status: Single, without dependents

Birth Date: 1925

Birth Place: Georgia

Source Box Number: 0104

Source Film Reel Number: 1.97

Conflict Period: World War II

Served for: United States of America

During World War II, he served a hitch in the Philippines with the Field Artillery, and reached the rank of First Lieutenant. A tropical illness led to his being furloughed home.

He returned to Cornell after his discharge and received his A. B. in zoology as a member of the class of 1947, rather than 1946, a year's delay because of his military service.

His interest in birds led to his zoology degree, and also to his work with Dr. Arthur A. Allen, who acknowledged Pete for "services rendered which have made the collecting of material for this book such a pleasant task" in production of his book *Stalking Birds with Color Camera,* National Geographic Society, 1951, 1961, 1963.

The *Cornell Daily Sun,* November 20, 1947:

Mr. and Mrs. Harry M. Moylan of New York City announce the engagement of their daughter Helen Mae to Stephen Bivins of Milledgeville, Georgia.

After his graduation from Cornell and his marriage to Helen Moylan in 1947, Pete went to Duke University where he earned his law degree in 1950. The couple then moved to Milledgeville, Pete's home town.

Pete devoted his free time to his interest in birds and to the youth of Milledgeville.

He was a member of the Georgia Ornithological Society, National Audubon Society and Bird-Banding Association.

His love of birds began in childhood and became a lifelong hobby he followed with the same or greater interest than his profession. He spoke often to groups about birds and taught biology one term at the local Georgia Military College; he participated in bird-banding for many years. A short time before his death he had completed the construction of facilities in his back yard which held more than 500 birds, including canaries, love birds, parakeets and other species.

He taught a Sunday School class of both boys and girls; served as Scoutmaster for a Scout troop and helped raise funds for the local Scout district. He was a member of the Moose, the Kiwanis and the Junior Chamber of Commerce. He also supported other civic organizations.

Pete had no children. His survivors include his wife, his sister Mrs. Floyd Jaggears of Florida, his mother, Mrs. P. N. Bivins of Milledgeville, and a step-brother Edward E. Livingston.

When plans began for the birthday events to celebrate Milledgeville's 150th birthday (Sesquicentennial), Pete served as co-chairman of the planning committee. He showed his support for the plans by being one of the first to grow the beard required the "laws" of the Sesquicentennial committee.

The then-new Civic Youth Center of Milledgeville was dedicated to him after his death, with the name Bivins Youth Center. It no longer exists in 2023, and Pete is remembered more for being a victim of Stembridge's anger than for his dedication to the youth of Milledgeville. I was pleased when I noted some "younger-than-I" Milledgeville natives posted online about remembering the Bivins Youth Center.

THE ALMOST VICTIMS

Sloan, Eva Lamb worked as secretary to Marion Ennis after her arrival in Milledgeville. She later became his partner in the law office. She held his hand as he died. She told me later she could not recognize a photograph of Marion Ennis because all she could see with her mind was the blood on his face as he died. She is a major source of information for this book, and this is my personal memory of Eva Sloan and her husband Bob. I adored Eva Sloan and admired Bob. I cannot remember not knowing them.

Eva was unique: An adult who treated teenagers as adults and not as children; a woman who sparkled with joy that she scattered around her wherever she went; and a lawyer dedicated to her profession.

When Stembridge went on his rampage, she was an attorney working in partnership with Marion Ennis. Her route from secretary to attorney differed from that of most attorneys in the twentieth century. She did not go to law school. Encouraged by her "boss" Marion Ennis, she studied law, and Ennis, Judge George Carpenter and Judge Ed Hines mentored her. She took the bar exam and passed on her first try.

One of her first cases came by way of Frank Bone. Stembridge loaned an employee of Frank Bone $50. By the time the man asked for Bone's help, Stembridge had collected $550 from the man. Bone hired Eva Sloan to research the transaction. Due to Sloan's work, Stembridge was ordered to repay the overcharge of $500.

Eva then became the favorite go-to attorney for the black residents of the county who needed help with their dealings with Stembridge.

At the first meeting after Stembridge murdered her boss, the County Commissioners asked Eva to replace him as county attorney and clerk, a job that she had technically been involved in since Ennis had been county attorney; she began working for him in 1940.

Only after her death did I know what a brilliant woman she was. The first female lawyer in Milledgeville and one of the first in Georgia. She was a member of (that is she could take cases in these courts) the Ocmulgee Circuit Bar Association, the

Georgia Court of Appeals, the Georgia Supreme Court, the U. S. District Court and the U. S. Supreme Court. She was also a member of the Georgia Trial Lawyers Association, the American Bar Association, the Georgia Association of Women Lawyers, the Georgia Association of Criminal Defense Lawyers, and the American Judicature Society.

Eva was also involved in organizations not related to her profession. She worked with the local Girl Scouts, and was a member of the Milledgeville Business and Professional Women's Association and a member of Quota International.

Who's Who of American Women recognized her in 1972-73, 1974-75, 1977-78 and 1981-82.

When my sisters and I witnessed an accident, we were delayed in town for more than an hour before we began our errands, so we went by Eva's to let her know in case our parents got worried and called her. When we mentioned the accident, she immediately began to question us for details. A white guy on a motorcycle tried to pass us and the left-turning vehicle in front of us; he slammed into the car in front. She represented the driver of the car, a black man.

Eva and her husband Robert (Bob) Glenn Sloan had been on Stembridge's hate list since shortly after they moved to Milledgeville. While still in South Carolina, Bob worked for Roses Five and Dime; his job was to find ways to increase sales. So he travelled. Eventually they settled in Milledgeville as the center of his travels for Roses. He initiated their Lay-Away plan.

On arriving in town, the couple rented an apartment from Stembridge. When they moved, Stembridge filed a suit against these newcomers for nonpayment of rent. Unfortunately for Stembridge, Eva worked for Marion Ennis, and Ennis took the claim to a jury and to victory for the Sloans. See Appendix 1 for details of the case.

After Stembridge hired Ennis to defend him in the 1949 murder case, he had to come to the office to discuss matters with Ennis. Stembridge never again spoke to Eva.

Over the years, Bob worked several jobs, and I got to know him well as a personal friend and a chaser of the cattle thieves and moonshiners who were active in the late 1940s and early 1950s, not only on our farm but throughout the county.

Bob managed to get fired when he raided a still in the back yard of one of the county commissioners. Undaunted, he opened and successfully operated a recreational facility on the edge of Lake Oconee.

These pictures reveal the Eva I knew and loved. Her laughter floated like stardust scattered by a thousand fairies.

Susan Lindsley

Photos provided by Tony Sloan Brown.

Baldwin, Carter Shepherd (Shep), Jr. was the solicitor (district attorney) who prosecuted Stembridge for the 1949 murder of Emma Johnekin.

The son of the long-time sheriff of the same name, Shep was born in Morgan County on August 22, 1896. After high school, he earned his AB at the University of Georgia in 1917.

He joined the army August 27, 1917, and was discharged as a First Lieutenant on February 3, 1918. Shep entered Mercer University in Macon and received his law degree in 1921.

During World War II, Shep again joined the U. S. Army, and rose to the rank of Colonel. He was often referred to by that rank after he became a civilian. His oldest son, Carter Shepherd Baldwin III, was killed at Guadalcanal.

When the war ended, Shep moved to Milledgeville to practice law. He was listed in the Milledgeville telephone book as "Col. C. S. Baldwin" with his office in the "Doctors Building" on Hancock Street.

He soon ran for Solicitor of the Ocmulgee Circuit. He won, and remained solicitor for about 24 years. Once, he challenged Representative Carl Vinson for his seat in Congress, but lost; Carl Vinson was unbeatable.

He was successful in obtaining a "guilty of voluntary manslaughter" against Stembridge from an all-male white jury in 1949.

Shep was rumored to be on a hit list carried by Stembridge. But Stembridge missed him on two visits to Shep's house and trips to his office.

Shep died of natural causes on November 24, 1963 and was buried in Madison, Georgia; pallbearers were members of the Baldwin County Bar Association.

Rumors still surround Shep Baldwin and his beard. Shep and Stembridge met on the street on May 2 (the date of the shooting) and Stembridge did not recognize him with the beard.

Shep Baldwin (left) and Tom Moore were caught by a cameraman in downtown, and it is easy to see why Stembridge would not have realized he was meeting the solicitor. The sailor does not seem to be the same man who faced Stembridge in court.

In an online post, Shep Little wrote:

Here is my sweet Aunt Kat and Uncle Shep Baldwin... Kat is obviously the better fisherwoman... isn't she cute... that pic really shows off her darling personality... they lived in the family farmhouse right after we quit farming for a living...

According to my family (Kat, mama, and daddy) Uncle Shep was the other lawyer that Stembridge was looking for to shoot; this picture was taken either right before or right after he grew the beard for the Sesquicentennial that saved his life...

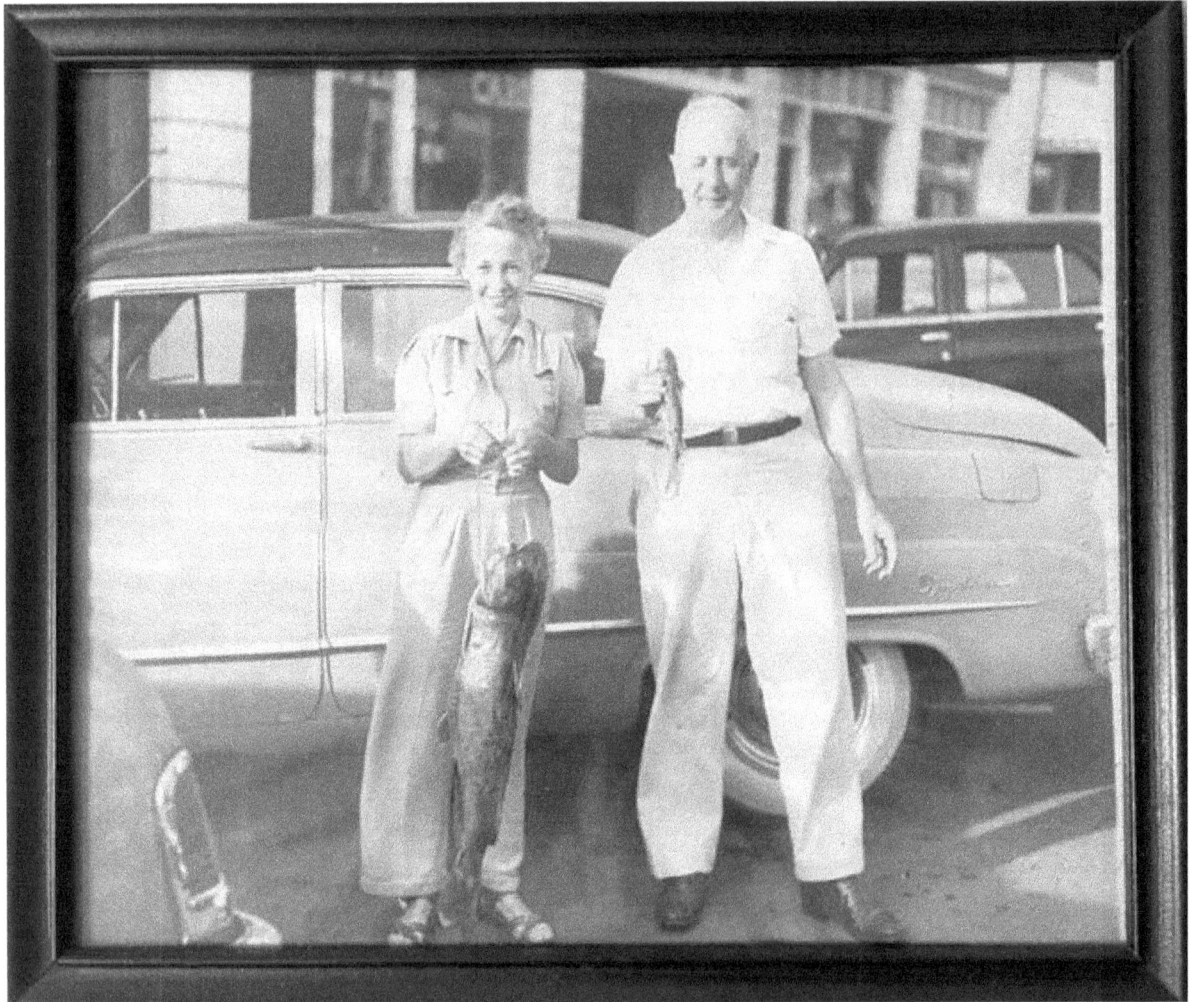

Personal note: *Shep was known for his social events, and a moonshiner who once ran a still on my family's farm told me of his relationship with Shep, prosecutor of moonshiners. Shep was having a social event in Nesbit Woods, a 16-acre park owned by the then Georgia State College for Women (GSCW) and located at the southern dead end of Columbia Street and bordered by Greene and Clarke Streets. The park had a lodge for indoor social events and plenty of outdoor space and horse-back riding trails.*

(The park has been replaced by the Centennial Center, and Napier Hall, Parkhurst Hall, Foundation Hall and Sanford Hall.)

My moonshiner friend received a message from Shep that he needed a couple of gallons for the party. The bootlegger told Shep he was asking the wrong person. Shep said, "I know you haul and I don't care as long as you don't get caught." (In other words, "Don't make me prosecute you for hauling whiskey to me.")

So to North Georgia went the bootlegger and back to Milledgeville with 10 gallons of moonshine. He unloaded it about a mile away and went to check on the party. The park was filled with people.

Shep hurried toward him. "Here's Santa Claus," he shouted.

The deliveryman replied, "It's not Christmas. I don't have gifts for anybody."

Shep's disappointment echoed in his voice. "You don't have my whiskey?"

"No, but I think I can find some." He went back to the hidey-hole and delivered the goods. No questions asked. No arrests resulted.

The same local provider informed me he also supplied State Representative Culver Kidd for his upstairs events and his victory parties in the courthouse.

(Isn't hidden history fun?)

WIFE # 2: A DIFERENT KIND OF VICTIM

On August 24, 1947, Stembridge married Sara Hunter Jordan Terry, the widow of John Thomas (J. T.) Terry.

Sara herself...

Sara Jordan from Whigham, Georgia, was actually born in South Carolina on May 25, 1896. She finished high school in Whigham in 1917 and entered Georgia State College for Women in Milledgeville. She received her Bachelor of Science Degree at GSCW in 1923 (Student Number 2843).

Sara and John Thomas (J. T.) Terry married on December 30, 1925. The wedding was announced in the *Macon Telegraph* a few days later:

January 3, 1926, *The Macon Telegraph*

~excerpt~ *Miss Sara Jordan Is Bride of Mr. J. T. Terry*

An event of much interest was the marriage of Miss Sara Jordan, of Whigham and Mr. J. T. Terry, of Milledgeville, which was solemnized at the Whigham Methodist Church at high noon Dec. 30. Rev. J. C. Walker performed the impressive ceremony in the presence of a large assembly of relatives and friends.

Mrs. Terry is the youngest daughter of Mr. and Mrs. E. C. Jordan and a young woman of rare personal attractions and talent. She is a graduate of Georgia State College for Women and has been a member of the faculty for a number of years.

Mr. Terry is the son of Mr. and Mrs. S. L. Terry, of Milledgeville. He was educated at the University of Georgia and is a promising young business man. After being entertained at a luncheon at the home of the bride's parents, Mr. and Mrs. Terry left in their car for a short wedding trip, and upon their return will be at home in Milledgeville.

The couple appear to have spent a lot of time apart, since she went to Columbia University and obtained her Master's degree in 1937.

It was common practice for women from Milledgeville to take the train from nearby Macon to Savannah and then a boat to New York to go to Columbia.

She continued her post-graduate work at Columbia during 1938-1941 and earned a Supervisor Certificate in Business Administration. She spent much of World War II (1943-1946) at the Army Air Base in Bainbridge, Georgia.

J. T.'s parents, Samuel L. and Frances Mills Terry, were both natives of Baldwin County. Samuel L. Terry served Baldwin Country as sheriff for 22 years. He won his eighth term while on his death bed, and when he died in 1928 John Thomas was appointed to replace him. J. T. served only until his father's term ran out and chose not to run for office.

J. T. attended Georgia Military College (Class of 1918) and the University of Georgia law school (Class of 1928). He returned home to Milledgeville and opened a law office. Governor Eugene Talmadge appointed J. T. County Judge, a position he held until his death.

J. T. did not sit idly on the bench. He studied law enforcement under the Federal Bureau of Investigation and in 1937 he helped organize the Georgia Department of Public Safety. A veteran of World War I, he also served as Lieutenant in the Navy in World War II. He was attached to the Naval Station in Pensacola, Florida, as legal advisor to the civilian council for the Navy Department in the Base Extension Program. He was a member of the Baptist Church, The Georgia Bar Association, Shrine, Elk, American Legion, and the Indian Island Club. He died February 2, 1945 and was buried in the Milledgeville Cemetery with all the honors the associations and societies he belonged to could confer.

Sara herself led a full life.

Her jobs over the years varied; Sara spent most of her work years at what is now Georgia College and State University, working as bookkeeper, assistant bursar, head of accounting, executive secretary to three presidents, director of personnel and services, assistant professor of business education. Other work included Supervisor of Training and Instruction, general accounting office Atlanta Audit Division, head of the business department at Lanier High for Boys (1945-1947); Director of Occupational Therapy at the Milledgeville State Hospital, 1949-1952); head of the business department of Dublin High School 1952-1953; Supervisor of Vocational Office Training and Counselor at the DeKalb County School System (1953-1954).

She was an active member in numerous organizations, including the First Methodist Church, the American Legion Auxiliary, the Daughters of the American Revolution, the American Association of University Women (A.A.U.W), and both Pi Lambda Theta and Kappa Delta Pi of Columbia University.

Nor did she stay home when she was not working. She travelled extensively in the States and in both Canada and Mexico.

Sara was recognized by *Who's Who in Education* for her contributions. She retired in 1962.

Sara Hunter Jordan Terry, Assistant Professor of Secretarial Training, Georgia State College for Women (GSCW) 1937 year-book *Spectrum* (p. 21)

By 1951 the 1947 marriage between Sara and Stembridge had degenerated. She remained in the house and he moved into the Baldwin Hotel.

THE BALDWIN HOTEL, MILLEDGEVILLE, GA

Sara filed for divorce from Stembridge in April 1953. The divorce petition details the abuse she suffered during the marriage. The divorce never reached court since he died May 2, 1953.

Sara died October 5, 1964, and is buried in Whigham, Georgia. It is interesting that her final last name, Stembridge, is not on her gravestone.

SARA HUNTER JORDAN
WIFE OF
JOHN THOMAS FERRY
MAY 25, 1896
SEPT. 7, 1964
AT REST

WHO ELSE INHABITED STEMBRIDGE'S LIFE?

Allen, Dr. Edwin Whittaker, Sr., Owner/operator of mental hospital, Allen's Invalid Home for the Treatment of Nervous Diseases, where Stembridge committed himself. He was also committed here by the sheriff when he was arrested on a lunacy warrant. (Date unknown)

Photos provided by Allen family.

Some online posts state that Stembridge's mother committed him to the Central State Hospital, but I have not found confirmation of his ever being in Central State Hospital, only at Allen's.

Beckum, Jack, Assistant Police Chief under Eugene Ellis.

Beman, Edward, Husband of Stembridge's sister Mildred and co-executor of Stembridge's will.

Beman, Mildred, Stembridge's sister and with her husband she served as co-executor of his will.

Bone, Frank, Business man whose employee still owed Stembridge the full amount of a $50.00 loan but had paid $500.00 in interest. Bone informed Eva Sloan, who took the employee's case against Stembridge and won in court.

Bootle, W. A., Attorney who represented Stembridge in his trial for attempted bribery of federal officers in April 1953. On May 4, 1954, President Eisenhower nominated Bootle to the United States District Court, to the seat vacated by Judge Abraham Benjamin Conger, who presided over Stembridge's bribery trial in which Bootle represented Stembridge.

Carpenter, George, Superior Court judge for Stembridge's 1949 murder trial who sentenced Stembridge in 1949. Granted bond pending appeals. He served as mayor of Milledgeville in 1936-1937.

Stembridge blamed Carpenter later for his troubles, and if he truly had a "hit list," Carpenter would have been on it. Stembridge studied the upper-floor windows of the courthouse before he went inside, probably to check on the possibility of Carpenter being in his office.

Judge Carpenter married Inez Lord on October 12, 1920. The marriage announcement stated, "The groom entered with his uncle, Mr. J. C. Cooper." (Cleve Cooper served as Clerk of Superior Court for many years).

They had two children: Martha and George Junior.

Conger, Judge Abraham Benjamin, (1887-1953) Federal judge who presided over Stembridge's bribery trial. When he died, he was replaced on the bench by W. A. Bootle, who defended Stembridge in his bribery trial.

Conger received his law degree from Mercer University in 1912 and later served on the Mercer Board of Trustees at the same time Marion Ennis served.

A.B. Conger, 1912
From the *Mercerian*, 1943

Cooper, Joseph Cleveland (Cleve), Clerk of Superior Court, Baldwin County. He was rumored to be one of the people on Stembridge's "hit list." There is no family relationship between Cleve Cooper and the Cooper family involved in the 1949 killing.

Cooper, Johnny and Richard (with their mother Mary Jane Harrison), Owed Stembridge money for a car. They witnessed the events leading to the death of Emma Johnekin and testified in the Stembridge murder trial.

Edwards, W. Sam, One of the attorneys for Sara Jordan Terry Stembridge in her court case to break Stembridge's will.

Edwards, Yancey, Internal Revenue employee who audited Stembridge and was one of two agents who testified against him in his tax-evasion/bribery trial.

Ellis, Eugene, Police chief in 1949 whose appearance on the stairs resulted in Marion Stembridge's suicide, was a Maine native but spent most of his life in Milledgeville law enforcement after his military years. While in the U. S. Army, he served in the Military Police as a Criminal Investigator; in Milledgeville, he joined the police force in 1946 and became chief on January 1, 1949. After thirty years with the Police Department, he retired as Police Chief. He then worked as Chief Deputy Sheriff for Baldwin County for ten years. He was active in numerous social and professional organizations.

Source, Randy Ellis　　　**Source, Donna Ellis Turner**

Evans, Frank O., Member of Stembridge's defense team in the 1949 murder trial. He did much of both direct and cross examination of witnesses.

Gautier, J. J., Assistant U. S. attorney who prosecuted Stembridge in his federal bribery case.

Gardner, Milton F., Attorney in Milledgeville, later state court judge. I remember him best for his actions toward a black church. The building burned, and members began rebuilding; the local lumber company delivered construction materials, but overnight someone uploaded the lumber and hauled it off. The villains were never discovered. Milton did not know any of the members, but when he read about the theft in the newspaper, he made a sizeable donation to the church to help them rebuild.

Harrison, Mary Jane Cooper, Shot by Stembridge, witness at the 1949 murder trial. Mother of Richard Lee and Johnny Cooper. Married to George Harrison. In his appeals Stembridge claimed she committed perjury because her trial testimony did not agree with her "death bed statement." Although he seriously injured her when he shot her, she survived. His claim of her perjury, however, was eventually used to acquire his freedom.

Johnekin, Emma, An eighteen-year-old black girl, killed by Stembridge in 1949 when he was collecting for a debt. Stembridge was tried for her murder, convicted of voluntary manslaughter; jury was all white and all male. I could find no information about her grave other than its location is unmarked.

Lingold, Buford Thomas, Deputy sheriff in 1953, later sheriff of Baldwin County (Milledgeville).

Mills, Vic, Name given me by Bob Sloan for an FBI agent who helped him raid stills, including one in the yard of a local government leader. Bob and Vic discussed Stembridge.

Stembridge thought Marion Ennis suggested the IRS investigate his income tax. The tip may very well have come from Eva to Bob Sloan and then to Vic Mills who promoted the investigation.

Nottingham, George, Witness to Stembridge's will.

Nottingham, Harry E., Witness to Stembridge's will.

Odom, Julian R., Internal Revenue employee who audited Stembridge and was one of two agents who testified against him in his tax-evasion trial.

Perdue, Ethel M., Witness to Stembridge's will.

Rowland, J. Roy, The judge who granted the writ of habeas corpus that released Stembridge from the manslaughter conviction and nullified Stembridge's conviction of manslaughter for the death of Emma Johnekin. He nullified decisions of the local Superior Court traverse jury, the Georgia State Court of Appeals and the U. S. Supreme Court.

Sibley, Judge Erwin, Witness to Stembridge's suicide. He replaced Bertie Stembridge as the probate judge for Marion Stembridge's will August 27, 1954.

Photo provided by Allen family.

Sloan, Robert (Bob), Eva's husband and co-defendant against law suit brought by Marion Stembridge against the Sloan couple for nonpayment of rent. Marion Ennis defended them and won the case.

Stembridge, Bertie, County Ordinary (now called Judge of Probate Court). She was Marion Stembridge's cousin and would have been responsible for the probate of his will. She was replaced for that hearing. As Ordinary, she had the power to commit anyone to the local Insane Asylum without a court order from a higher court judge.

Personal comment: *I was in her office when a black lady came in and complained her husband was drinking again and beating up on her; Miss Bertie said she would have him put in the asylum.*

Stembridge, Roger, Marion's brother. He served in WWI. He was wounded while in France, and twice decorated for bravery.

Roger's engagement was announced on September 28, 1920, in the local *Union-Recorder*:

*DAVIS-STEMBRIDGE. Announcement has been made of the engagement of **Miss Ella Davis** to **Mr. Robert Stembridge,** the marriage to take place Sunday, October 3rd, at the home of the bride's parents at Ella Gap, Ga.*

Roger's son also provided a lengthy letter to David Stembridge, his cousin, in which he offered much hand-me-down information about Marion's life.

Stembridge, **Thelma,** Marion Stembridge's sister and heir.

Terry, John Thomas (J.T.), Milledgeville born, son of Sheriff Samuel L. Terry (who was elected to eight four-year terms) and brother of Sam Terry who worked for Stembridge. When his father died, J. T. served out Samuel's last term. He was first husband of Sara Jordan (Terry Stembridge). He graduated from the local Georgia Military College (1918), served in WWI, graduated from University of Georgia, and practiced law in Milledgeville. Governor Herman Talmadge appointed him County Court Judge. He served in the Navy during WWII as a Lieutenant attached to the Pensacola Naval Station. After the war he returned to Milledgeville and resumed his position as County Court judge until he died on February 2, 1945. He was a member of several professional and social organizations.

Terry, Samuel L., Sheriff of Baldwin County from 1907 until his death in 1945. Father of Sam Terry who worked for Marion Stembridge and father of John Thomas Terry who married Sara Jordan. John Thomas (J. T.) was appointed to replace his father as sheriff, and he served out that term but did not run for office again.

Terry, Sam, Son of Samuel L. and brother of J. T., he stated in court he was coroner of Baldwin County and brother of the sheriff. He went with Stembridge in 1949 to collect money from Richard Cooper and was present when Stembridge shot and killed Emma Johnekin, an eighteen-year-old black girl. The grand jury investigating the shooting returned a *no bill* against Terry, that is he was considered innocent and was not to go to trial in connection with the shooting.

Watts, Jimmy (J. M.,) Jr., (1916-1995) **Vice-president of Stembridge Banking Company** and one of the three-man attorney team defending Stembridge for murder in 1949. Jimmy later served as prosecutor in Baldwin County State Court. Jimmy was a graduate of Mercer University and the Walter F. George School of Law. He served on the board of the Georgia Prosecuting Attorneys Council and as chairman of the board of the Baldwin County Department of Family and Children Services. He practiced law in Baldwin Count for 55 years.

Whitman, R. C., Attorney on the team before Judge J. Roy Rowland.

OTHERS WITH CONNECTIONS TO THE EVENTS

Dexter, Pete, Author of *Paris Trout*. From his grammar school days in Milledgeville, he remembered the Stembridge shootings and returned to gather information for his novel. His major source of information was Robert (Bob) Green. His book was loosely based on the 1953 murders. It won the National Book Award.

Kindergarten Christmas play, 1949 Peabody Elementary School, Milledgeville, Georgia. Photo provided by Anne Overstreet Walden.

1st row: Charles Hodges, Charles Pennington, unk, unk, Marion Robinson, Diane Sims. 2nd row: Ella Grace Elliot (Woods), unk, Martha Marion Garner (Kingery), John Ferguson, Steve Peacock, Kay Morris (Holmes). 3rd. row: Marie Mille (Adams), Thurza Whitaker (Strag), Richard Vincent, Joyce Goddard (Oxenrider), Angela Freeman (Prosser), Charlotte Eakins (Watkins), Ennisc McDade (Burke), 4th row: Anne Overstreet (Walden), Tommy, Pete Dexter, Rusty Smith, Jack Thornton, Penny Peabody, Warren "Punky" Reid, Joanne Cooper (Battle).

Third from left on back row, Pete looks as if he were already telling some tall tale.

Green, Robert (Bob): Rumors said Bob hid under his desk when he heard the gunfire. As a State Court Judge, Bob twice faced misconduct charges filed with the State Judicial Review Committee (once for ethical misconduct and once for threatening another judge with a pistol in the courthouse) and was temporarily suspended. He once served in the state legislature, and during that time faced a civil suit for sale of cattle not belonging to him. The case never went to trial; Green had it continued continuously. He is best known as the attorney for Francis Gary Powers, pilot of the U-2 spy plane shot down over Russia and who was tried in Russia as a spy. When Powers was swapped back to the Unites States in exchange for a Russian, Green was present for the swap.

O'Connor, Flannery, Award-winning author and local resident who also wrote of the Stembridge events in a short story, "The Partridge Festival." Her work and life are widely known.

THE MARCH 7, 1949, SHOOTINGS

Marion Stembridge went to the home of Richard and Johnny Cooper, their mother Mary Jane Harrison and her then husband George, and a teenaged Emma Johnekin who had resided with them for only a few months. Stembridge brought Sam Terry with him, to add a bit of "enforcement" for collecting on a debt.

Details of the visit came out in the murder trial in the July term of court.

EXCERPT FROM TRIAL TRANSCRIPT, July 1949

Stembridge and Sam Terry went to collect money owed by Johnny Cooper for a car loan. They arrived at the house to find Richard sitting on the porch railing. They sought Johnny, but he was not home.

Johnny lived with his brother Richard on one side of the duplex, and the other side was occupied by Mary Jane and George and a teenaged Emma Johnekin who had resided with them for about three months.

On each side the rooms were aligned, from the front room (a sitting room) to the back one (a kitchen). Bedrooms stretched between. Stembridge got a bit physical with Richard. He gripped Richard by the collar at the back of his neck and demanded he sign a note for the balance due. The youth refused.

The youngsters' mother Mary Jane Harrison arrived, together with Emma Johnekin. The situation "went South" and the two women were shot.

Emma died. Mary Jane took several bullets, but survived. Stembridge and Terry were charged with murder; the grand jury returned a no bill for Terry, but a true bill for Stembridge.

The dying declaration given by Emma was accepted in the testimony of J. E. (Jimmy) Jones, a GBI agent who interviewed her shortly before her death. He also took a dying declaration from Mary Jane Harrison, but she did not die.

Stembridge later claimed in his appeals that Mrs. Harrison's dying declaration and her sworn testimony were not the same, that her sworn testimony was perjury. The testimony of these two women formed the core of the case against Stembridge.

DYING DECLARATION OF EMMA JOHNEKIN

Solicitor Shep Baldwin established the credentials of Agent Jones, who took down Emma's dying declaration.

My name is J. E. Jones. I am an operator with the Georgia Bureau of Investigation and my duty is to assist the Sheriffs and municipal governing authorities and superior court judges in the investigation of any criminal case in which we are invited. I was called on this case on March 7ᵗʰ, the night it happened, and I went around to the hospital that night and talked to Emma Johnekin and while I was there, I noticed three wounds on her. There could have been more. There was one in the right arm; there was another one in the abdomen and there was another burned mark on the back on the left side. There was a bullet hole in the shoulder but I couldn't swear which side of the body it was on. It seemed as if the burned mark on her back had been caused

(Page missing from trial transcript)

the hospital or Mr. Beckum had already been to the hospital, one or the other and that they were in a critical condition and they wanted me to go up and talk with them.

(Legal chatter)

Q. Did you write down what she said?
A. Yes.
Q. What did she say?
A. May I read it?
Reply. Yes. (Witness reads)

When Mr. Stembridge and Terry came there all of us were on the porch. He asked about Richard and Johnny told him Richard was not here. "Where is Richard?" "He is working." And Johnny changed the subject, Johnny said, "I will pay you, Mr. Stembridge, for what I owe you. I went to work at the State." "Haven't you been working there all the time?" "No, sir." Then he asked Johnny, "Will you sign a paper for Richard?" "No, it doesn't seem right." And she spoke up, "Lord have mercy," said, "He has got on brass knucks," and turned to Mr. Stembridge and said, "Haven't you?"

(Legal chatter, and witness continues reading.)

"He has got on brass knucks – haven't you?" He turned to go in the house. "God damn it, what is it to you?" And he grabbed me and hit me with his knucks. He hit me on the head. Mary ran where I was and pulled him loose from me. He shot me in the hand and he shot at Mary. I went on inside the house and sat on the trunk. He came to the door and shot me in the shoulder and in the stomach. I didn't have a gun, neither a knife and Mary had neither gun nor knife. I swear this information is true. When he hit me I grabbed him, and Mary pulled us apart. He had a gun and started firing. Signed, Emma Johnekin.

"This was signed in my presence and signed in the presence of Deputy Sheriff Buford Lingold and Louvenia Harrison and Johnny Cooper, the latter two being relatives of the deceased." I saw Mary Jane Harrison that night. She seemed to be in the same condition as Emma. She had been shot also. I talked to her that night.

During cross-examination by Evans, Jones stated:

"I had 2 years of pre-med at Mercer University. I have not had medical training.

"Emma Johnekin had a hole in her elbow. She had an abrasive wound on the right side of her head. I am positive the one I saw was on the right and if there was one on the left, I didn't see it. I couldn't swear who her doctor was. I was new in this town at that time, he was introduced to me, I don't remember his name. As to my consulting with her doctor as I was going to take this so-called dying declaration, the doctor was in the room and I asked him in her presence her condition and that was when he put a 12- or 14-inch-long probe into her stomach. He never did answer one way or the other. As to whether he didn't answer as to her dying condition, I say he didn't answer my question. He came in while I was taking the statement. I don't remember the name of the doctor. As to whether I could anticipate that, as an investigating officer, I should know that the identity of the doctor would come up on the trial of this case, I say I know who the witnesses are that were there during the entire time, the doctor came in when I was about half way through with the statement and left before it was finished. I couldn't swear to the name of the doctor. As to my knowing the attending physician when I take a dying declaration as an investigating officer, I say I can't always get a doctor. Even though the doctor was available, I didn't think it was necessary. I didn't turn to the doctor and tell the doctor to tell her she was fixing to die because at the time I was in there, the doctor was making an examination and when I was taking this statement, talking to her about this, the doctor left immediately to go to see the other woman. I have been in cases before where dying declarations were involved. The doctor was in the room. I asked him the question. I had been told what he had said, he or some other doctor, as I have told you before, being a stranger in town, I didn't know which doctor had made the statement to Mr. Ellis. He simply told me they were in a critical condition and desired me to go up there. I wrote down the names of those present during the entire time.

"It is not necessary that it should only be through a doctor that she would be conscious of a dying condition. There were other people in the room that heard her make the same groans and when I asked her the question did she realize the seriousness of her wounds and she said yes and when I asked her if she knew she would probably not live through it and she said yes and when I asked her to be very careful and not to leave out anything at all, I explained to her, I even told her I was sure she didn't want to go on to her reward and have the blood of some innocent person on her because she failed to make some statement and she said yes and then she began to talk and I began writing and during that time the doctor came in and he put the probe into her abdomen about 14 inches down into her abdomen and as soon as he took it out I asked him what was her condition. He did not answer my question one way or the other, he went on out to the other room.

"I did not go and talk to the doctor when he was there available and ask if she was in a dying condition because the Chief of Police had told me that the doctor had made the statement to him. It is true that I had heard that the other negro woman was in a dying condition too. She didn't die but she made a statement to me, though, as if she had. I believe that the other negro woman thought that she was going to die. I turned that statement over to the Chief of Police. My only copy is in Atlanta. I couldn't swear the exact words of the statement but it said virtually the same thing. I took it down. I don't remember every word she said."

DYING DECLARATION OF MARY JANE HARRISON

She said she was next door at the time Mr. Stembridge came up and she saw them on the porch and came over. When she arrived there on the porch there was a scuffle. She heard Emma say that Mr. Stembridge had on brass knucks. I asked her if she saw the brass knucks; she said she did. She said she heard Mr. Stembridge make a statement to her, "What business is it of yours?" She said she saw Emma go into the house, Mr. Stembridge followed her and she came in behind. She told me she was shot in the back by Mr. Terry. She put all of that into what she thought was her dying statement the night that I talked to her, the same night she was shot.

She said she tried to get to them, to the people that were fighting, and was shot again. She said she went out to the back door and saw a car.

"If there was that big a conflict between the two witnesses in their so-called dying statements where one said that, *I got in a tussle in there and Mary came through and pulled the fellow off me with the gun and he then shot me in the hand and turned and shot at her*, "and if the other made the statement, *No, I walked in there and was shot in the back and was shot again in the back and didn't go around them and went and lay down on the back table,* as to this question whether or not I would notice that, as an investigating officer, I say that the other witness is here, you may question her as to what her statement is. I have the statement from her.

"I do not know whether Emma was under morphine or not at the time she made her statement. I did not ask the doctor whether she was under morphine, I was told by the nurse that nothing had been done to her. She was not a special nurse assigned to Emma, she was a general nurse. As to my seeing that a person is not doped up when I take a dying declaration from them, I say she was talking to me as any person that knew what they were saying. I have not said I had any medical experience."

MARY JANE HARRISON'S TESTIMONY IN COURT

She testified she had been downtown and returned to visit next door, about 30 feet from her home. When she came out of the neighbor's house, she saw Terry and Stembridge on her porch, and saw Stembridge hold Johnny's collar. Stembridge kept his left hand in his pocket. Mary Jane called "Johnny, what's the matter with you all?"

"I walked on over and got near-about to the door step and went up the door step and asked Johnny, "why don't you get up from there?"

He said, "Mama, Mr. Stembridge has got a thing for me to sign."

Mr. Stembridge said, "Ma, hell," but neither looked back and when I come up on the porch Mr. Stembridge had those brass knuckles on his left hand and he was holding Johnny with his right hand and Emma got up there, said, "Lord have mercy, look at the man standing up here with brass knuckles on and his hand on little Johnny's collar." He made a rake to hit her and she dodged. Before he hit at her he said, "What in the hell God damn you got to do with it." Those are the words he said. She tore off in the house and he tore off in there behind her like he was tearing down a panel. I come up the steps.

I didn't use any curse words or bad language and Emma Johnekin didn't call him anything. I didn't make any threats and nobody got mad but him. Emma ran in the room. When I entered the door, they were right by the foot of the bed in the second room. *They were holding each other and I saw a place on her head where he had hit her with the knucks. He had burst the skin.*

Q. What did you do when you went in?

A. When I went on in there, I didn't do anything because I couldn't do anything but when I went in, just about the time I got right in the middle door –

Q. Middle door of what?

A. Just about the time I got out of the living room, the front room and went in the second room door, got right in the second room door Mr. Sam Terry come right on behind me off the porch and he shot me in the back. A little before I got to Mr. Stembridge and Emma I was shot again right there. I kept right straight by them, I didn't do nothing.

The bullets went in my body. I could feel them and the shock of it. I went right on by Mr. Stembridge and Emma and never did get hold of them. I went on in the kitchen and went to lay on the kitchen table and dropped on my knees and was shot twice. While I was on that table, Emma come out of the room and sit down on the trunk. Mr. Stembridge had shot her in the arm. Yes, she came out of the second bedroom and sit down in the third bedroom, which is a part of the dining room. She sat on the trunk after she was shot in the arm and hit on the head. After she sit down, I know Mr. Stembridge shot her twice, I only know that and he shot 3 times. While I was on the table, Emma said, "Lord have mercy, Mary, he has hit me in my stomach" and I raised up and went to turn around to look at her and just as I went to turn around Mr. Sam had got middle way of the dining room and bedroom and when I went to turn around to look at her, I just twisted because I was paralyzed in the shoulder, he ran out there just a little piece and I was at the table and he just shot me right there and I said, "Come on, Emma" and she got up and me and her went on out the back door. When I went out of the back door I started to the other house and I saw a car parked. I didn't have a gun after them. Emma Johnekin didn't have a pistol. We didn't go in there trying to get a pistol. I have never shot a pistol in my life.

The shooting started about that second door (referring to diagram) in the second room. I was shot 3 times there. There are 2 bullet holes in the wall and one in the door facing. There was a bullet on the top of the bed cover. There is a bullet hole in the dining room right over the trunk where Emma was sitting. They found a bullet behind the stove. Three bullet holes is all that we could find.

Q. Can you show the jury any of these holes in you – show me where the first one was – can you pull up your dress?

Mr. Ennis: I object to any wounds being shown the jury that are on this particular witness. It is not the deceased and it would not be admissible in this case. If he has any evidence to show as to the nature of the wounds on the deceased, for which this defendant is on trial, that would be admissible but it would not be admissible to show it to this jury here.

BY THE COURT: Well, Mr. Baldwin, I don't think you can make an exhibition of those wounds without subjecting the witness to a rather embarrassing position.

Mr. Baldwin: I won't have to disrobe her. I want to show some of them. All she has to do is to pull up her dress.

Mr. Ennis: I would like further for the record to show that my objection is, it is for the purpose of prejudicing this jury. It is highly prejudicial to the defendant and improper and irrelevant and not germane to the issues involved in the particular case.

BY THE COURT: I will let it in for the present time, if he can show those wounds without undue embarrassment.

Q. Where did the first bullet hit you – right in the middle of the back?

A. Yes, sir.

Q. Where did the next bullet hit you (witness shows on body); hit you right in the side there?

A. Yes, sir.

Q. Where is the next one (witness shows); hit you right in that shoulder?

A. Yes sir.

Q. Where is the next one (witness indicates on body); hit you right in the breast?

A. Yes, sir. None of us at the house cursed Mr. Stembridge or Mr. Terry. Neither Emma nor I had any kind of a weapon, nor did we try to get any kind of weapon. Emma Johnekin was the first who went into the house, she was running; the second one, right behind her, was Mr. Stembridge; I went in then and Mr. Sam Terry came in behind me. All my little children were right there; they were right there in those bedrooms while the shooting was going on. They came in behind Mr. Terry. All that shooting happened in just half a second; all the shots were fired in a short length of time. After they finished shooting, both of them ran out of the house; when I looked around both of them were just running. Emma and I went on out of the back door and I saw his car parked behind the house.

I don't know how many times Emma Johnekin was shot but I saw 3 holes in her. I don't know how many shots were fired in all. The shooting that killed Emma Johnekin took place in Baldwin County.

Immediately after the shooting, Emma and I walked out to the back and I started around the house but Johnny met us and said, "Don't you all try to walk, you all go inside the house and lay down." We went in Johnny's side from the back. Johnny went over to the next door and told those people to come over there and do something for us while he was going to the store and call the Sheriff, police and the doctor. He went running to Mr. Hardy's.

The police came right immediately, time he called them, looked like they were already coming. I estimate it is about 300 yards to Mr. Hardy's store from the front of the house. When the police got there, I was lying on the bed and he asked me what had happened and I just couldn't tell him nothing. I was in bad condition. They did not look around the house. The police carried me to the hospital right then and also carried Emma. My little girl and three policemen went with me.

We own a pistol. We always kept it around there in the living room-bedroom. In the third room back. It was not there that day. I didn't know where the pistol was, I didn't know it was around there. I was not making for that pistol when I went in the house. I can't shoot a pistol. Emma lived three days, I think, after she was shot.

They never got that bullet out of me. I am still carrying it around.

Mr. Ennis: ...I ask that the court exclude from this jury all evidence on the part of this witness with reference to any wounds that may have been inflicted on her by Sam Terry. The witness testified that Sam Terry shot her. Sam Terry is not on trial. The defendant is not on trial for shooting this woman.

(Legal chatter)

Mr. Ennis: I think the highest and best evidence on this particular question is the indictment itself. The Solicitor General has drafted a joint indictment against Marion W. Stembridge and Sam L. Terry. It may have been at one time the state was basing it on conspiracy but the grand jury on this indictment finds a no bill against Mr. Terry, as far as this trial is concerned.

Mr. Baldwin: That doesn't make any difference what the grand jury finds because he can still be indicted by a second grand jury and that does not make any difference anyhow. Mr. Terry is a witness, sworn here. Their contention as they outlined to the jury is that nobody had a pistol but Mr. Stembridge. We have got a right to see if that is true and show the fact that he shot, but I never dreamed of a proposition where you couldn't present wounds in a case, all in one transaction, all part of the res gestae of the case. Certainly you can present the wounds to show, if nothing else, how many shots were fired.

BY THE COURT: Well, I will adhere to my former ruling, Mr. Ennis; I will leave it in for the present time.

Mr. Ennis: In other words, I still have a right to renew my objection at any time before we go to the jury.

BY THE COURT: Yes.

SAM TERRY'S TESTIMONY

(Johnny moved toward the other apartment)

He (Johnny) kept making his way, he stepped back until he got even with the other door. Then he made a dive for it and slammed the door to and locked it.

He didn't go through over me because he figured possibly I had a gun, I had my hand in my pocket and stuck my finger out, he couldn't tell whether I had a gun or not and he backed up. He went in the door to the apartment on the South. That is not the one the shooting took place in and I did not see him anymore.

After he went in the South apartment door, for a second I kept my eye on that door. I didn't know whether he was coming back out there or not, I didn't know what he was coming out with. I had given up, I knew that they had the advantage of me but he didn't come out and I turned around and as soon as I heard him going back towards the back of the house I turned around and when I turned around and I observed Mr. Stembridge holding a negro woman's hand up. Which one it was I don't know. And she had a gun in her hand. They were weaving from room to the door, the middle door leading into the back, and about that time I hollered out, I said, "Look out, Marion, look out, he is coming around the other way." I saw them stop, and about that time they started shooting. I didn't know who was doing the shooting, whether Mr. Stembridge was doing the shooting or whether the negro was doing the shooting or who was getting shot. I was tied up by the door, I couldn't leave there because there were two other negroes supposed to have been there, her husband and her other son, which I knew were very bad, mean negroes.

The shooting was done so fast until I couldn't keep up with them, in fact, it excited me, I didn't know how many shots it was, couldn't tell you to save my life. Immediately, I saw one of these women go down as if she had stepped off into the back, as if she had stepped on an uneven step, from one room to another. Marion came bouncing out then and before he got there he hollered to me at the front door, said, "Go on, Sam, go ahead." I didn't move. He got almost to the door and said, "Go ahead, Sam, there is going to be more shooting." Well, I left there then in a big hurry. We came on down to the car as quick as we could possibly get there.

The jury found Stembridge guilty of **voluntary** manslaughter; Judge Carpenter sentenced him to one-to-three years. Stembridge remained free while he appealed. He never served a day.

The indictment and the Brief of Evidence (not a full transcript) are given in Appendix 2.

Stembridge appealed. His Bill of Exception as filed with the Court of Appeals of Georgia is given in Appendix 3.

The trio who defended him in trial submitted the Bill of Exception. The reply of the Court showed only James M. Watts as receiver of the reply. The Court decided on June 5, 1951 and denied a rehearing on July 17, 1951. Their one-sentence summary: *The trial court did not err in overruling the motion for a new trial.*

The full reply of the Court is given in Appendix 4.

The U. S. Supreme Court heard arguments on April 22, 1952, and decided the case May 26. The documented syllabus reviewed the Georgia Court's report and the U. S. Supreme Court dismissed the appeal on May 26.

Although Stembridge was convicted of **voluntary manslaughter**, for some unknown reason, perhaps simply a typographical error, the U. S. Supreme Court in its decision on Stembridge's appeal, stated:

*Having been convicted in a Georgia state court of **involuntary manslaughter** and his conviction having been affirmed by the Court of Appeals of Georgia...*

That typographical error was interpreted as the lower court's finding and was repeated often by the press.

The full summary of the Supreme Court's decision is given in Appendix 5.

NEW ATTORNEYS AND THE ROAD TO FREEDOM
or
GOOD OLE-TIMEY SOUTHERN JUSTICE

The events that freed Stembridge so he never spent a night in jail actually began when Judge J. Roy Rowland lost his bid for reelection in the Johnson County Democratic primary in July 1952.

Stembridge hired a batch of attorneys to tackle this aspect of his conviction as appeals failed and jail time approached: Victor Davidson of Irwinton, GA, T. Arnold Jacobs of Macon, the law firm of Jackson and Jackson of Gray, GA, and *E. L. ROWLAND, BROTHER AND LAW PARTNER OF THE JUDGE.*

> **Attorneys representing Stem-bridge in the case, according to the court records here, included Victor Davidson of Irwinton, T. Arnold Jacobs of Macon, E. L. Rowland, a brother of the judge, and the law firm of Jackson and Jackson of Gray.**

J. Roy Rowland and E. L. Rowland had jointly defended individuals accused of various felonies in the Johnson County Superior Court and also in appeals to the State Court of Appeals. Since they were brothers and law partners, for one of them to represent an accused in the court of the other violated legal ethics. Brothers support each other because they are brothers; brothers who are law partners support each other to an even greater degree. Shared money is usually involved.

Stembridge's petition for release was a continuation of his claim of perjured testimony that formed the basis of his appeals through the courts: That Mary Jane Harrison made a dying statement, but did not die and her trial testimony conflicted with the dying declaration. He claimed he did not know of the "dying declaration" until long after the trial, but that the prosecution did know.

> **Stembridge's petition for release said he was convicted on perjured testimony of Mary Jane Harrison, a Negro woman who also was shot at the time Emma Johnekin was fatally shot. It claimed the woman had made a statement while she believed she was dying**

from the injury and that she made statements during the trial which conflicted with that "dying declaration." He said the earlier statement did not come to his knowledge until long after the trial, although it was in possession of officers who assisted the state in prosecution of the case.

This claim of perjured testimony also was the basis for Stembridge's extraordinary motion for a new trial which was denied by the U. S. Supreme Court.

Judge Rowland granted a writ of habeas corpus on July 17, but dismissed it when the State Attorney General's office moved to quash it. Rowland filed a new writ on August 20, essentially the same as the original one, and Stembridge remained free under a bond order signed by Rowland and approved by Sheriff Dewey F. Hall of Johnson County. Roy Hodges signed as principal for the bond.

Newspaper reports state that Stembridge arrived in Wrightsville at Sheriff Dewey F. Hall's office, with papers from the State Department of Corrections assigning him to the Johnson prison. Hall called Ben Hill Webb, warden of the prison camp, to Hall's office to pick up Stembridge, and when Warden Webb arrived, Stembridge presented him with the papers assigning him to the Johnson prison. (Webb reported to the Department of Corrections later that he never received the commitment papers by mail, only from Stembridge.)

Sheriff Hall immediately presented the warden with the habeas corpus petition, issued by Judge J. Roy Rowland that day and filed in the clerk's office that same day (July 17), and Hall took control of Stembridge. A few minutes later he was released again on bond pending a hearing before Judge Rowland.

WHAT WAS GOING ON?

Robert E. Warren, state director of corrections, later stated that although some proceedings had unusual aspects, "if there was any collusion, it certainly was not with any intentional co-operation on our part."

On July 17, 1952, a lot happened re Stembridge that overlapped time:

The Baldwin County Clerk of Court certified Stembridge's conviction after his appeals were turned down by both the State Court of Appeals and the U. S. Supreme Court. The certification was mailed from Milledgeville to the corrections department in Atlanta on July 17.

The corrections department orders for Stembridge to be assigned to the Johnson prison were issued on July 17 and were **mailed** to Warden Webb. "He (Stembridge) might have had a copy of the court order, or something, but I can't believe he could have had that commitment order." If he had the orders, how, and from whom, did he get the orders or a copy of the orders when the papers were in the mail?

The writ of habeas corpus petition was filed and Judge Rowland released Stembridge under bond pending a hearing. He held the hearing and on September 6 released Stembridge from all charges.

The document that freed Stembridge:

```
Filed in office Aug 27, 1952.
C. B. Harrison
          Clerk
     Motion to quash this writ is overruled and denied.
     This Sept. 6, 1952.
                                                    J. Roy Rowland
                                              Judge S. C. D.C.

MARION W. STEMBRIDGE,              *      JOHNSON SUPERIOR COURT
                                   *
        PETITIONER                 *      HABEAS CORPUS
                                   *
    vs.                            *      NO.   4        .
                                   *
B. H. WEBB, WARDEN                 *
Johnson County Works Camp,         *
        Respondent.          OF*
                        ORDER/COURT
     Upon hearing evidence in the above-stated case and both parties having closed on August
27, 1952, and this court having taken said case under advisement and reserved it s decision
until September 6, 1952, it is therefore considered, ordered and adjudged, that this writ of
habeas corpus is granted and sustained, and it is the order of this court that petitioner,
Marion W. Stembridge, is hereby discharged and freed from custody as prayed in his petition;
and the said B. H. Webb, respondent, is hereby ordered and directed to release petitioner
from custody.
     It is furthered ordered that the costs of these proceedings be paid by Respondent.
     This 6th day of September, 1952.
                                                    J. Roy Rowland
                                        Judge Superior Court Johnson County, Ga.
```

The records of the Johnson County Superior Court relating to the Stembridge's appeals and eventual freedom are given in Appendix 6.

HOW DID THESE EVENTS OCCUR?

How did Stembridge get copies of the commitment assignment?

Did Stembridge somehow arrange to be assigned to the Johnson Prison, located in the home town of his attorney?

Did Attorney Rowland's representing Stembridge influence his brother and law partner Judge Rowland? The judge was leaving office as of January 1, so he had nothing to lose. What did he have to gain? Part of his brother's income in their partnership? How much did Stembridge pay Brother E. L. Rowland to handle his legal troubles? A bonus perhaps offered by Stembridge for a free pass from prison?

Why was no one aware of the unethical relationship of these brothers in this case? Why did the state attorney not challenge on the grounds of judicial misconduct?

Ole fashioned Southern justice prevailed.

Details of these events were published in a lengthy news article on May 6, Monday after Stembridge's shot the two attorneys. Rowland publicly defended his actions. (Appendix 7)

On May 7, reports appeared in newspapers quoting Attorney General Cook defending his staff. "Everything possible was done to appeal Rowland's court order." But only one reporter noted the list of attorneys on the Stembridge team. See Appendix 8 for details.

OVERLAPPING PROBLEMS FOR STEMBRIDGE

September 6 was not the end of his problems. He had been digging himself into a hole since early 1951. Uncle Sam was not someone to expect to outwit, or to bribe.

The Internal Revenue sent him a mimeographed notice—an agent would make a routine visit in February 1951. The "routine" became a steadily increasing problem for Stembridge, who had filed the tax forms but indicated he owed no taxes for several years.

As the tax investigations dug deeper into his finances, Stembridge dug himself deeper—he postponed meetings time and again, but when the agents were getting close, he offered money for the agents to go away. His trial was set for April 1953.

Sara filed for divorce March 21, 1953.

Meanwhile, Milledgeville was wrapped up in plans for the biggest party a town could have: Its own 150th birthday party, with the nation invited.

SARA'S DIVORCE PETITON

Sara married Marion Stembridge on August 24, 1947. They lived as husband and wife until July 31, 1949, when he moved to the Baldwin Hotel. She filed for divorce on March 21,1953. Pete Bivins was one of her attorneys, as was the firm of Nelson and Nelson from Dublin. The preliminary hearing was originally set for the morning of May 2, 1953 but for some reason was rescheduled for May 22.

Her details of her reasons for the divorce reveal Marion to have been a cruel and abusive husband.

From her petition for divorce:

3) Your petitioner (Sara Jordan Terry Stembridge) *and the defendant were duly and lawfully married on August 24, 1947, and lived together as husband and wife until July 31, 1949, on which date the defendant separated himself from your petitioner, and they have not lived together as husband and wife since that date.*

4) During the two years of their married life, your petitioner made the defendant a true, loyal, affectionate and devoted wife; she performed all of her domestic duties while living with the defendant as his wife, and gave him no cause whatsoever for complaint. In addition to performing her household and domestic duties, your petitioner worked in the defendant's office, store, and place of business; worked long hours daily and many hours at night, as bookkeeper, secretary and clerk—doing any and everything within the scope of such work – and she made every possible contribution to the defendant's business and material success during that period.

5) Notwithstanding the foregoing facts, the defendant treated your petitioner in a cruel and inhumane manner, inflicting all sorts of cruelty upon her, both mental and physical; he became involved in a criminal enterprise, and was convicted of a crime involving moral turpitude, and finally he deliberately and willfully abandoned and deserted your petitioner.

6) Your petitioner brings this suit for divorce on the grounds of (a) cruel treatment, and (b) conviction of the defendant for an offense involving moral turpitude, and (c) willful and continued desertion.

7) The acts of cruel treatment are specified as follows:

(a) The defendant nagged, abused, cursed and threatened your petitioner almost continuously during the last ten months they lived together; used sharp and inhumane words, abuse and profanity towards her, repeatedly and on numerous occasions;

(b) Defendant insisted, demanded, and virtually forced your petitioner to work long hours in his office, store and place of business daily, and often at night; and denied her social privileges;

(c) Defendant was cold and indifferent towards your petitioner, and deliberately and willfully refused to show her the affection, love, care, respect and recognition to which a wife is entitled; but maintained the attitude toward her of a cold-blooded and hard-boiled employer toward an employee;

(d) The defendant has an unusually temperamental, eccentric and queer personality; he is extremely egotistical, has a high and uncontrollable temper, and on numerous occasions he would fly into fits of temper and rages of anger—and thereby caused your petitioner to live in a constant state of fear and dread of him;

(e) On numerous occasions the defendant made false and ridiculous accusations and charges against your petitioner, and did everything within his power to embarrass and humiliate her; and forbade her to visit relatives and neighbors, and heaped abuse, profanity and vilification upon her whenever she would attempt to do so;

(f) On numerous occasions the defendant would strike, slap and kick your petitioner, and shove her around, and commit other acts of physical cruelty on her;

(g) The defendant carried a pistol, slept with a pistol under his pillow or by his side, conducted a reign of terror, and kept your petitioner in a state of virtual slavery throughout their married life.

8) The aforesaid acts of physical and mental cruelty committed by the defendant upon your petitioner, was such willful infliction of mental and physical pain and suffering upon your petitioner, as reasonably justified her in apprehension of danger to her health and life.

9) At the July 1949 term of the Superior Court of Baldwin County, Georgia, the defendant was convicted of voluntary manslaughter, for the fatal shooting of Emma Johnekin, and was sentenced to a term of imprisonment in the State Penitentiary; and the said conviction, judgement and sentence of said Court was affirmed and became a final judgement. The said crime was involving moral turpitude, and is an absolute ground for divorce.

10) On Sunday night, July 31, 1949, the defendant abruptly and deliberately left the home where he and your petitioner were living, moved to the Baldwin Hotel, and has never returned to live with your petitioner as husband and wife since; thereby deliberately and willfully abandoning and deserting her.

The divorce never happened. The marriage was still in effect on May 2 when Stembridge committed murder and suicide. But he had written his will in January 1951, and left her only $1.00, to meet the requirements of the law that a spouse/wife could not be omitted from a will.

MILLEDGEVILLE PLANS BIRTHDAY PARTY

Milledgeville, like Washington D. C., had been laid out to be a capital, and it assumed that title in 1803. The original capitol building is still in use, now as an administration building for the junior college Georgia Military College. The associated high school is still a military-style school and the students now include both young men and women, who wear uniforms and earn ranks.

North gate, GMC, November 5, 2013. Photo by author.

Talk about town for more than a year had been about how to acknowledge the 150th anniversary of Milledgeville becoming the capital of Georgia.

The year 1953 was to be one of celebration, and the town leaders planned a week-long series of events. But citizens were excited about the pre-birthday goings-on. A Queen of the Sesquicentennial would be chosen from a group of high-school-aged young ladies. *The Union-Recorder* shared the picture.

ONE WILL BE QUEEN OF THE SESQUI-CENTENNIAL. Contestants being sponsored for the title of Miss Milledgeville and Queen of Milledgeville's 150th Birthday Celebration, are shown at Sesqui-Centennial headquarters. Front row, from left to right, they are: Misses Sue Herndon, Louise McKnight, Sallie Moore, Nancy Mudge, Emily Hodges, Ria Bouchillion, Joe Ann McCluney. Back row, left to right: Misses Nell Lawrence (who since has withdrawn from the contest), Dennise Cox, Caroline Fowler, Marianne Berry, Thulia Lindsley, Essie Mae Prosser and Betty McMillan. Contestants not present when the photo was made are Misses Mary Joyce Pritchard, Virginia Veal and Gloria Ann Erwin.

Bonnets, parasols and long skirts could be seen in downtown Milledgeville when ladies gathered just to show others that the Sesquicentennial was a time for fun.

The Union Recorder, Milledgeville, Georgia, April 2, 1953

HEADQUARTERS SESQUICENTENNIAL 1803 ·· 1953·

SWISHY IS AS SWISHY DOES—The committee in charge of the Sisters of the Swish practice what they preach. They were caught by the photographer as they swished out of the Sesqui-Centennial headquarters during the week-end· From left to right, they are: Mrs. Roland Dickinson, Mrs. William Tennille, Sr., Mrs. Stephen Bivins, Mrs. James Tillman, Mrs. Sue A. Brooks, Mrs. Bill Fowler and Mrs. J. G. Lunsford.
                                                                    —Staff Photo

This group did not wait for the opening day of the party to stroll about town; they were a solid month early as they dressed to the nines in their 1803 gowns and visited the Sesquicentennial headquarters. The group includes Mrs. Pete Bivins (third from left), our only image of her. Second from right is Mrs. Bill Fowler, whose daughter Carolyn was on the Queen's Court.

For the men to not be outdone by the ladies, the committee in charge of the celebrations dictated that clean shaven men would be "arrested" and fined, the fines to be used to cover expenses of the whoop-de-do.

BROTHERS OF THE BRUSH, exemplifying the true spirit of the Sesqui-Centennial and the best spirit of cooperation, gathered last week for their first meeting and the Union-Recorder camera caught this group as they listened to the proceedings. They are, left to right: Gus Dunn, Sidney Logue, M. M. Bonner, Jody Watts, Roland Dickerson, and W. T. Long. The Brothers of the Brush plan a lot of cutting up during the week of the Sesqui-Centennial.

APRIL, 1953: THE BRIBERY TRIAL

While Milledgeville residents became more and more excited about the pending party, Stembridge's problems with the Internal Revenue Service increased. The conflict began in 1945 when he received a printed letter that an agent would stop by for an informal discussion.

Stembridge postponed discussions as long as possible, but eventually he and two agents met, and met again. When Stembridge let the agents know he was willing to pay them to go away, he faced charges in Federal court. The trial for attempted bribery of Federal agents ran four days in April 1953.

It ended with Stembridge convicted and facing time in federal prison. Monday, May 4, 1953, he would be sentenced in federal court.

Before the trial began in the Federal Courthouse in Macon, a lengthy argument ensued in the Judge's chamber. Stembridge faced perjury charges in another case, in Milledgeville. He had used his need to prepare for that trial as an excuse to postpone meetings with the IRS officers.

His defense attorney, W. A. Bootle, insisted if the jury knew the true reason for some of the delays, the jury would be prejudiced against Stembridge. The judge offered a solution:

I am not judging him at all, but I think if there was a conscientious effort to delay the investigation, that would be admissible. I would think, Mr. Gautier, that it would be best for you to ask your witnesses when they reach this point to substitute for indictment for perjury that there was a pending case. . . .. However, I am not going to make any ruling on it until it is presented to me.

MR. GAUTIER (prosecutor): "Of course, you are asking me, Your Honor, please, to tell my witnesses what to say. I don't like to do that."

The discussion continued about the relationship between "delaying tactics" with respect to submitting his accounting information, the pending perjury trial in Milledgeville, and the eventual alleged offer of bribes.

The judge finally suggested the IRS agents be brought into the discussion. He informed them:

I think it would be prejudicial for you to repeat that he said he wanted a delay because he was under indictment for perjury. That is a case separate and distinct and apart from our case. He is being tried here for an alleged offer to give a bribe.

I suggest to you that when you come to this point in your evidence, you state that he said he had a matter in court for which he would have to prepare, rather than state what the offense was, although an indictment is not admissible at all because he may come clear. Counsel have brought that to my attention and I think it is a legitimate matter. So when you reach that point in your evidence, just state that he said he had a matter pending in the court for which he had to prepare and you would have to come back. Don't say what it was. I believe that would be in the interest of justice. Very well.

With that matter settled, the defense brought up its concern about the IRS agents mentioning that Stembridge had not paid any income taxes since "1941 or 1940." The defense argued that tax matters in those years were not relevant. The prosecution stated that his not paying taxes for those years was the reason for the investigation that led to these charges. The judge ruled for the prosecution.

The prosecution called Julian Odom of Macon as its first witness. He had been an IRS agent since December 17, 1945, and was stationed in Macon, in the federal building.

Odom mailed a customary mimeographed letter requesting an appointment, but in his reply, Stembridge requested that for personal reasons the examination be delayed until a later date. Because he was in Milledgeville a couple of days later, he stopped in the store to see Stembridge "to discuss the matter and see if we couldn't settle upon a convenient date for the examination."

Odom carried Stembridge's personal and corporate tax returns for 1949 with him.

Stembridge however, insisted he had personal matters to attend to and asked that the examination be delayed until October. Odom informed Stembridge such long delays were unusual, but Stembridge insisted he had matters out of his control to attend to. Odom accepted Stembridge's reasons for the delay and granted him an extension until October for the examination.

After a couple of years attempting to investigate Stembridge's finances and determining why he had not paid income tax, the investigation turned into a case of attempting bribery of two IRS officials.

Testimony by the officials covered the months of delaying by Stembridge; he was always busy at the time the investigators wanted to interview him and review records.

Testimony of Julian Odom, Internal Revenue Agent, Investigating Officer:

I again asked Mr. Stembridge if he still thought that he didn't owe any taxes and if he didn't want to get his tax liability straightened out with us. And he said-- reaffirmed his other statements that he didn't owe any taxes. And from that point he said, "Well, now, I can give you some leads"—he said it would take us two years to make a full check-out.

Q. Take you two years---

A. Take us at least two years, a minimum of two years to give him a complete check-out.

Q. Of his tax liability?

A. That's right. And then from that point he went in and said that he could give us some leads and some things to check and at the end of two years we would be better off by $10,000. I didn't know what Mr. Stembridge meant at that time, whether he was trying to say that the--that he could give me some leads on other people to check where me, the Government, representing the Government, would be better off, I could get a $10,000 tax liability against someone else. I didn't know what he meant, but that's what he said, that you would be---

Q. What did he say? Go over that again.

A. What he said? He said, "Both of you would be better off at the end of two years." And I said, "Well, how would we be better off?" He said, "Just by knowing me, just having known me." He also said that he knew certain influential people, *bankers and so forth, and that we could make trips together, and that at the end of two years we would be better off by $10,000.*

I said, "Mr. Stembridge, if what you're trying to tell us--tell me that you can give me leads to check somebody else, I'm not interested in that. I haven't got but one thing to do now and that's to determine your correct tax liability, not anybody else's. I want to determine your correct tax liability."

And he said he didn't mean that, and he said that we'd be better off at the end of two years--the end of the year--he first said it would take two years to check him out. Then he said we would be better off at the end of the year by $10,000 each.

I said, "Well, I'm certainly not interested in any proposition like that and I know Mr. Edwards is not interested, but Mr. Edwards can speak for himself. And at that time Mr. Edwards did speak. Mr. Edwards asked Mr. Stembridge again what he meant by that, and it was the same process, that we'd be better off by $10,000 at the end of the year.

Then I picked the conversation up again to try to clarify it. It was firmly established in my mind then what he meant. Nevertheless, I asked him--I brought the subject back to Mr. Stembridge, and I said, "Do you mean that $10,000 apiece, two times 10,000 is $20,000--do you mean that the Government--that you would have a $20,000 tax liability at the end of this examination?" Whereupon Mr. Stembridge says, "No, I do not mean that. The Government would be left out. That would be yours."

The entire transcript of this trial stretches to almost 150 pages. Therefore I am including the judge's charge to the jury in Appendix 9. It provides a shorter summary of testimony.

The jury found Stembridge guilty of two counts of attempted bribery on April 27, 1953.

Judge A. B. Conger gave Stembridge time to get his affairs in order and scheduled sentencing for Monday, May 4. Stembridge posted bond, remained free and went home.

But Stembridge was not idle. On Thursday, April 30, his attorneys filed an appeal. (Appendix 10)

He, however, began his scheme to change the world and began a slow easy start on his pathway to revenge on Friday, May 1.

MAY 1953: PARTY TIME AND MURDER TIME

MAY 1, 1953, FRIDAY

Few people paid any heed to Marion Stembridge that May, 1953. Even fewer knew the facts of his illness. Some called him insane, perhaps a crude explanation for his paranoia that he himself had sought help for by checking himself into Allen's Institute for two weeks in November 1933. The law officers of the community knew Stembridge had been jailed on a peace warrant and lunacy warrant in 1942 and taken to the same mental health institution for treatment, and released before the year's end.

On Friday, May 1, Stembridge wrote a note and carried it in his pocket when he went to town the next day with "justice" his goal.

Stembridge drove to Shep Baldwin's house, where he was seen wandering around in the yard with a pistol. Shep was not home.

He also visited "attorney hall" three times to try to open Ennis's door but found it locked. Fortunately both Ennis and Eva Sloan (his law partner) were away that day.

Ennis was in Macon, with others on the Sesquicentennial committee, finalizing plans for the grand ball, scheduled for Saturday evening, May 2, as the opening event of the celebrations.

MAY 2, 1953

The first Saturday in May 1953 dawned with typical Southern warmth and excitement. The greatest horse race of the year would be broadcast on the local radio stations nationwide from Lexington, Kentucky, and bring fame and glory to the horse and rider winning the Derby. In the Georgia countryside, farmers' children scattered across the land to pick the first of the season's wild strawberries.

In Milledgeville, the day meant Herty Day, an annual event at the women's college to honor the leading scientist in the South. The honor carried the name of the Milledgeville native who developed paper from pine pulp and thereby established the South as a pulpwood land; Charles Holmes Herty also designed the cup used to tap pines without killing or damaging the tree, to collect the sap for producing turpentine. At the University of Georgia, he was a football coach and the man who re-shaped the football itself.

Opening day of the party, locals and out-of-towners dressed like Milledgeville residents of 1803 as they enjoyed the excitement of the first day of the big party.

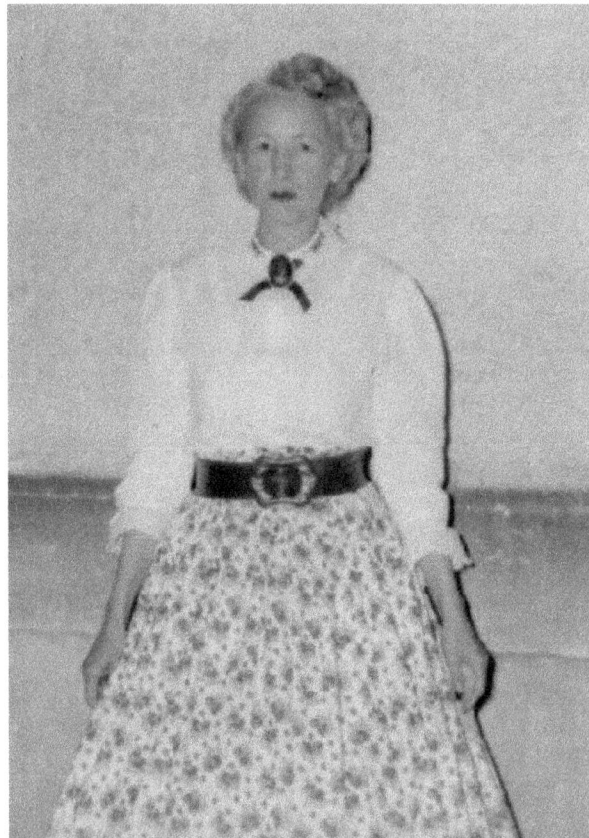

Katherine (Mrs. Shep) Baldwin
Photo provided by GMC Archives.

Martha Glover Humphrey and Homer Humphrey were typical of everyone joining in the fun. With them are the children of their son Thomas Humphrey (Highway 212 is named for him). The children are L to R, Phyllis, Robert, and Jimmy.

Picture provided by Phyllis Humphrey.

The afternoon events for Herty Day went on that afternoon and evening in spite of the morning's event. So did the Kentucky Derby.

Life events for Stembridge, however, went from apparently peaceful to premeditated murder the morning of May 2. He began his activities with a visit to his 87-year-old mother. They talked for about an hour that morning, and she reported him to be in good spirits.

Personal comment: *Stembridge had made his decision about the coming events when he visited his mother. When we are in a quandary we suffer; once our decision is set, the internal stress ends. Stembridge knew exactly his course of action when he left his mother's home. Many articles in the press state he was in a murderous frenzy or uncontrollable anger, but I believe he was in total control of his actions, knew what he was doing with the clarity of an executioner. He plotted his sequence of victims and cleared his pathway to exit the courthouse by propping the back door wide open. Leaving the car door open and the motor running show he figured to* *escape. Or die. A soldier leaving on what he considers his last, fatal, mission might say to his mother as his final words: "Have to run some errands. Bye, Mother, and remember I love you."*

Eva Sloan told me they figured since Stembridge had missed locating Shep the day before, he planned to begin his mission by killing Shep first on May 2. She shared with James S. Owens the details of Stembridge's attempt to locate Shep that morning. James shared the details; Shep lived northeast of town. Stembridge lived downtown in the Baldwin Hotel on South Wayne Street, across from his store.

By James S. Owens, October 7, 2016

Marion Wesley Stembridge drove northeast along the Oconee River banks the morning of 2 May 1953, making his way to Shep Baldwin's home located on Furman Shoals Road. Marion is said to have aimed to kill Baldwin, first thing. Although Shep was inside the Furman Shoals home watching television, Marion didn't see Shep's car. His wife had driven the car to town before the Sesquicentennial crowd hit the streets. Maybe Shep's wife went to town for groceries, perhaps at the Piggly Wiggly. I doubt anyone will ever know, but she likely saved her husband's life.

Since Marion didn't see Shep's car, he turned around in Shep's driveway, and left County Solicitor Carter "Shep" Baldwin, one of the primary targets on Marion's alleged hit list, enjoying whatever television program Shep tuned to the morning of 2 May 1953.

Stembridge turned west from Jefferson Street onto Hancock Street, turned right onto Wilkinson Street and parked near the entrance to the Piggly-Wiggly grocery and the Sanford Building. The courthouse clock showed almost 10:00.

He stepped out, reached inside for his briefcase. It held a Colt. 45 with a full magazine, plus three more loaded magazines, and a Colt 380 with three extra magazines.

Personal comment*: The 380 is a popular choice for self-defense; its compact size makes it ideal to carry concealed.*

None of the Saturday-go-to-town crowd paid him any mind, although he left the driver's door open, the key in the ignition and the engine idling. A farmer might have noticed if the mule that pulled his wagon to town caught a breath of exhaust and snorted.

Stembridge stood by the car a moment.

All of Milledgeville was throbbing with excitement over the coming events. Dances and parties were being held in Milledgeville and also in nearby Macon where the available facilities were larger. A parade was planned, and a pageant presenting the 150 years of history was scheduled to run for a week. Banners and flags flew all over town, and the entire community was in a party mood.

Stembridge faced the courthouse and looked up at the open windows of Judge George Carpenter's office.

Saturday and celebration day, but Milledgeville was still a country town, and country people came to town on Saturday. So the courthouse, post office and businesses stayed open on Saturday morning, making up the half-day lost by closing on Wednesday afternoons.

Stembridge surely concluded Judge Carpenter was in office this Saturday morning with the whole week to be taken up by the towns' birthday whoop-de-do.

He crossed the street, walked up the steps toward the side of the courthouse, and turned right onto the porch toward the front door.

He had to pass near the "jail' set up for a "policeman" to arrest any man who came to the area with a clean shave. To make "bail' from this cell, a man had to make a financial contribution to the Sesquicentennial Committee to help defray costs. Some men would stop by, shaved, just to make a contribution and brag they had been arrested by the committee. Stories later circulated that the "policeman" had started toward Stembridge, but backed down when he realized there was no joy or cooperation in the expression.

Stembridge entered the courthouse. He passed the tax receiver's and the tax collector's offices. Halfway down the hall, he paused at the open door to the clerk's office, made eye contact with Cleve Cooper the Clerk of Superior Court, and continued to the back door. He propped the door open with a wooden wedge kept for that purpose. With the summer heat already building up, the door was often left wide open to catch any breeze that might be stirring, and no one paid any attention to any open door in the 1950s.

Stembridge re-crossed the street with his briefcase, turned right on Wilkinson and left on Hancock, passed Trapnell's shoe store and Nelson's appliance on his way to the Campus Theater. He passed children scooting here and there.

Had the boys been shooting off cap pistols, the later gunfire might have been considered just more children's play. Downtown, everyone was in the mood for a party—except Stembridge.

Behind and to the east side of the ticket booth, a door opened to stairs to the second floor.

Photo by author, March 2013.

Attorneys' offices lined the left side of the hall, where their windows overlooked Hancock Street. Spittoons and chairs lined the other side. A few lawyers were tidying up their desks, getting ready to join the festivities. Some doors were locked.

Briefcase in hand, Stembridge approached the stairs.

Eva Sloan and Marion Ennis were at work, preparing for the next Tuesday's County Commissioners meeting that had been moved to that Saturday morning because of the Sesquicentennial events. The change had been announced in the local weekly paper on Thursday to be sure everyone who might want to attend would be aware of the change. Eva left Ennis's office about the time Stembridge left the courthouse. She signaled Ennis to hang up the phone, they were late for the County Commissioners meeting. She patted the armload of files she carried to indicate she had the papers they would need.

As she stepped into the hall, she spoke over her shoulder. "Hurry up, Boss. We're already late." She strode down the hall and toward the stairs to the street. Later she realized she avoided death by only minutes, but at the moment her thoughts were on the work across the street at the courthouse and the grand ball in Macon that evening.

As she neared the end of the hall, Lee Partis, a young lawyer, called to her and she turned into his office to chat and wait for Ennis. While she was gabbing away, Stembridge came up the stairs.

Lee asked her what she thought the federal judge would do to Stembridge at the sentencing next week, and she said, "I hope the judge burns him," when footsteps sounded in the hall.

Lee waved her to silence. She turned toward the door and peeked out. Stembridge, carrying his briefcase, pushed through the door into the men's room.

She turned back into the office. "It's just Marion Stembridge going to the men's room. What's to worry about? My boss has a pistol in his desk, and Shep's door is locked, so there's nothing to worry about. He's scary, and crazy, but I don't think…"

A loud *blam* rolled down the hallway. Eva shook her head and grimaced. "Somebody sure did slam Marion's door wide open and made it hit the new copy machine." She reminded herself she ought to move the machine before it got damaged. They bought it only a week before and hadn't rearranged the office to have a place for it.

Seconds later, she heard a shot, but her mind could not register that it was gunfire. More shots close together. Partis rose from behind his desk and asked, "What the hell's going on?"

She said, "Oh, that must be Jim (Jim Smith) playing with his musket. He puts a firecracker in the end of it and then lights it up for the noise. I've had to tell him more than once not to point that thing at me. I don't want a firecracker jumping at me."

"I guess he set off a whole pack?" Lee asked.

Eva remembers footsteps running by and hurrying down the stairs.

Then silence fell, a silence louder than all the noise itself, as if the walls themselves listened.

Still thinking the noise was nothing more than a game the attorney was playing with his musket, not letting any idea other than the fun planned for the sesquicentennial to penetrate her mind, Eva mentioned again the need to get Ennis going to the meeting and stepped into the hall. They couldn't be late; he was clerk and attorney for the Commissioners, and his father was Chairman.

As she neared their office, Marion Ennis staggered into the hallway, his white shirt smeared as if he'd wallowed on the dirty floor, playing dead in the game of firecrackers/shoot-em-up. "Don't you think y'all are carrying this too far?" she said as she neared him. He slid down onto the floor.

She thought for only a second, *Why was he lying on the dirty floor—people put out cigarettes on the hall floor, some didn't bother to aim at the spittoon, the floor doesn't even get swept every week.*

But something was wrong. Eva rushed down the hall, squatted beside him.

He rolled his eyes, looked into hers, and grabbed her arm, his tight grip nearly breaking it. He tried to lift his head and speak, but no words, only blood gurgled and gushed out, all over his beard, his white shirt, his face, and splashed onto her. Eva screamed. And screamed. And screamed.

Ennis died. Even in death he held onto her arm.

Other attorneys burst out of their offices. Eva could not move. One attorney pried Ennis's fingers from around her arm. She bore a red image of his grip for hours, and the bruise remained for more than a week.

Two attorneys lifted her up, but she couldn't stand. She was in such deep shock she stayed in that squatting position and they settled her into a chair.

Eva said the hardest thing for her was she forgot what Marion's face looked like, that when she saw a picture of Marion Ennis later, she did not recognize him because all she could remember was his face as he died—bloody all over.

As Eva was being comforted and cared for, she was not aware of what was going on around her, other than Ennis had died from the gunshot wounds.

Eva told her daughter Toni that Ennis appeared to be coming out of his office when Stembridge fired the first shot. The bullet missed Ennis, passed through the bookcase and lodged in the wall. The second shot hit Ennis and he fell. Stembridge fired a third shot into Ennis as he lay on the floor; the bullet went through him into the floor. Toni said a carpet was laid over the hole in the floor.

Another report stated Marion was shot in his arm, in his back, and, while on the floor, had taken a third bullet between his shoulders.

Eva said she couldn't believe he'd been able to get to the door.

Personal note*: I have tried to get medical information from autopsy and ballistics reports but these are no longer available in either the Baldwin County Courthouse records or with the Georgia Bureau of Investigation. The Coroner's Report has also been lost or destroyed.*

Across the street, a teenaged Carolyn Fowler (Smith) was shopping and recalls the morning.

Yes, I was down town shopping for a new dress in Ms. Lawrence's Dress Shop across from the building where the event took place. I heard the gun shots and I called my mother and she screamed to me, "Get on the floor at the shop."

I watched the unfortunate men being brought out on stretchers.

The party that I was planning to attend and needed a new dress for was in Eatonton and it was cancelled because of this sad event. The party was for the girls in the "Miss Milledgeville Pageant." I was asked to be the DeMolay representative.

(The DeMolay organization is part of the Masonic "family" and is devoted to helping boys become men of outstanding character through dedicated mentorships and unique, hands-on life-skills. It derives its name from Jacques de Molay, last grand master of the Knights Templar.)

As Stembridge reached the street, a child pointed to him and said, "That man has a pistol." His mother replied that a lot of the men were toting toy pistols as part of the celebrations. The ticket taker at the Campus Theater later reported he had seen Stembridge with a pistol.

Stembridge hurried some fifty feet west along Hancock Street, past the appliance store and shoe store, and turned north on Wilkinson Street to the entrance to the Sanford Building. Many people on the sidewalk saw him with the pistol, but no one paid him any attention. With the Sesquicentennial underway, everybody thought it was simply another part of the celebrations and that the pistol was only a toy.

Johnny Mercer, who passed away in 2015, was a 17-year-old working at the campus theater at the time. Mercer told 13WMAZ-TV, "I was face-to-face with him [Stembridge], like that, and he had dropped the pistol, and he picked it up and turned and ran to the Sanford building."

Stembridge's car still idled and the door remained open as he entered the door to the stairway. He scurried up the stairs to the hall where Pete Bivins, his wife's divorce attorney, had his office.

Jean Stockum, Bivins secretary, was quoted on Monday in one of the many newspaper reports:

When Stembridge reached the office, Bivins was dictating to her, and he looked up. Bivins greeted him with, "Good morning, Mr. Stembridge. What can I do for you?"

Stembridge's reply was five shots.

Four hit Bivins in the chest, but he sprang up and managed to wrestle the pistol and a clip of ammo from Stembridge in the hall. Bivins collapsed with the pistol in his hand.

Stembridge pulled another gun from his briefcase, and, newly armed, started down the hallway to the stairs. Possibly, he saw Police Chief Eugene Ellis who was coming up the stairs, because Stembridge turned, retreated back down the hall, and shot himself in the head with the Colt 380, so the bullet roared through him and up into the ceiling.

Originally, the story released was that Pete had killed Stembridge. Pete died at his office door with a gun in his hand; Stembridge lay dead only a few feet away. The general layout of bodies and a bullet hole in the ceiling generated the early rumors that Pete shot Stembridge as he himself died. That theory was the first version of events I heard, and the version that ran the rumor mill in town for weeks if not years.

Erwin Sibley and his secretary verified later reports that Stembridge killed himself; he committed suicide just outside their office door, with them watching.

Chief Ellis said, "I saw him lying face down on the floor in front of Judge Edwin Sibley's office. I thought he was playing possum." Stembridge still gripped his pistol; Chief Ellis kicked it away.

Jay Arvis in his book *Georgia's Crime Doctor* (about Dr. Herman Jones) writes that Dr. Jones determined (by ballistics) that the bullet in the wall in Ennis's office (one that missed Ennis) was fired from Stembridge's weapon, as was the bullet removed from Pete Bivins. There was no doubt about who shot the two men.

Without the legal reports, I cannot confirm, but have found reports that his briefcase held seven magazines/clips, and each clip held eight cartridges. Seven bullets remained in the 380 pistol he used to kill himself.

Personal Thoughts: *I wonder if he did plan to kill himself at that point. I think he planned to return to the courthouse, kill Carpenter and Cooper, reach his car and escape. He had parked his car close to the door to the Sanford Building, left it running and the driver's door open. His plans seemed to be for a quick getaway. Stembridge was thwarted when Chief Ellis came up the stairs, and there was no escape. His written note indicated he would do as much justice as he could; he saw no way to "do more justice" and ended his quest.*

CHIEF ELLIS'S INVESTIGATION

When Chief Ellis went into the room Stembridge rented at the Baldwin Hotel, he found evidence of Stembridge's paranoia. Each corner of the room housed a pistol, rifle and shotgun and a supply of ammunition for each. Ellis said, "If he had ever gotten back to that room, he would have given us a hard time."

Also in the room on a nightstand beside the bed were two books: A *Bible*, and a copy of *How to Win Friends and Influence People* by Dale Carnegie.

At Stembridge's store at 135 South Wayne Street, Ellis found two safes, one containing a gallon of what was identified as Stembridge's urine, with a note that if anything happened to him the specimen was to be taken to a specific doctor in the state crime lab to determine what was being used to poison him.

There was a refrigerator in his store said to contain small bottles of urine. A friend of mine, Patricia Bass (Riner) told me of seeing it when she went to the store to get something for her mother; she happened to open the refrigerator and saw the containers and Mr. Stembridge yelled at her to close the door.

Eva told me the police informed her they did find a hit list, with six names. Two were the attorneys he killed, and she was number three. Everyone on the list was either an attorney or in law enforcement. Also on the note he wrote the day before,

"I don't know how much justice I can do but I will go as far as I can," implied he planned to kill more than the two attorneys. During his trial in Macon for tax evasion, he commented on his "enemies, the courthouse crowd in Milledgeville."

Ellis said that Stembridge did not get along with lawyers—he would hire a lawyer one day and fire him the next. Eva said both Ennis and Bivins kept guns in their law offices because of the implied threats.

Mildred Stembridge, his sister, said there was a paper in his pocket but not a hit list; it stated "I refuse to be incarcerated for another crime I did not commit."

Many people spoke their minds about Stembridge, some good, some not so good.

He was handsome and always well dressed and charming.

Bob Green, local attorney, said he was "brilliant, intelligent, bordering on genius."

His sister Mildred said he had mental problems from the time he was in the military in World War I, and he received a medical discharge. She also said he thought he was the *crown prince* of the family. She also said he had alienated himself from everyone in the family except his sister and his mother.

His cousin Bertie Stembridge was County Ordinary and had the power to send anyone to the State Asylum without any other judge's or physician's orders; Marion Stembridge, however, admitted himself to Allen's Institute once; the sheriff admitted him to Allen's the second time. I found no indication he was ever in the Milledgeville State Hospital.

EVENTS AFFECTED BY THE MURDERS

The sesquicentennial event for the night of May 2, the grand ball, was cancelled.

The Herty Day events went on. The barbecue supper for the attendees was held on the lawn of Georgia State College for Women; the honoree received the gold medal in Russell Auditorium and gave his speech as planned. The scientists from around the Southeast continued their informal socializing in and around the auditorium. The shootings might have been mentioned but the Herty Day events went on in spite of the morning's event.

The first Saturday in May was also a time for a nationally awaited event: Kentucky Derby Day. Horse lovers in Milledgeville crowded around their radios to hear the two-minute-plus action from Lexington, Kentucky. (For those interested, Native Dancer, the favorite, was upset.)

Some Saturday-evening newspapers ranked Lexington, the Kentucky Derby and the dramatic upset of Native Dancer to be less important to the nation than the

Milledgeville events when they put Stembridge not only as the major headline but also above the fold and on the right-hand column of the front page.

Word of the murders also reached across the nation when *Newsweek* carried this story: A double murder and suicide involving only white people was unheard of in 1953.

GEORGIA:

Carnival of Death

Milledgeville, tradition-soaked Southern community of white-columned mansions and ancient green trees, capital of ante-bellum Georgia, observed its 150th anniversary last week. Visitors from all over the South flocked in for the sesquicentennial and agreed that Milledgeville had outdone itself in Southern hospitality, recapturing the spirit of the romantic past. But there was something wrong. The civic-minded citizens, sharing a secret among themselves, had tacitly agreed not to tell the outsiders any more than they had to about the tragedy that hit Milledgeville on Saturday afternoon as the first visitors were moving into town.

Marion Stembridge, 63-year-old private banker and moneylender, had been known as a queer one for a long time. In his rooms at the Baldwin Hotel, where he ate all his meals alone, there were locks on everything, even the icebox. In the old days when he had his own house in town he had removed the knobs from the outside doors so nobody could get to him. He had a list of people in Milledgeville whom he believed "had been plotting against him" and he had two guns, a .45 automatic with sights painted white for sharper aiming and a .38 which had been rebored to take a heavier cartridge.

Death Stroll: Saturday afternoon Stembridge pocketed his guns along with four extra clips of cartridges and went hunting. No party to the anniversary nonsense, he ignored the bunting and the banners along Hancock Street. He marched straight to the office of Marion Ennis, 45-year-old attorney, county political figure and centennial planner, and killed him with three shots from the .45.

Down a flight of stairs to Hancock Street again clomped Stembridge and up another flight of stairs to the law office of 27-year-old Stephen Bivins, co-chairman of the centennial committee. Bivins had stopped four bullets, one through the heart, when he seized the .45 and held on to it, dying. In the corridor, with pursuers pounding up the steps toward him, Stembridge drew his .38, put the barrel in his mouth and killed himself.

Stunned townsfolk agreed without saying it that the thing to do was to put on a cheerful front and receive the visitors just as if nothing had happened. Among themselves they sought motives, recalling that Ennis had defended Stembridge in 1949 when he was convicted of manslaughter for shooting a Negro woman; that Bivins had acted in a divorce suit against Stembridge.

~On Thursday afternoon, as the celebration neared its climax, there was a hilarious kangaroo court ruling Milledgeville. Citizens were being "arrested" wholesale by make-believe cops and a mock judge was sentencing them all to the public stocks. Two Waves, for instance, were convicted of willfully wearing lipstick, and a young bridegroom of failing to kiss his wife good-by that morning. To the uninitiated it seemed that gaiety reigned supreme. But the minds of most of the townsfolk were not on the fun but on the tragedy. In a lunchroom the manager said it was all the community's fault for allowing Stembridge to remain at large after the 1949 killing. A waitress dabbed at her eyes. A taxi driver looked out at the show and growled: "They ought to cut this damn celebration out."

□ **Newsweek, May 18, 1953**

The parade marched on Monday afternoon, rescheduled to begin after Pete's funeral, and the pageant began Monday night. After all the horror of the weekend and the grief over the loss of two of the celebration's hard-working leaders, a bit of humor occurred at the GMC football stadium. Several of the horses scheduled to appear in the pageant escaped; two of the wranglers who captured them were teenage girls. The crowd cheered when they realized the pageant would continue with all livestock on hand.

MARION STEMBRIDGE REVEALED AFTER DEATH

Stembridge was a business man who ran a grocery store, and most folks did not know about his loan-shark business. Eva Sloan represented several members of the black community to end their interest payments that over time exceeded the face value of their loans.

Stembridge's net worth rose to more than a half-million from the loan-shark business. He also gained real estate by lending money to landowners and when they did not pay the loan, he foreclosed. The Baldwin County Index to Deeds for 1946-1948 show two and a half pages of security deeds granted to Stembridge. See Appendix 11.

Strange stories came to light after his death. Chief Eugene Ellis let it be known what he found during his investigation.

Stembridge had left his wife and moved into the Baldwin Hotel. His room was secured with several locks. Ellis reported Stembridge had a collection of firearms, enough to prevent his arrest if the police had to enter his room. Everyone found it strange that Stembridge had two books in his room and wondered at the side of him perhaps seeking comfort and advice from the Bible and from Carnegie. There had to be some good there, somewhere, and it appeared he hoped to better himself with faith and behavior toward others. He knew he was mentally ill and had tried to get help.

Ellis in later interviews did not mention sheets of metal above and below the bed, nor did his wife in her divorce petition.

In her attempt to break his will, however, Sara stated he had fits of temper and rages of anger which left her in constant fear. He also slept with a pistol under his pillow, and a film of metal under the mattress on his side of the bed.

Years later, Eva laughed about attorney Bob Green, who heard the shooting and crawled under his desk, the only bit of humor associated with the events of that morning.

A story that circulated from that morning through the years is that law enforcement officers found a "hit list" in Stembridge's pocket. Rumors varied as to who was on the list. As well as the two men he had killed, Stembridge had apparently planned to kill Shep Baldwin, who prosecuted him; Eva Sloan, who helped the blacks regain excessive interest Stembridge had charged. Also on the list were said to be both Cleve Cooper and Judge George Carpenter.

Frank Bell was said to be on the list also, because he too had handled lawsuits for some of the blacks against him. Stembridge had tried to open Frank's door between the time he killed Ennis and the time he reached Pete, but the door was locked. Frank had gone around to the bank and was talking to his brother Buck at the time. Frank had planned to be in his office for an appointment that morning, but the client had postponed the meeting by a phone call.

The only paper officially reported to be in Stembridge's pocket that May morning was his handwritten note that he didn't want to be sentenced for a crime he did not commit, written the day before.

His sister Mildred also said the note about serving justice was the only written item in his pocket. The statement included: "I will not be able to do my full duty. I can do only the best that I can."

That sentence was taken to mean he had a planned-inside-his-head list of those he would kill. His note included a statement that he was innocent of any crime and was framed. It was dated the day before the shooting.

That early rumor still lives in Milledgeville, and apparently is more than just a rumor. Eva told me she learned from a police officer there was a list, but in Stembridge's briefcase. She was on the list.

Pete Bivins and Ennis each kept a loaded gun in his office after Stembridge started berating them and accusing Ennis of bribing the jury and of not putting on a defense. But Ennis had not been able to reach his weapon that day. Neither had Pete. His secretary confirmed reports that he wrestled a pistol from Stembridge as he died.

Some considered him paranoid, especially since he collected his own urine and stored it in the cooler in his grocery, to have it tested for poison. Rumors also indicated he would eat only canned food so no one could poison him, and that he suspected his wife of trying to poison him. Sara herself stated he had sheets of metal installed under the mattress so no one could kill him with X-rays while he slept. He was known to carry a pistol.

Culver Kidd said when Stembridge lived in the house, "You had to go through about ten locks and chains he had on the door."

Sara turned some of the rumors into facts when she challenged the will. She testified that he slept with a pistol and that there was indeed metal sheeting under the mattress. He was afraid of being poisoned so ate only canned food and refused what she cooked. He also feared his sister was trying to poison him, but included her in his will. Chief Ellis acknowledged finding the collected urine in the store refrigerator.

Some people who knew him described Stembridge as "plain, ugly and big framed." Some considered him still handsome in his fifties. His draft papers described him as *blue-eyed* with *brown hair*.

Others, however, considered him a real charmer, always impeccably dressed, always excessively polite. Some thought he had bad eyesight because of the "Coke-bottle-thick" glasses he wore.

As late as 2023 stories circulated that he was buried seven feet down to have a head start to hell. But Moore's Funeral Home was in charge of the burial, and the funeral home's reputation alone is enough to put that rumor away.

TRUE OR *FALSE* WORD AROUND TOWN THEN AND NOW

Many stories circulate even in 2023 about the actions of Stembridge, his wife and local residents. These stories may or may not be true, but each one is interesting when we consider Stembridge's unpredictable behaviors.

Stembridge met someone on the street he planned to kill but did not recognize him because the intended victim had grown a beard for the Sesquicentennial. **Probably true**. Believed to have been Shep Baldwin.

Stembridge's mother had him committed to the Georgia Insane Asylum. **Not so.**

Sara Stembridge, then teaching at a public school in Dublin, supposedly was asked on Monday May 4, if she wanted the day off, wasn't that her husband who was killed over the weekend. She is said to have replied, "No I don't need a day off. I married him for his money and he never shared any and I am not going to lose a day's pay over his death." **True or not, unknown**.

Marion Stembridge was insane. **True**, but today we call it "mentally ill," and consider his condition an illness rather than a crime, until a crime is committed. Legally, the culprit is likely to be found "not guilty by reason of insanity" **IF** the accused does not know the difference between right and wrong. Stembridge's note about doing justice indicated he thought killing his victims was an act of justice, not a crime.

Stembridge had a law degree from University of Georgia. **Not so.** He had a college degree from a small state college—the Georgia College of Agriculture—that was later absorbed by the University. But UGA has no record of his attending either UGA itself or its associated law school.

He married Sara Terry to have someone to do his books. **Perhaps so**, since she worked long hours at his store according to her divorce petition, but Stembridge himself was said to be brilliant with math.

In the Milledgeville *Union-Recorder,* September 5, 2008, Johnathan Jackson reported that according to published accounts, Ennis grew uncomfortable with the case and ended his legal representation of Stembridge. Stembridge was tried again and convicted, but was released again. **NOT SO.** Jimmy Watts, **vice-president of Stembridge Banking Company,** received the response of the State Court of Appeals, but Ennis was still on the three-man team for the appeal; there was no second trial for that shooting. Stembridge's second trial was for tax evasion and attempted bribery of federal officials. A third trial, never held, would have been for the perjury charges in a case involving a mortgage.

After his conviction for manslaughter, Stembridge accused Ennis of using the retainer he'd paid to bribe the jury to convict him. One story I have not been able to verify is *Stembridge asked Pete to appeal the case and Pete had taken the job because he was new in town and needed some business so he'd have some income.* Pete's name did not appear on the Bill of Exception for the appeal, however, so he was not on that team. Only the original three were listed: Frank O. Evans, James Watts and Marion Ennis.

Gracie Childers wrote online in October 2021: *Marion Ennis, Baldwin Country's district attorney, decided to reopen the case against Stembridge, as he wasn't comfortable with the fact that Marion had escaped without consequences. Ennis enlisted the help of another Milledgeville attorney, Stephen T. Bivins, to help bring justice to Stembridge.*

Personal response: *Ennis was not the county's district attorney but a member of the three-man defense team who sought to have him found not guilty. Ennis's name does not show on the appeal response document, so he apparently was not the primary attorney, but not being the primary did not indicate he wanted another trial. Stembridge was not getting off "without consequences," even though the sentence seemed light. Stembridge was appealing the verdict. I cannot believe an attorney with even the lowest ethics would attempt to have his own client re-tried for a different verdict; "retrial" is handled as an appeal, not as a new procedure before a traverse jury.*

Federal authorities learned and later successfully proved in court, that Stembridge had not paid federal taxes for several years. It was a widely held belief at the time that Ennis and Bivins uncovered evidence that resulted in Stembridge's conviction on tax evasion charges. Stembridge himself also held that belief.

They may all have been wrong, however. In his conversations with the FBI agent he introduced to me as Vic Mills, Bob Sloan might have suggested Vic get his friends in the Agency to investigate Stembridge. Bob and Eva knew Stembridge was well-to-do from his loan shark—cash—business.

MAY 2, 1953

THE SESQUICENTENNIAL

MILLEDGEVILLE'S 150TH BIRTHDAY PARTY

With the town in shock the Sesquicentennial committee decided to cancel the entire celebrations. The wives, now widows, of both Marion Ennis and Pete Bivins said no, continue the events. But the committee made changes.

They cancelled the period ball set for the evening of May 2. Attendees were to dress in clothing as worn by the well-to-do, elite of 1803. Long dresses and formal wear of the times. How long does it take a committee to call on landlines, some having to be connected by operators, to reach those who had purchased tickets, with some of the dancers not local but visitors? To cancel the orchestra? To notify the ballroom there would be no dance? But the men managed, I am sure with a lot of help from wives and friends…while the ladies wept for their friends who died and tried to offer sympathy to their families.

CHURCH SERVICES
May 3, Sunday

As part of the Sesquicentennial celebrations, Sunday had been designated *Interfaith Day.* All churches were encouraged to celebrate homecoming and the founding of their churches.

CONCERT
May 3, Sunday, 3:00 p.m.

The GMC band was to hold a concert at Davenport Field (drill field and football field). At 4:00 p.m. the Al Sihah Temple Band from Macon would perform on the same field. I do not know if these concerts were held or cancelled.

FUNERAL FOR MARION ENNIS
May 3, Sunday, 5:00 p. m.

By AGNES McCARTY
Constitution Staff Writer

MILLEDGEVILLE, May 3—Shocked and grief-stricken citizens paid final tribute Sunday to Marion Ennis, 45, attorney, one of the victims of a double murder and suicide Saturday which turned this historic Baldwin County community from a festival mood to one of tragic mourning.

Ennis and Stephen T. Bivins, 27, another attorney, were slain by Marion Stembridge, 63, grocer and banker, who then ended his own life on the eve of the city's sesquicentennial observance, a coroner's jury ruled.

Simple rites for Ennis were held at 5 p. m. Sunday at the Hardwick Christian Church, with the Rev. Roy Barnett and the Rev. John Houghston of the Milledgeville Baptist Church officiating. The board of deacons served as pallbearers and burial was in Memory Hill Cemetery.

Funeral services for Bivins will be held at 3 p. m. Monday at Milledgeville Presbyterian Church with Dr. H. Kerr Taylor and the Rev. Houghston officiating.

Ennis is survived by his wife, the former Antoinette Bonner of Morgan County; two children, Oscar Marion Jr., 15, and Marianne, 6; his father, Oscar Ennis of Milledgeville; a brother, Jordan Ennis of Tullahoma, Tenn., and two sisters, Mrs. Fred Couch and Mrs. Charles Tucker, of Anniston, Ala.

PETE BIVINS SERVICES
May 4, Sunday 3:00 P.M.

Pete's obituary, printed after the funeral, indicated how much the people of Milledgeville loved him. It began, "Hundreds of mourners filled the First Presbyterian Church, its vestibule and grounds Monday afternoon when funeral services were held for Stephen Thomas Bivins, 27-year-old native of Milledgeville who was one of the two victims in last Saturday's tragedy."

The church's seating capacity was 250, but a few more could squeeze into already full pews. The overflow crowd outnumbered those early enough to find a seat inside.

Pete's obituary was also carried by the *Cornell News,* Vol. 55, No. 17, p. 20, June 1, 1953.

'46, '47 AB—Stephen Thomas Bivins, attorney in Milledgeville, Ga., was shot by an insane person, May 2, 1953. During World War II, he was a first Lieutenant, US Army, for three years in the Philippines. His address was Pendale, Milledgeville.

The *Journal of the American Ornithology Society* (The Auk), Vol 71, Issue 4, July 1954, carried an announcement of his death.

STEPHEN THOMAS BIVINS, an Associate of the American Ornithologists' Union since 1946, died at Milledgeville, Georgia, May 2, 1953. Death resulted from the action of an insane person. He was born in Milledgeville on October 30, 1925. After graduating with first honors from Georgia Military College, he entered Cornell University at the age of sixteen and in due course obtained a degree in zoology. Majoring in ornithology under Professor A. A. Allen, he accompanied the latter on many of his photographic trips. Subsequently he took a degree in law at Duke University. His education was interrupted by a call to the Army in 1943. During his service as First Lieutenant in the field artillery in the Pacific and in the Philippine Islands, he contracted a tropical disease and was invalided home. He began the practice of law in Milledgeville in 1950.

His interest in birds, shown at the age of six, continued throughout his life. On the average he lectured on birds once a month. A talk for young people stressed "shooting" birds with a camera instead of a gun. He taught biology for one term at Georgia Military College and engaged in bird-banding for many years. Always interested in young people, he devoted much time to the Boy Scouts. He was a member of the Georgia Ornithological Society, National Audubon Society, and Bird-Banding Association. Unfortunately he had not reached the stage where sufficient leisure was available to commit his bird studies to print. In remembrance of his pleasing personality and other admirable qualities, the new Civic Youth Center of Milledgeville was dedicated to him.—A. W. SCHORGER.

TOUR OF HOMES
May 4, Monday

The Tour of Homes included 13 homes and public buildings, all but one erected before the War Between the States. The Governor's Mansion, the official residence from the years Milledgeville was the capital, was on the tour; in 1953 it was the residence for the president of the Georgia State College for Women.

Also on the tour was the Rockwell Mansion, which had served as residence for the Georgia Governor during the building of the official Governor's Mansion.

In 1953, the Rockwell Mansion was home of the Marion Ennis and his family. It was immediately taken off the tour after his death.

Personal Note: *The house was home to my great-grandfather S. P. Myrick and my grandfather was born there. In 1953, the Ennis family was friends with my family, and their son, Buddy, was classmate with my sister Lil.*

The house was built for Samuel Rockwell about 1832 by Joseph Lane, Sr. Other owners include Governor Herschel V. Johnson. The fence enclosing the grounds is said to have cost almost as much as the house itself. The fence was cast by Dugal Fern and Brothers of Milledgeville.

PARADE
May 4, Monday, 4:30 p.m.

The grand parade was scheduled to begin at 3:30 p.m. Monday, but the start time was moved to 4:30 so as not to overlap with the funeral services for Pete Bivins.

The Queen's Court, with Betty McMillian Sesquicentennial Queen, highlighted the parade. Members of the court were Sallie Moore, runner-up, which automatically made her Miss Baldwin County. Other members were Mary Joyce Pritchard, Gloria Ann Erwin, Thulia Lindsley, Essie Mae Prosser, Joanne McCluney, Nancy Mudge, Virginia Veal, Mary Anne Berry, Emily Hodges, Denise Cox, Sue Herndon, Carolyn Fowler, Ria Bouchillon, and Louise McKnight.

THE HILLS OF HOME

May 4, Monday Evening

Opening presentation of the pageant *The Hills of Home* began on schedule Monday evening. A cast of 500 local citizens presented the history of Milledgeville, from its "origin through a century and a half of glorious history." The pageant was held nightly at Davenport Field, the parade ground for the local Georgia Military College.

Whatever tears the cast shed for Pete and Ennis stayed hidden from the audience and the show went on.

Not scheduled was the escape of the horses, which fled down toward the Oconee River, into Hamp Brown Bottom, named for, a blacksmith/preacher/real estate investor. Once a thriving social and business area for the black population, the area has now been cleared of all human habitation and has become a park/walkway known as the Greenway. Lil Lindsley (James) was one of the wranglers who chased and returned the horses to their backstage "green room."

The pageant cast included town folks from youngsters in grade school to the older citizens; the Crack Squad from GMC performed; those with musical voices sang; the history of a town flowed across Davenport Field nightly for a week. Classmates, neighbors, politicians, store keepers, country residents performed for others, and also for each other as they united a town torn apart on Saturday morning.

Peabody High School classmates, childhood friends and neighbors who took part in the events remained friends throughout life. A few cast members are shown here.

June Kitchens (Smith)   **Ria Bouchillon (Veal)**   **Dollie Hardee (Brookins)**
                                   On the Queen's Court

Patricia Bass (Riner)

Thulia Lindsley (Bramlett)
On Queens Court

Aubrey Nelson

Selma Fennell (Adams)

Carolyn Fowler (Smith)
On the Queen's Court

THE OLD CAPITAL HISTORICAL SOCIETY

presents

"The Hills of Home"

A JOHN B. ROGERS PRODUCTION

Davenport Field, G.M.C.   Milledgeville, Georgia

May 4, 5, 6, 7, 8, 9, 1953 — 8:00 P.M.

Lloyd West, Managing Director   Edmund Najaimey, Associate Director

Mrs. Edward Bass, General Chairman

SESQUICENTENNIAL COURT OF HONOR

HER MAJESTY, SESQUICENTENNIAL QUEEN, MISS MILLEDGEVILLE,

MISS BETTYE McMILLIN AND MISS BALDWIN COUNTY,

MISS SALLIE MOORE

PRINCESSES OF THE ROYAL COURT:

Mary Joyce Pritchard	Marianne Berry
Gloria Ann Erwin	Emily Hodges
Thulia Lindsley	Dennise Cox
Essie Mae Prosser	Sue Herndon
JoAnne McCluney	Carolyn Fowler
Nancy Mudge	Ria Bouchillon
Virginia Veal	Louise McKnight

Narrators: Joe Dukes, Mrs. W. C. Battle, John H. Gore, Mrs. M. R. Bell

At The Baldwin Console: Mrs. Bill Oxford

Sesquicentennial Choir Under Direction of Dr. Max Noah

Choreographer: Dr. Barbara L. Page Beiswanger

Synopsis of Scenes

Prologue—

Dedicated to THEIR MAJESTIES, MISS MILLEDGE-

VILLE — MISS BALDWIN COUNTY

1. A fanfare of trumpets herald the arrival of Our Sesquicentennial Queens, Miss Milledgeville and Miss Baldwin County as Their Majesties, surrounded by The Sesquicentennial Princesses, The Ladies-In-Waiting, Pages and Color-Bearers make their entrance .... Down through the Avenue of Flags of The United States and The United Nations comes the Royal Entourage, as the United Nation Representatives and The Patriotic Ensembles pay homage to The Queens .... All bow in attendance as Their Majesties step forward for the Ceremony of Coronation.

INDIAN SEQUENCE—

2. An early representative scene of the Creek Indians who considered this area as their favorite hunting ground. A friendly White-Trader pauses in his travels and shares in the Indian Ceremonial, Passing of the Peace Pipe.

3. McGillivary and His Chiefs were lavishly entertained and bribed into a treaty which extinguished the Indian title to all land east of the Oconee, but which reaffirmed the Creek's claim to all lands west of that river.

EARLY MILLEDGEVILLE Sequence—

4. Land Lottery of Georgia was conceived and used with great success as a most democratic way of disposing of tracts of land.

5. JOHN MILLEDGE, whose name our famous city bears stands out for his many contributions and devoted loyalty to his state.

6. Abraham Baldwin not only established the first State University but was chosen president of the body of trustees for Franklin college, holding this position for 14 years.

7. A great Military Ball was planned to climax the visit of General Lafayette to Georgia's Capital in 1825.

8. The Red Old Hills. Soil exhaustation and the ease of migration formed a vicious combination which threatened early calamity to ante-bellum life in the community.

9. Early Church. The early settlers expressed their fervent need for the strength of God.

War Between the States Sequence.

10. Abolitionist — There began to blow a dark wind from the North .... it was the breath of the abolitionists, whispering rebellion in the night.

11. GEORGIA SECEDES FROM THE UNION. After a long and heated debate, Georgia proclaims herself a free and sovereign state.

12. Confederate States Rally To The Cause. The men in Grey march away to war. The widows and the old stay at home only to witness the tragedies and heartbreaks left in the pathway of a nation at war.

13. Reconstruction Days— "The South was left a helpless, shattered prey under the carpet baggers cruel sway.

14. Gay 90's SEQUENCE. The day of the high-wheel bike, the barber shop quartetes, Nostalgic memories make the oldsters cry, "Those were the Days!"

15. PARADE OF THE LOVELIES — "May I go out to swim?" Ladies rarely did, but the bathing suits—what a sight!

TURN OF THE CENTURY—

16. G.M.C. and G.S.C.W. A scene to emphasize the contributions these two institutions have made, not only nationally, but to Milledgeville itself, a contribution of leadership and high ideals.

17. WORLD WAR 1. Our respects to the memories of those who served in the first World War.

18. Roaring 20's—The "Flapper" and the "get rich quick." Oh, yes, remember the Charleston!

19. World War II. Where were you that Sunday, December 7, 1941? War was declared the next day. Final results?—Peace, but at what a cost!

20. Finale. The entire cast presents a spectacular finish in a vast human Wheel of Progress. This is climaxed by a tremendous fireworks display each evening.

Prologue

COLOR GUARDS—

G.M.C.—
Franklin Cason, Roy Alford, Jr., Donald Gibbs, William D. Kennedy, Jr.

Baldwin County National Guard—
SFC M. A. Eubanks, Sgt. Charles H. Sloan, Sgt. James R. Adams, Pvt. Charlie C. Grimes.

Girl Scouts—
Rebecca Worsham, Ginger Bell, Jarnette Reynolds, Mary Elizabeth Bailey, Janice Jordan, Margaret Giddings, Page Bonner, Shirley Reeves, Beth Houghston, Barbara Ashfield, Barbara Green, Glenna Thompson, Martha Baum, Valette Jordan, Faye Powell, Carl Franklin,, Dolores Bailey, Sandra Stone.

Boy Scouts—
Johnnie Parker, Perry Walker, Johnny Holland, Harry Stevens, Pat Rogers, Miles Golden, Jim Tillman, Tillman Wyatt, Walker McKnight, Billy Manning, John McMillan, Ramsey Parker, Emory Buffington, Ronny Holmes, Wilton McGowan, Calvin Rice, Billie Peabody, Johnnie Overstreet, Jr., Donald Falvey, Kenneth Moody, Joel Curry, Charles Cary, David Gore, Tom Banks.

4-H Girls—
Harriet Gillman, Sandra Brantley, Patricia Reynolds, Anne Dorrough, Patsy Brown, Kay Ward, Marcia Farmer, Charlene Deason.

4-H Boys—
Ray Harris, Jimmie Meeks, Clement Pennington, Roland Miller, Jordan Flourey, Wendell Veal, Jimmy Fountain, Clifford Pennington.

Miss Columbia — Margaret Bass

States—
Sara Frances Powers, Adelia Torrance, Virginia Hollis, Nancy Carrier, Jonnie Lewis, Louise Brookins, Judith Kemp, Leslie Hardee, Gail Bradley, Margaret Jones, Caroline Logue, Sandra Combes, Susan Kaler, Doris Garland, Patricia Bass, Patsy Williams.

Nations' Queen —
Pat Davis, Selma Fennell, Lucille Humbert, June Kitchens, Beverly King, Ruby Towns.

Cadets—
Marjorie Polk, Ann Owen, Marion Williams, Sue Albert, Harold Joe Mays, Faye Teague, Patsy Smith, Freeda Mac Arthur, Mary Ethridge, Joyce Huff, Virginia Layfield, Mary Jo Holloway.

Jackies—
Jacqueline Hercin, Gwendolyn Lewis, Dorothy Ezell, Coressa Veal, Janice Segars, Jeanette Prather, Mary Anna Worsham, Amelia Adams, Jean Grace, Eleanor Seals, Myrna Mathews, Joyce Henry, Louise MacDonald, Pinkie Wilson, Peggy Sessions, Betty Jo Faulkner, Millie Dunn.

Trumpeters—
Margaret Stapleton, Dollia Hardee, Mackey Brown, Alice Scott, Leah Renfroe, Inez Layfield.

Episode 1. INDIAN, Sequence—
Alexander Mc Gillivary, Chief of the Creeks—
Major C. W. Crawford
A local Chief — Major David Black
White Trader — Larry Willoughby

Indian Villagers—
Laddy Rogers, Benjamin Roberts, Harold Freeman, Joseph Brown, Pat Parker, Frank Evans, Jr, Edward Robinson, Jr., Linda Smith, Diane McDade, Imogene Tanner, Genelle Mixon, Yvonne Janes, Shirley Hines, Kathleen Layfield, Janet Adams, Juanita Sauls, Martha Ann Adams,

Diane McCoy, Faye Tanner, Jimmy Chandler, Edgar Chambers, Tommy Moore, Beau Farr, Hank Falvey, John Barron, Becky Payne, Maggie Ann Brookins, Jeanine Tyre, Norma Dodd, Erin Turner, Dixie Dixon, Pat Porker, Betty Blizzard, Jackie McCluney, Laveda McMullen, Mary Janette Avant, Bill Curry, Bob Sheppard, Robert Smith, Eddie Harrison, Joe Digby, Barbara Ann Layfield, Don Neal, Hal Scott, Wilma Janes, George DuPree, Mike Brooks, Mark Hodges, Jr., Virginia Sadler, Elizabeth Brannen, Cecelia White, Nat Smith, John P. Baum, Jr., Samuel M. Goodrich, Phylis Veal, Eunice Wilson, Jack McCluney, Louise Brown, Wadad Khazin, Abla Kawar, Dido Christian.

EARLY MILLEDGEVILLE

Araham Baldwin — Arnold Parker
John Milledge — Robert H. Green
General LaFayette — Guy Roberts
Samuel Carswell — Royce Smith
Augustus B. Longstreet of Richmond County — George C. Dupree, Sr.
Elizabeth Floyd of Chatham County — Mrs. J. L. Hitchcock
Auctioneer of Lottery — Reynolds Allen
Minister — Hugh Y. Cook
Plantation owner — George Powers.

Other Settlers—
Mrs. Hansell Hall, Miss Martha Thomas, Mrs. J. L. Sibley, Sr., Mrs. J. G. Lunsford, Mrs. Boyd Butts, Jr., Boyd Butts, Jr., Mrs. George C. Dupree, Sr., Mrs. Royce Smith, Mrs. Charlie Pennington, Mrs. W. H. Johnson, Mrs. M.M. Crooms, Mrs. E. Y. Walker, Sr., Mrs. E. Y. Walker, Jr., Mrs. Marion McMillan, Mrs. Hugh Y. Cook, Mrs. O. L. Mills, Miss Alice Hardee, Miss Mildred Hardee, Mrs. Sarah Lloyd, Reginald Hatcher, Mrs. Binion Wood, Mrs. Joby Edgar, Joby Edgar, Mrs. J. B. Knowles, Mrs. J. L. Blackwell, Mrs. Jere N. Moore, Jere N. Moore, Mrs. Marion Ennis, Marion Ennis, Mrs. George Powers, Sr., Mrs. W. M. Martin, W. M. Martin, Katherine Spassell, Davie Lyon, Frances Miller, Imogene Hanson, Ann Overstreet, Martha Marion Garner, Catherine Garner, Wade Hughston, Sara Ann McMillan, Aubrey Nelson Darenda Lunsford, Janel Pennington, Jerry Mills, Edward Lloyd, Carol Ann Rice, Marcelyn Edgar, Larry Edgar, Garland Overstreet, Dale Dupree, Edwina Moore, Madge Bell.

LAFAYETTE BALL DANCERS

Girls—
Jackie Anderson, Helen Barnhill, Ruth Dixon, Anne Hodges, Mary Fayne Hicks, Vivian James, Joan Klecan, Jackie Lankford, Patricia Miller, Hannah Ray, Sally Robison, Betty Jane Rogers, Romana Sims, Mary Margaret Spottiswoode, Peggy Ann Von Pippin, Lee Lee Wheeler.

Boys—
Max Faulk, Dick Rhine, Tom Hall, Raymond Molina, Mack Davis, Don Taylor, Allan Drake, Eddie Toler, George Hearn, Bill Beck, Charles Sloan, Tony Esquivel, Jim Foster, Johnny Martin.

THE WAR BETWEEN THE STATES SEQUENCE
General William T. Sherman — Stewart Barnes, Sr.
Abraham Lincoln — Otto C. Morrison

Yankee Soldiers—
Claude Brookins Beck, Glen Phillips, James Tyson Radford, William Aaron Gibson, Eddie Clyde Toler, Jerry Roach, Carlton Ellington, Miss Frances Williams, Mrs. John Baum, Sr.

Prologue

(Continued)

Confederate Soldiers—

SFC Robert Tredway, SFC James Vinson, M/Sgt. Charles Cheeves, 2nd Lt. Bobby Jones, Pvt. Mack Bryan, M-Sgt. Thomas Stephens, SFC Ronnie Parker, M-Sgt. Max Faulk, 2nd. Lt. Walter Toulson.

Citizens of Milledgeville—

T. E. Owens, Sr., John Baum, Sr., Mrs. C. S. Baldwin, Miss Bertie Stembridge, Mrs. Aubrey Jones, Mrs. George Carpenter, Miss Alice Hall, Mrs. Ben Wade, Ben Wade, W. F. Mudge, Hoyt Brown, Mrs. Otto Morrison, Mrs. Roland Dickinson, Roland Dickinson, Dick Moore, Jake Nash, Pete Cheeves, Mrs. Joe H. McKenzie, Joe H. McKenzie, H. H. Payne, Mrs. Steve Dillard, Carol Hooks, Beth Brown, Charlotte Brown, Mary Vinson, Joe Dewberry, Kenneth Aikins, Pat Teague, Herbert Meyer, Russell Walden, Ray Bouchillon, Frank Hines, Alling Jones, Joy Dickinson, Mrs. Linton Fowler, Jacqueline Marsh, Jane Spooner, Sallie Howell, Ann Adams, Norma Teele, Mrs. Jon Hutchinson, Mrs. T. P. Allen, Ennise McDade, Mrs. Clara McDade, Mr. W. A. Hemphill, Jr., Joe F. Specht, Mrs. Guy Wells.

RECONSTRUCTION DAYS—

Uncle Remus — C. S. Baldwin
Aunt Minerva Ann — Miss Sandra Sammons

THE BEAUTY SPECIALS OF G. N. & I. C.

Imogene Hanson, LaVance Clement, Betty Powell, Betty Jo Caruth, Betty Jo McCormick, Ann Waters, Mary Elizabeth Mosely, Barbara Batchelor, Carolyn Cloats, Jean Manning, Ann Adams, Jeanne Brannan, Carmen Davis, Barbara Shellhorse, Margaret Bean, Etta Lee McDaniel.

CRACK SQUAD OF G.M.C.—

SFC Robert Tredway
SFC James Vinson
M-Sgt. Charles Cheeves
2nd Lt. Bobby Jones
Pvt. Mack Bryan
M-Sgt. Thomas Stephens
SFC Ronnie Parker
M-Sgt. Max Faulk
2nd Lt. Walter Toulson

FIVE-PIECE BAND

Buster Smith
John Roberts
Donald Sikes
Morris Watkins
Billy Hammond

THE GAY NINETIES—

Mrs. Evelyn Boone, Mrs. Jane Waldhauer, Bill Waldhauer, Allen Drake, Lorine Sauls, Mrs. W. C. McFarland, Mrs. Sue A. Brooks, Jeanine Rich, Peggie Ann Von Pippin, Dorothy Alford, Huie Alford, Polly Daniels, Phyllis Spivey, Margaret Ivey, Dean Rogers, Mrs. Robert Pursley, Robert Pursley, Gus Dunn, Patricia McMullen, Beverly Horton, Kay King, Mrs. V. C. Johns, Ann Adams, Melody Merritt, Marie Johns, Helen Ann Taylor, Linda Miller, Mrs. Joseph Muldrow, Col. Joseph Muldrow, Charles Pennington, John Ferguson, Charles Hodges, Jimmie Powell, Dee Fuller, Peter Dexter, Mrs. Reyna Williamson, Reyna Williamson, Mrs. Bill Carrier, Bill Carrier, Mrs. Edwin Scott, Dr. Edwin Scott.

THE ROARING TWENTIES—

Millionaire — Pete Bivins
Flapper — Helen Bivins

Dancers—

Gene Tate, Dixie Dixon, William Curl, Dorothy Nell

Fann, Hank Falvey, Barbara Batchelor, Jane Waldhauer, Bill Waldhauer.

World War 1—Doughboy
SFC. J. W. Mathews.

World War II—

Mother—Mrs. Robert G. Sloan
Father—Robert G. Sloan
Son—Will Rogers
Daughter—Patsy Daniel

Iowa Jima—

Sgt. W. M. Holsenbeck, Sgt. E. R. Holsenbeck, PFC J. M. Holsenbeck, Pfc. Walter Johnson.

Navy—

Lt. Commander Benjamin E. Harrison

Army—

Frank Davis

Marines—

Austin Duckworth
Air Force—H.W.Thompson
WAVE—Mrs. John Kidd
WAAC—Mrs. Jim Kidd
Marine—Miss Edith Horn

Finale—

ENTIRE CAST—

COMMUNITY CHOIR MEMBERS—

Mrs. Olin Banks, Mr. Jack Birchall, Mrs. Stephen Bivins, Mr. John Black, Miss Ruth Carroll, Mrs. J. R. Curl, Mrs. Arthur Dunlap, Mr. Arthur Dunlap, Miss Frances Epps, Mrs. Manley Eskin, Mrs. Hines Ennis, Mrs. A. E. Falvey, Mr. A. E. Falvey, Mrs. Fairfield, Mrs. Lee Fuller, Mrs. Alma Giles, Mr. Herbert Green,, Dr. Frances Hicks, Mr. J. Belton Hammond, Mrs John Holloway, Mrs. Harold Hunter, Miss Maggie Jenkins, Dr. Clyde Keeler, Mrs. Gussie T. King, Mr. J. B. Lindsley, Mrs. R. E. Long, Mrs. Ray Nesbitt, Mrs Max Noah, Mr. John Parker, Mrs. Clayton Peacock, Mrs. J. R. Rogers, Dr. J. R. Rogers, Mr. Harris Rogers, Mrs. R.T. Shreve, Mrs. Thomas Stembridge, Mrs. Charlie Simpson, Mr. W. T. Thompson.

—A CAPPELLA CHOIR—

Julia Frances Adams, Myra Louise Bagwell, John A. Barron, Helen Elizabeth Ball, Melton Monroe Bonner, Cornelia Bostick, Mary Webb Bradbury, Gayle Elizabeth Christensen, Betty Churchwell, Mary Carolyn Cook, Frances Elizabeth Crawford, Barbara Ann Driver, Patricia Ann Dunaway, Ida Jane, Elrod, Pauline Jones Farr, Latham Webb Faulk, Thomas Felix Fendley, Thomas S. Freeman, Rita Garner, Jacqueline Garrett, Lucy Berry Gay, Patsy Griffin, Shirley Ann Hall, Helen Ward Harrell, Natalie King Harrison, Robert Edward Harrison, Jane Henderson, Nan Smith Hoover, Eddie Gilford Hollingsworth, Saralyn Ivey, Edith Ramona Johnson.

Patricia Ann Johnson, Wesley Law, Patricia Long, James Hyman Lyons, Harriet May, Ella Jean Mitchell, Jimmie Mae McConnell, Ann Louise McKnight, Margueicia Ann Dunaway, Ida Jane Elrod, Pauline Jones Farr, Ann Smith, Lattie Elizabeth Stancil, Jean Lemos Starr, Carol Stone, Mary Byrne Stover, Ora Eugene Tate, Florence Alma Taylor, Patsy Thomas.

Barbara Grace Thompson, Mary Gail Thompson, Laura Dell Trapnell, Barbara Claire Unglesbee, Charlotte Frazia Warren, M. Carolyn Webb, Elinor Jeanne Williams.

Celestine Sibley of the *Atlanta-Journal-Constitution*, the South's leading columnist, wrote a raving review of the opening-night performance. She did not hesitate to refer to the events that almost cancelled the weeks' celebrations.

No mother saddened by tragic death in the family in the midst of preparations for a beloved child's birthday party ever rallied more bravely than did the old town of Milledgeville as it hid its grief over the Saturday slaying of two of its leading citizens and put its best foot forward to receive the first of 10,000 visitors to attend the week-long sesquicentennial celebration.

The death of attorneys Marion Ennis and Stephen Bivins before the blazing gun of banker-grocer Marion Stembridge Saturday was still uppermost in many minds, but as soon as the second funeral, that Bivins, was over at 4 p. m., the town turned resolutely to staging "the finest 150th birthday party for the finest town in the U. S. A." (Rites for Stembridge who killed himself after the double murder will be held privately Tuesday.)

TUESDAY, MAY 5, STEMBRIDGE SERVICES

Marion Stembridge's funeral rated two paragraphs in the local paper.

Rites Held For Mr. Stembridge Tuesday Morning

Private funeral services were conducted Tuesday morning for Marion W. Stembridge, the rites taking place at 10:30 a.m. at the home of his sister, Mrs. L. N. Callaway. Burial was in Memory Hill Cemetery.

Mr. Stembridge, who was 60 years of age, is survived by his mother, Mrs. J. W. Stembridge, who makes her home in Laurinburg, N. C.; one brother, Roger Stembridge of Milledgeville, three sisters, Mrs. Callaway of Milledgeville, Miss Thelma Stembridge of Arlington, Va., and Mrs. Edward Beeman of Laurinburg, N.C

It was a time for family, not for visitors or the press or angry locals to curse them. In such a situation, family unites, remembers the good and prays the evil will be buried with their brother.

Graveside services were conducted by Joe Moore of Moore's Funeral Home. He asked some friends to attend so there would be someone besides the undertaker at the burial. A boy was asked if he wanted to go; he did, and years later he wrote a moving essay about the burial ceremony (Kelley Kidd, The Most Important Story of My Long Life: Part II, *journalofpubliclaw.org/ page 2/* December 27, 2020).

Jere Moore of *The Union-Recorder* also wrote a lengthy editorial about the events and the effects on the community (Appendix 12).

Marion Stembridge was buried in the east side of Memory Hill Cemetery, section B, lot 22.

MAY 5

The Baldwin County government could not function without legal advice for the Commissioners. They selected Eva since she had served them in partnership with Ennis. She was no longer his secretary, but had been his partner and an attorney for years.

Mrs. Sloan Gets Ennis' Place

MILLEDGEVILLE, Ga., May 6 (P)—Mrs. Eva Sloan, secretary to Marion Ennis who was slain last week in a double murder and suicide, was elected yesterday to succeed Ennis as county attorney and clerk of the Baldwin County Board of Commissioners.

She was selected by the three-member board of commissioners.

Mrs. Sloan, 43, studied law with Ennis and was admitted to the bar in January, 1952. She is the mother of four children and grandmother of two. Her husband, Robert G. Sloan, is a county employe in the Alcoholic Beverage Revenue Department.

STEMBRIDGE'S WILL

Stembridge wrote his will in longhand in January 1951, after he moved out of the home he shared with Sara, abandoning her on July 31,1949. His handwriting was not easy to read, but it stood up in court.

The will in readable form:
January 1951

Georgia, Baldwin County

I, Marion W. Stembridge, of said county and state being of sound mind but realizing the insecurity of life, do make this my last will and testament. I made a previous will some years ago but this previous will was made void by my later marriage.

I am informed that it will be necessary for me to give to my legal wife a certain share of my estate and I am sorry that this is true. I am not able to avoid the thought that if she had brought to our marriage the love, the enthusiasm, and the willingness to work that I felt; our answer would have been different. After neater consideration, it is my unqualified belief that she married me for what she hoped to get out of the marriage in a financial way.

I give and bequeath to my legal wife the minimum that the law requires, one dollar.

To Mrs. Veta H. McKastley, who works with us, I give and bequeath the sum of $500.00

To Miss Vera Puckett, who works with us, I give and bequeath the sum of $1000.00

To everyone who owes me directly or indirectly, I give to them everything that they owe me.

To Mr. L. A. Puckett, who works with us, I give and bequeath the entire stock of groceries and all fixtures therewith that shall be in our grocery department at the time of my passing with the provision that he is to pay all outstanding debts of this department. This grocery stock does not include the above [$20,000] worth of merchandise in our wholesale department. (The upstairs in our building is set aside for our wholesale store).

The balance of my estate consisting of only and every kind whatever, I give and bequeath to my sister, Thelma.

I appoint my brother-in-law, Edward Beman and my sister Mildred Beman, as executors of this will. They are to serve without bond.

Marion W. Stembridge (Seal)

Published, declared and executed by Marion W. Stembridge as his last will and testament on the 8ᵗʰ day of January 1951 he signing in our presence and we signing in his presence and in the presence of each other and at his special interest and (?).

Ethel M. Perdue   *address Macon, GA. Persons Bldg.*
Harry E. Nottingham   *address   "   "   "   "*
Nottingham

Needless to say, as soon as the will was filed for probate, Sara Stembridge challenged the validity of this will. Rumors said he deeded the house to her when he left her, but he did not part with any possession willingly. He died owning the house. She continued to live there and was able to purchase it in 1955—at public auction.

PROBATE

Probate of will, before a jury and Judge Erwin Sibley, Baldwin Superior Court. August 27, 1954:

W. S. Edwards, George Jackson, Whitman Whitman, R. C. Whitman, Jr., for plaintiffs in error.

Milton F. Gardner, D. D. Veal, contra.

Marion W. Stembridge executed a will on January 8, 1951, and died on May 2, 1953. His wife, Sara J. Stembridge, was his only known heir at law. (An online post said he had five children, but I found no further documentation for any of them.) Mrs. Mildred Beman, Edward Beman, and Thelma Stembridge filed for probate in solemn form, in the Court of Ordinary of Baldwin County (Bertie Stembridge), the will in which Marion Stembridge named Mr. and Mrs. Beman as his executors, and in which he bequeathed one dollar to his wife, made provision for named employees, and left the residue of his estate to his sister, Thelma Stembridge.

Mrs. Marion W. (Sara J.) Stembridge filed a caveat on the grounds that at the time the will was executed: (1) the deceased was not of sound and disposing mind and memory; (2) the deceased was suffering from monomania or insane delusions toward his widow (Mrs. Sara Jordan Terry Stembridge), in that he believed she was trying to poison him or kill him with X-rays in order to get control of his money and property; (3) the deceased suffered from monomania and thought his wife was trying to get his money, and his will was the result of and connected with his monomania; (4) the deceased was laboring under a mistake of fact, in that he thought his wife did not love him and was against him, which was not true; and (5) that, after the execution of the will, the deceased made material changes and alterations with the intention to revoke the same and did revoke the instrument.

WITNESSES TO THE WILL AT PROBATE

George Nottingham, an attorney in Macon; Mrs. Ethel M. Perdue, Harry E. Nottingham, Macon attorney: All signed in presence of each other and in presence of Marion Stembridge. All witnesses thought he was of sound mind.

OTHER WITNESSES AT PROBATE

Dr. Edwin Allen, who operated Allen's Institution, testified for Mrs. Sara Stembridge: In November, 1933, Marion Stembridge was disturbed mentally and was treated two weeks in witness's institution. Stembridge had delusional ideas that people were trying to hurt him by putting poison in his food or medicine, and he involved his sister, Mrs. Leon Callaway, and the local doctor. At times Stembridge had hallucinations that people were shooting X-rays into his genital organs. He came to Allen's Institution voluntarily and was quiet and orderly for a while. Then he barricaded himself in his room and they had trouble getting his meals to him. Witness ate part of the food to demonstrate it was not poisoned, after which the testator ate. His condition improved and he got tranquil. He was in a panic state, which is more or less a temporary type of reaction. In November, 1942, the sheriff brought Stembridge, who had been placed in jail on a peace warrant and a lunacy warrant, to Allen's Institution and instructed Dr. Allen to keep him until he called for him. Dr. Allen considered Stembridge to be psychotic or suffering from mental illness. Money was important to him. He operated his business while he was a patient. The last time he was doing a brokerage business and he carried that on. He was not suffering from monomania about his money, but had delusional ideas on other subjects, particularly the idea that someone was trying to harm him. He was in a fear state. When his fears subsided to where he was fairly tranquil, he left the hospital. The last time witness saw the testator professionally was in 1942.

Mrs. Marion W. (Sara J.) Stembridge testified: She and Marion Stembridge married in August, 1947, and separated in July, 1949. In 1948 they were on a visit to her old home in South Georgia. She had not been back since her mother was buried in August, and asked Stembridge to stop at the cemetery. He said he had to get back because he was losing important money. When questioned he became very angry, saying he was building a cathedral and if he built it strong they would not need friends, if you had money you had friends, money was your best friend. On their return home he began to tell her of Mrs. Callaway and Roger Stembridge trying to poison him so they could get his money, and that she was not to have anything to do with them; that she was his protection and as long as he had a wife they could not get his property. Any associations she had with his family upset him greatly. He admonished her frequently not to have anything to do with Mrs. Callaway, Roger Stembridge, and Miss Stembridge. Shortly thereafter he shot a Negro woman, thus making it necessary for her to be associated with his family. He was still very much upset and under the fears and delusions that they were against him and that she (his wife) expected to send him to prison so she could get his property. He left her after his trial (1949, the murder trial, but she was in touch with him on January 7 and 8, 1951, and right along. He still persisted in the delusion that she was a part of a conspiracy to get his money. He was upset about the trial and wanted her (Sara) to get out of the house. When he did not get a new trial, he accused her of interfering with his case and trying to send him to prison. He told her she would never get a penny of his money. He never ate with her down town in Milledgeville. They went in a restaurant one time and ordered dinner, but he never touched it. At that time everything he ate came in cans. He never drank any water or ate anything she gave him. He did eat with her a time or two when they were first married. From time to time she loaned him money, totaling about $17,000, some of which was paid back before and some after the separation, and $4,000 has not been repaid. From her contact with him over the telephone on January 8, 1951, he was laboring under the delusion that she was trying to do him harm in his trial and in his business. From 1948 until his death in 1953, based on witness's contact with him over the telephone, his condition was progressively worse. Shortly after he left her, she found double rows of sheet lead between double rows slats on the side of the bed where he slept, and found **films between the mattress and spring** underneath the pad. She did not give him any reason to believe she was trying to take his money. She worked for him constantly in the business and did everything she could to help him. At the time the will was executed, the employees referred to therein were not working for him.

On cross-examination, she testified she could not swear she talked to testator over the telephone January 6 or 7, or maybe the 8th. In January 1951, he was having the house painted, and was suffering with a delusion that a Negro painter was stealing his paint. She called Stembridge when the painter was going to quit, and he accused her of interfering with the painter. The painting of the house was finished in the summer of 1951. After they had been separated nearly four years, she filed suit for divorce, in which she sought to recover the $4,000 that had not been paid back to her. She was supporting herself and was in trouble and felt she was entitled to it.

W. S. Cox, a former bailiff, testified: About 1949 Mr. Stembridge was in the loan business and Cox handled many papers for him in the Justice of the Peace Court. On one occasion after Stembridge obtained a judgment against a Negro, the latter reached an agreement with Stembridge by paying part of the debt and executing new notes for the balance. When the negro defaulted on the new agreement, Stembridge took the fi. fa. off of the old judgment and demanded that witness levy it on the negro's property. Cox told him that he had made a new contract and his judgment was no good. Stembridge was upset and threatened to come into court and demand his money from Cox. About January 7 or 8, 1951, Cox did not remember the exact date, Stembridge was having his house painted. Stembridge had the idea that the negroes were stealing his paint and wanted Cox to put on old clothes and crawl under the house and watch to see if they stole any paint, which Cox declined to do. Previously Cox had had a violent dispute with testator about the fi. fa. On the question of the testator's mental condition in January 1951, in the witness's opinion, he was a hard man when it came to business affairs, who would not stop at anything if you crossed him up, and a man who thought he was right and you were wrong. Cox resigned the bailiff's office because he did not care to have any further trouble with Stembridge. After the run in about the fi. fa., Cox could not see any difference in Stembridge's attitude. Stembridge always acted normally and was just as courteous and nice as could be and always paid his costs promptly without any argument.

C. S. (Shep) Baldwin, Jr., Solicitor-General Emeritus, testified: In 1941 Stembridge brought samples of food and drink to his office and said his sister and her husband had been trying to poison him to get his money. Subsequently, upon being shown a report from the F. B. I, Stembridge had the appearance of thinking deeply, and then said: "Well, I will tell you what has happened. I have got enemies in the post office. Undoubtedly the samples were switched in transit." About 1943, Stembridge brought more samples of food that he wanted the witness to send off to be analyzed. He had been at Allen's Sanitarium and involved Dr. Allen. Baldwin mailed the specimens to J. Edgar Hoover. He did not have much to say when the report came back, but he then got the G. B. I. and a private detective and worked on that case for six months. After making reference to the trial in 1949, when the testator was accused of killing a negro woman, Baldwin testified that in his opinion the testator had delusions of persecution, that people were trying to kill him, that his folks were trying to poison him, and that somebody substituted the samples in the mail. There was no doubt in witness's mind about testator being off. He was abnormal when it came to money matters. He could make money better than any of them. He would really go after it and he would get excited more over his money than anything else. From 1948 until Stembridge's death he was under delusions of persecution and he was worse at the time of his death.

*A **personal observation**: A group of legal personnel and store keepers, including Sonny Goldstein who owned a department store on South Wayne Street in the same block as Stembridge's store, met almost daily for coffee before going to their offices or places of business in the 1960s. If this group were meeting back in the early 1950s, and if Stembridge were aware of it, he would probably have thought he was their subject of discussion and that they plotted against him.*

Paul Cox, a police officer, testified: In May, 1953, he was called to the Baldwin Hotel to unload some guns. He found five automatics, and unloaded four. One was already unloaded. They were cocked or in position to fire. A refrigerator there had a padlock on it, and some of the bookcases had locks on them.

Robert J. Ashfield testified he put a padlock on the refrigerator for Stembridge, who said that the boys who ran the hotel were stealing his hair tonic. Ashfield declined to express an opinion as to whether testator's mind was sound or unsound on January 8, 1951.

G. D. Beck testified he borrowed $6,000 from Stembridge on three trucks about 1949. Afterwards he thought he paid most of the money back. He paid Stembridge so much a week and got a receipt from him. Stembridge claimed that Beck still owed $4,400 and did not like it when he procured another finance company to take the loan up. When the matter was being closed, Stembridge claimed Beck owed him an additional 75 cents which he paid. Thereafter Beck saw Stembridge on the street once or twice a week, but he never spoke to Beck, and on one occasion Stembridge crossed the street when Beck wanted to see him about a driver who owed Stembridge some money. Beck traded at Stembridge's store every week. Based on the transaction with reference to the loan on the trucks, in Beck's opinion Stembridge was a little off, he was of unsound mind.

Jesse Alvin Gilmore, an attorney who was appointed administrator of the Stembridge estate before the will was offered, testified: He found five safes in Stembridge's office, one of which he had not been able to open. The safe which was used by Stembridge was a heavy magnesium-steel screw-type safe, in which Gilmore found, among other things, an automatic pistol, a series of notes, various keys, and papers including the will.

VERDICT

The jury returned a verdict in favor of Mrs. Stembridge, but the legal conflicts continued.

APPEAL BY STEMBRIDGE'S FAMILY

The co-executors, Mr. and Mrs. Beman (Stembridge's sister Mildred and her husband Edward) appealed the local court's decision to the Supreme Court of Georgia on November 8, 1954. The Court rendered its verdict on January 10, 1955, in favor of the Bemans. The will would stand as written, with Sara to receive only the designated $1.00.

The opinions of the three witnesses to the will were considered evidence that Stembridge was of sound mind and knew what he was doing at the time he signed the will. The erratic and paranoid behaviors demonstrated by Stembridge over the months and longer were considered signs of emotional disturbances rather than the inability to think straight; he ran his business successfully until the day he committed suicide.

As a result, the Georgia Court of Appeals upheld the will and Sara received only the one dollar. She bought the house at public auction to remain in her home. (The Court's reasoning is given in Appendix 13.)

THE STEMBRIDGE HOUSE

SALE OF THE HOUSE

Sara received the deed to the house she lived in as the wife of Marion Stembridge on June 11, 1955. Her having the house may not have been the wishes of Marion Stembridge, but nevertheless he would have approved of the way she had to fight to obtain ownership.

Jesse Alvin Gilmore, administrator of the Stembridge estate, advertised in the local paper the required four weeks and the house went on the auction block the first Tuesday of June, 1955. Sara was the highest bidder, at eight thousand, five hundred ($8,500.00).

The property was described as Part of Lot No. One (1) in Square No. seventy-one (71), fronting eighty feet on Columbia Street and running west on Montgomery Street 142 feet. Purchased by previous owner (Marion Stembridge) from Mrs. Katie Cone Alfriend, July 17, 1928. (Deed Book 28, p 114, Baldwin County Courthouse).

THE HAUNTED HOUSE ON THE CORNER

The house remained a rooming/apartment house until it was purchased by the Theta Chi Fraternity at the local college, then named Georgia College and State University, but known as Georgia State College for Women when Sara was a student and employee there.

Many who drove by the corner of Columbia and Montgomery streets never thought of Stembridge or heard the stories of his ghost that was supposed to haunt the house. In 2013, the house looked like any normal home in the community. But some said the house was haunted. Stembridge's brother Roger E. Stembridge wrote,

The house has been reputed to have his ghost roaming the halls since his demise back in 1953. ... That house is for sale because all prospective buyers get run off by some unknown entity stomping through the house.

A former college student wrote: *I also lived in the boarding house as a college student. I just read that the house burned down in 2019. It had a dark and ominous presence for sure. I lived in the downstairs right apartment for 3 months, then got out. I slept at a friend's house many nights because of all the scary stuff that happened in that apartment. I don't think Marion ever left that house.*

Another stated "It was a beautiful house, just filled with bad energy."

March, 2013. Photograph by the author.

Word spread quickly the night of February 10, 2019, as the house burned and many came to photograph the last breaths related to Marion Stembridge. Some of the pictures cast an eerie view of the Stembridge residence.

Susan Lindsley

Reposted online without information on photographer.

In 2019, when the house burned, some said the last of Stembridge had finally gone to hell. The rising smoke provides a profile as if his spirit were leaving the remains of the house.

Photographer Scott Little.

Perhaps, however, he still haunts Milledgeville. A close friend reports her granddaughter worked for the store located on the site where Stembridge's store stood, and she has heard chains rattle. The granddaughter never heard of Stembridge or his haunts. Perhaps the new store could increase business if customers were to come in not just to purchase but to listen for the chains.

Although Milledgeville tried to return to normal after the murders in 1953, the stories never stopped and normal never fully came back to Milledgeville. Seventy years later, Stembridge may no longer have a house to haunt, but he still lurks in the memories of the old and the young who lost both a past and a future when an angry paranoid man went on a preplanned military-style operation, hustled from place to place and killed normalcy.

APPENDIX 1

COURT OF APPEALS, JUNE 17, 1942

Stembridge vs. Sloan

DECIDED JUNE 17, 1942. REHEARING DENIED JULY 27, 1942.

Complaint; from Baldwin Superior Court — Judge Jackson. October 22, 1941.

Marion W. Stembridge, Smith, Smith Bloodworth, Croom Partridge, **for plaintiff.**

Marion Ennis, **for defendants.**

The evidence, viewed in its most favorable light to upholding the verdict in favor of the defendants, authorized the jury to find that there had been an open running rental transaction between the plaintiff and the defendants from the time they entered the premises on August 12, 1939, until they moved therefrom April 24, 1941; that the occupancy was continuous; and that all advancements made, even though there were overpayments made during the first year of the occupancy, were but branches of the main rental transaction, and these advancements became constituent parts of the main rental transaction.

2. "Ordinarily a promissory note contains only the maker's obligation to pay." Where the occupancy of the rented premises was continuous and for more than one year, the mere giving of the note reciting that, "... after date I promise to pay to the order of Marion W. Stembridge three hundred dollars, payable as follows: twenty-five dollars on Sept. 1, 1940, and twenty-five dollars on the first day of each month thereafter until the full amount is paid, for value received..." even though it was for the second year's rental did not necessarily show that the second year was not an integral part of the entire running rental transaction which also included the first year.

3. The plaintiff, by basing his action on this note alone, could not deprive the defendants of their right to show, if they could, that all payments of rent during the entire period they continuously occupied the rented premises, under the continuous running transaction, were elements from which the final balance was to be ascertained.

4. The judge did not err in overruling the demurrer to the amendments to the defendants' counter-affidavits.

5. The evidence authorized the verdict.
DECIDED JUNE 17, 1942. REHEARING DENIED JULY 27, 1942.

Stembridge had a dispossessory warrant issued against Mr. and Mrs. Sloan. In his affidavit he deposed: "That the said tenant fails to pay rent now due on said house and premises (or that said tenant is holding said house and premises over and beyond the term for which same were rented or leased to him); that the said owner desires, and has demanded possession of said house and premises and the same has been refused" by the said tenants.

The tenants filed counter-affidavits and denied that the rent claimed was due, and subsequently amended alleging that the plaintiff wanted $35 per month for the apartment but agreed to rent it for $25 per month if the defendants would renovate the apartment if they desired any improvements; that the defendants accepted the plaintiff's proposition and immediately had the living room and bedroom floors sanded, varnished, and shellacked, the ceilings and walls in four rooms and the woodwork in the living room painted, and paid the plaintiff $25 for the month of August, 1939; that the defendants occupied the apartment from August 12, 1939, to March 18, 1941, the date of the issuance of the dispossessory warrant, paying the total sum of $540.50 in rent during that period; that the defendants had continuously occupied the premises from August 12, 1939, to March 18, 1941, and which aggregated a period of nineteen months and eighteen days, and that at $25 per month the total accrued rent was $490, and that the plaintiff's own receipts as held by the defendants totaled $540.50 and gave the defendants a credit of $50.50 with the plaintiff and the rent paid until May 18, 1941; that the defendant R. G. Sloan, a traveling salesman, working on a commission basis, when commissions were large in order to provide for his family in the months when the commissions would be small, would pay as much as $35 some months by way of keeping his rent well paid in advance; that the defendants are not asking for recoupment, offset, or endeavoring to recover any overpayments, but are merely asking that a proper credit be had, and that when the payments they have made as rent on the same premises that they had continuously resided in are credited they will have a credit as of March 18, 1941 of $50.50; that the defendants are hereby attaching receipts that were given in the handwriting of the plaintiff, August 12, 1939, $25; September 1, 1939, $25; October 6, 1939, $35; November 11, 1939, $35; December 7, 1939, $35; January 1, 1940, $25; February 16, 1940, $35; March 16, 1940, $35; April 6, 1940, $35; May 13, 1940, $35; June 14, 1940, $30; July 29, 1940, $15; August 3, 1940, $35; September 2, 1940, $25; October 5, 1940, $20; October 11, 1940, $5; November 2, 1940, $25; December 7, 1940, $25; January 11, 1941, $18; February 8, 1941, $12.50; February 15, 1941, $10; totaling $540.50; that though the rent was not due and even though it was paid until May 18, 1941, they moved out of and vacated the premises on April 24, 1941; that the plaintiff swore out a distress warrant on March 18, 1941, alleging that the defendants owed $44.17 as past-due rent; that the defendants filed a counter-affidavit and an amendment alleging that they had paid their rent until May 18, 1941, and that a verdict was awarded in their favor in the justice's court of the 320th G. M. of Baldwin County; that the defendants did not ask for recoupment or offset or request to recover any of the overpayments, and specifically asked the jury not to award them a judgment for the overpayments, and the defendants state that although the overpayments were more than enough to pay the rent from March 18, 1941, to April 24, 1941, because the rent was paid up to May 18, 1941, they are not asking for a recovery of the difference. The defendants contended that they merely pleaded payment and did not ask for any judgment over and against the plaintiff.

The plaintiff demurred to the amendment on the ground that the alleged overpayments made during the first year the defendants occupied the premises could not be allowed as against a dispossessory warrant seeking to collect the rent under the second year's rent contract, even though the tenants' possession had been continuous from the time they entered the premises until after the issuance of the warrant. The plaintiff also demurred on the ground "that as against the dispossessory warrant no plea of overpayment of any kind under a previous rent contract may be allowed." The judge did not err in overruling the demurrer.

On the trial the plaintiff introduced a note signed by the defendant R. G. Sloan, the material part of which is as follows: "8/10/40. 19 — ... after date I promise to pay to the order of Marion W. Stembridge three hundred dollars, payable as follows: twenty-five dollars on Sept. 1, 1940, and twenty-five dollars on the first day of each month thereafter until the full amount is paid, for value received, payable at ____, with interest after maturity until paid, at eight per cent. per annum." The remainder of the note is in the customary form providing for collection of attorney's fees and with waiver of homestead exemption. The plaintiff testified: "On August 10, 1940, I rented to R. G. Sloan an apartment at 208 North Columbia Street in the City of Milledgeville for one year from September 1, 1940, to September 1, 1941, for $25 per month to be paid in advance. I took R. G. Sloan's note for $300 to be paid $25 per month beginning September 1, 1940, and $25 each month thereafter until paid." On cross-examination he testified: "The receipts from August 12, 1939, through September 2, 1940, were given by me under a previous rent contract, and the other receipts were given by me under the contract upon which I am suing."

The defendants introduced evidence which in effect substantiated the allegations in their counter-affidavits. The receipts introduced by the defendants which were in the handwriting of the plaintiff showed payments in excess of $25 per month for the whole period during which the tenants occupied the apartment. The plaintiff objected to all receipts tending to show payment or overpayment of rent for the first year the defendants occupied the premises on the ground that the contract for each of these years was a separate contract. The objection was overruled. If these receipts had been ruled out, the evidence would have shown rent due on the two years' rentals at the time of the issuance of the dispossessory warrant.

MacINTYRE, J. (After stating the foregoing facts.)

The plaintiff contends that the two questions now before this court are: (1) "May a plea of alleged overpayment under a previous rent contract be made as against the dispossessory warrant?" And (2) "May evidence intended to set up a claim for overpayment under a previous rent contract be admitted as against the dispossessory warrant?" The defendants contend that their plea is one of payment, and that the written receipts of the plaintiff, when taken as a whole over the period that they continuously occupied the premises, showed that they had paid the plaintiff in full, and that the evidence of the defendants sustained their plea. Under the rule of law as we understand it, after verdict we must construe the evidence in the most favorable light to the upholding of the verdict (*Vandeviere* v. *State,* 58 Ga. App. 18 (197 S.E. 338), and where the evidence is conflicting, while the trial judge may grant a new trial in the exercise of a legal discretion this court must accept the findings of fact of the jury below if there was any evidence to support them. *Smith* v. *State,* 91 Ga. 188 (17 S.E. 68). And the evidence viewed in its most favorable light to the defendants authorized the jury to find that there was an open running transaction between the plaintiff and the defendants from the time they entered the premises August 12, 1939, until they moved therefrom April 24, 1941. All the advancements made (even though they were overpayments made during the first year of the occupancy) were but branches of the main rent transaction, for in making the advancements the defendants recognized the existence of an unadjusted rent transaction, and not only assented to the application of the advancements thereon as one of the elements from which their final balance was to be ascertained, but that the plaintiff, by his acceptance of the overpayments during the first year, also recognized the existence of the unadjusted rent transaction during the second year. "Ordinarily a promissory note contains only the maker's obligation to pay. If the note does not purport to express the contract in pursuance of which it is executed, and the contract rests in parol, its terms may be proved by parol." *Anthony Shoals Power Co.* v. *Fortson,* 138 Ga. 460, 463 (75 S.E. 606).

The defendants' evidence was to the effect that the basis of the overpayment during the first year was not a wholly different transaction from the obligation to pay the rent the second year, which obligation for the second year's rent was evidenced by the note introduced by the plaintiff, and this note contained only the tenants' obligation to pay. The record does not disclose that the note contains the entire contract between the parties. The note does not state that it was for rent, nor does it describe or even refer to any particular premises rented. The record discloses that the defendants rented the premises in question and thereafter continuously occupied them until the dispossessory proceedings were instituted. The plaintiff, by basing his action on the note alone, cannot deprive the defendants of their right to show, if they can, that all the payments of rent during the entire continuous period that they occupied the rented premises were elements from which the final balance was to be ascertained.   Hubbard *v.* French,   1   Pa.   Super.   218; *Petit* v. *Teal,* 57   Ga. 145; *Thomas* v. *Mitchell,* 74 Ga. 797; *Sikes* v. *Carter,* 30 Ga. App. 539 (118 S.E. 430). To illustrate: suppose a part of the rent had been due to the landlord for some of the months during the first year and a part for some of the months during the second year for the premises which the tenants had continuously occupied, and the landlord had elected to introduce evidence to this effect, and the jury had so found, can it be said that the landlord could not have recovered under the dispossessory warrant and the other pleadings in the instant case the final balance for the two, or the part of the two, years which the tenant occupied the premises immediately preceding the dispossessory warrant? We think not. See in this connection *Johnson* v. *Klassett,* 9   Ga.   App.   733,   737   (72   S.E. 174); *Roberson* v. *Simons,* <u>109 Ga. 360</u> (2) (34 S.E. 604). The jury seem to have rejected the plaintiff's contentions as to the controlling facts, and to have accepted the defendants' evidence and found the facts to be as set forth in the defendants' counter-affidavits which were based on the payments they had made during the entire rental transaction, beginning August 12, 1939, and ending April 24, 1941, when the tenants moved out. We see no trace in the evidence of any purpose by either party to give or claim any sum by way of gratuity. This was a renting of the premises, and the jury were authorized to find, under the defendants' evidence, that there was an open running transaction of payments and overpayments by the defendants of various amounts on the rent, and that each party recognized the existence of the unadjusted rent transaction, and that each party assented (did a passive act of concurrence) to the application of the advancements of the amounts paid under the entire running transaction, and that all of the payments of rent during this period were elements from which the final balance was to be ascertained. Thus, if the jury found that the rental transaction was for $25 per month for the continuous period that the tenants occupied the premises, then they could find that the tenants were entitled to be credited with each and every payment or overpayment which they had made during their continuous occupancy of the premises, all of which were made on an open running rent transaction, and that they would not, under their plea and their evidence, be due the plaintiff any rent. And thus the jury were authorized to find that the plea of payment was 415; *Lufburrow* v. *Henderson,* 30 Ga. 482; *Willis* v. *Harrell,* 118 Ga. 906, 909 (45 S.E. 794); *Carter* v. *Sutton,* 147 Ga. 496 (94 S.E. 760); *Lamar* v. *Sheppard,* 84 Ga. 561, 569 (10 S.E. 1084); *Hayes* v. *Atlanta,* 1 Ga. App. 25, 26 (57 S.E. 1087); *Hill* v. *Federal Land Bank of Columbia,* <u>186 Ga. 889, 891</u> (199 S.E. 177).

The judge did not err in overruling the motion for new trial.

Judgment affirmed. Broyles, C. J., and Gardner, J., concur.

APPENDIX 2

INDICTMENT and BRIEF OF EVIDENCE

GRAND JURY INDICTMENT OF MARION STEMBRIDGE

INDICTMENT—Murder—No. 254.   Bennett Printing & Stamp Co., Atlanta

GEORGIA, *Baldwin* County.

IN THE SUPERIOR COURT OF SAID COUNTY

The Grand Jurors selected, chosen and sworn for the County of *Baldwin*
to-wit:

1	Ralph Summerson		FOREMAN
2	Grady Moore	13	Bob Watson
3	Geo Ross Sr	14	Tom Hall
4	G J Adams	15	Grady Hillyard
5			
6	Geo Powers	1?	Jackson
7	Floyd Veal	18	C ? Ray
8	E B Kuel	19	Stewart Barnes
9	Branson Chandler	20	Ja King
10	Carl Nelson	21	Will Brown
11	Guy Roberts	22	
12	Will Ivey	23	

In the name and behalf of the citizens of Georgia, charge and accuse
Marion W Stembridge and Sam L Terry
of the County and State aforesaid with the offense of

MURDER

for that the said *Accused*

on *7* day of *March*, in the year of our Lord Nineteen Hundred and *forty Nine*
in the County and State aforesaid, did then and there; unlawfully, and with force and arms, make
an assault in and upon one *Emma Johnston*

in the peace of God and said State then and there being, then and there unlawfully, feloniously,
wilfully and of his malice aforethought, did kill and murder, by *shooting*
the said *Emma Johnston* with a certain
pistol
which the said *Accused*
then and there held, and giving the said *Johnston*
then and there a mortal wound, of which mortal
wound the said *Emma Johnston* died

And so the Jurors aforesaid, upon their oath aforesaid, do say that the said
Marion W Stembridge and Sam L Terry
the said *Emma Johnston*
in manner and form aforesaid, unlawfully, feloniously, wilfully and of his malice aforethought, did
kill and murder, contrary to the laws of said State the good order, peace and dignity thereof.

Baldwin   Superior Court.   *Mattie Smith*
                                                              Prosecutor

July   Term, 19*47*   *C. S. Baldwin Jr*
                                                              Solicitor General.

THE STATE	Indictment for Murder
	Baldwin Superior Court
V.	Trial: Before
	Honorable George S. Carpenter
MARION W. STEMBRIDGE	and a Jury
	July Term, 1949

BRIEF OF THE EVIDENCE

Testimony For the State

RICHARD LEE COOPER, Sworn for the State

Direct Examination by the Solicitor Baldwin

I am Richard Lee Cooper. I bought a second-hand 1941 Chevrolet car from Mr. Marion W. Stembridge in June, 1948 and bargained to pay him $800.00 and insurance went to $227.00, making $1,027.00 for it. I bought the car and was the head of it and signed the paper for it. My mother and brother signed the note with me.

My mother is married to George W. Harrison and my brother, Johnny Cooper, signed with me. I don't know how old he was. I was supposed to pay $17.50 by the week. I was to pay the whole $17.50 and my mama was to pay $10.00 a month and my brother $5.00 a month, making a total of about $85.00 a month. I paid on it until September, making three months payments and paying all I was supposed to pay for those first months.

I stopped paying on it when a lumber truck ran into the back of it and tore it up and I went to Mr. Stembridge about the insurance, reported the wreck and he told me that he didn't have any insurance on it. The car would still run but the back of it was torn out. I took the car to the front of his store and he said he didn't have any kind of insurance on it, he didn't care if the lightning struck it and tore it up, that was my affair. I carried it back to the house and about three or four weeks later, he pulled it in and I reckon he sold it. I don't know who he sold it to, I don't know the boy.

After he had pulled the car in, he called for me to come up there but I did not go. I was not at my home on March 7th when this shooting took place and it was after the shooting, at about 8 o'clock that night, before I got home.

Cross Examination by Mr. Evans

I don't know exactly the day that this wreck occurred. The day I ran into Mr. Louie Veal was a different time from that. I was not in the car then; I was in a truck.

I don't know positively whether it was $800.00 or $850.00 that I was to pay for the car. When he carried me out there to look at it, he told me $800.00 and insurance ran it up to $1,027.00. The notes ran for 12 months and were $85.00 a month. I stopped paying on the car after I had the wreck and he would not fix it. I had had the car about 2 months or a little better when the wreck occurred. I paid him some after I had had the wreck because I thought he was going to fix it up. I paid him once in September and the car was wrecked sometime in August but I couldn't say whether it was the first part of August or the last part of August. I don't know how many weeks I paid Mr. Stembridge after I had the wreck in August. I paid him two or three weeks after I wrecked the car and during that time I drove it a little bit.

The car was to be mine and my mother's and my brother's but they were not using the car. I drove it all the time myself. My mother never did drive it any. She can't drive. My brother, Johnny, don't have a license. Yes, Johnny carried his wife to mama's house and back in the car.

I had borrowed some money from Mr. Stembridge before I bought the car to fix up other cars and I reckon I owed him about $25.00 at the time I bought this car. It was not put into the price of the car. I paid him along on that separately. I am not sure it was not over $100.00 but I owed him something about $25.00.

That pistol that Johnny had out there was my step-father's pistol. I don't know that Johnny had my step-father's pistol out there the day of the shooting, I was not there. Johnny did not have my pistol that day. I didn't have one. I have not done anything with a pistol, I have never had one. I was convicted for carrying a pistol in 1946 in this court house. That was my father's pistol I was bringing from Eatonton. I was convicted here. I don't know whether I was found guilty or not. I didn't get a two months sentence. I paid a $25.00 fine.

JOHNNY COOPER, Sworn for the State.

Direct Examination by Solicitor Baldwin

My name is Johnny Cooper. On March 7, 1949, I was at home when Mr. Stembridge and Mr. Terry came up. I was sitting there on the right of the house, side of the apartment house, on the porch, on the banister by the chair.

I was supposed to pay $5.00 each month on the automobile that Richard bought from Mr. Stembridge. I was 18 years old when the car was bought and I gave mama the payments to make for me. I made three $5.00 payments and stopped paying after we wrecked the car. He would not fix it up and we stopped paying.

That day went Mr. Stembridge and Mr. Terry come up on the porch, my wife was there and Emma and my two little sisters. Emma Willie Johnekin was the one that got killed. She was 18 then. When Mr. Stembridge first came, he didn't say nothing, he just walked on the porch and looked at me. I owed him $20.00 so I told him, "Mr. Stembridge, the little money I owe you, I will pay you on the 10th." I had just started with the State six days before. I owed him $20.00 besides the automobile. He said he was not talking about that money but about the car and what were we going to do about it. I told him I was not going to do nothing. He asked where Richard was at. I told him, "He at the box factory. Ain't that right, Emma?" She said, yes. He said "Where you working?" I said, "I work at the State now." He said, "Sam has got a blank and you going to sign it." I said, "I ain't going to sign a blank." So Mr. Sam got out the blank and when he walked over to Mr. Stembridge, Mr. Stembridge kind of standing back of me, I was sitting and never did get up, he walked to Mr. Stembridge and handed it to him and Mr. Stembridge took it and read it and handed it to him and Mr. Stembridge took it and read it and handed it to me. When he handed it to me I read it. While I was reading it Mr. Stembridge walked up and caught me back of the collar. When I got up – Mr. Sam never stepped back when he handed it to Mr. Stembridge and he put his hand right back in his pocket.

I identify this as the order that Mr. Stembridge told Mr. Terry to write for me to sign. I identify this as Mr. Sam's pen that he gave to me and told me to sign with. I didn't sign it. I told him I was not going to sign it. He asked what was I going to do about the car. I asked would we get it back. He said, "No, you are not going to get it back." At that time I refused to sign it, Mr. Stembridge had me in the collar. When I got up Emma said, "Lord have mercy, he got brass knucks." When she said that he turned me loose and broke at her. She was already standing by the door and she ran in the house and he went in the house behind her, caught her in the first room, she was going in the second room. When Emma said, "Lord have mercy, he got on brass knucks," Mr. Stembridge asked, "What the hell she had to do with it" and he turned me loose and broke in the house after her because she ran. He ran straight behind her into mama's side of the house.

There is four rooms on mama's side of the house and four rooms on the other side of the house. On the side of the house that Emma ran in, the doors between each room are in a straight line, one right in front of the other. In the first room there was just a bedroom suite, in the second room just two beds, in the third room a bed and table. There was no trunk or box just inside the third room sitting against the side, there was a table there. In the fourth room, there was a stove and a table. Mr. Stembridge caught Emma as she went back in the second room. He and her were tussling, he had her and she was running, he caught her in the back. I didn't see or notice any knucks.

After he went after Emma, mama had just got to the top step. She didn't run in behind them, she walked in behind them. After she went in Mr. Sam he backed back off me with his hand in his coat pocket and backed until he got to the door and turned to go in and I went to go in my side. I went in my side running out of the way. Just time mama went in behind Mr. Stembridge, Mr. Terry backed off from me and went in and before I could get to my door, ain't but three feet, the shooting had started. I couldn't tell how many shots were fired, looked like a bunch of firecrackers, all almost together, from the first shot to the last, it was only 4 or 5 seconds. After the shooting, I went to the back and the next people I saw was Mama and Emma both coming out the back of the room, Mama holding her breast and Emma holding her stomach. I did not see Mr. Terry and Stembridge when they left.

There was a pistol on my side of the house when the shooting took place, it was not on the side where the shooting happened. It was under my bed, under the mattress. None of us ever got that pistol, never even bothered it until next morning when they came out there after it. I got it and gave it to them then. I gave it to Mr. Ellis, the policeman.

I did not fight Mr. Stembridge any. I did not put my hand on him and he didn't have his hands on me but about 4 or 5 seconds. He had me in back of the collar – it was hot and I had my shirt open - my shirt was unbuttoned all the way down. My wife was in my side of the house when the shooting was going on; she came to the door while they were out there. My sisters, Louvenia and Martha, and my brother, Will, three children, were around there at the house.

Cross Examination by Mr. Evans

I do not drive a car. I drive sometimes out in the woods; I pull a load. I do not have a driver's license. I can't think of what day it was when Richard Lee had his wreck; as near as I know, it was on the 6th day of September. We bought the car from Mr. Stembridge in June and I had paid him three $5.00 a month payments. I did not make him any further payments after the wreck occurred. After the wreck, it would still drive and we drove it around a couple of weeks afterwards trying to see about having it fixed. The payments were all paid. When it got wrecked, he told him that if the lightning struck it and it got burned, he didn't have anything to do with it, that was his part, so he sit it out in his yard. I think Mr. Stembridge came and got it. I know that they come and got it from the front of his yard. Mr. Terry came and got it. We stopped paying on it when it was wrecked. We didn't make any payments after it was wrecked. That is right, I do remember making one more payment because the car was wrecked on Friday and he made a payment Saturday. I remember the payments now. It was not but one payment made, it was a weekly payment, after the car was wrecked. After Mr. Terry got the car, it sit in Mr. Hodges' garage awhile. I think it was sitting there last November. None of us got it from there. Mr. Stembridge or Mr. Terry didn't have to take that car away from us twice. I never saw Richard Lee with the car after that. When Mr. Terry took the car, it was wrecked, nothing wrong with it but all the back end knocked off of it. The piston was slapping.

When Mr. Stembridge and Mr. Terry came up, I was sitting on the banister of the porch talking to Emma toward the house but when I saw them, I was looking back there. I was sitting on the rail of the front porch a little better than the middle of the porch on the side towards Milledgeville. When they came up both came right on up there. Mr. Sam had his hand in his coat pocket and Mr. Stembridge had his hand in his pants pocket. They came on up and stood up, neither one said nothing. I owed him $20.00. So I told him about the money I owed him I would pay him on the 10th. I had just started working at the State. I thought he had come to see me about the money that I owed him and which was supposed to have been paid. I was behind with it. I was sitting down. I did not stand up. Well, after I told him that he said, "Where is Richard?" I told him at the box factory. I had just come from work at the State. She said "Yes, he at the box factory." He said, "What you all going to do about the car?" I told him I wasn't going to do nothing. He said, "Where you work?" I said, "I am working at the State." He said, "Write it out, Sam, he is going to sign it." Mr. Sam walked against the porch an wrote a blank and handed it to Mr. Stembridge and Mr. Stembridge read it and handed it to me and I took it and read it. Mr. Stembridge was standing kind of side of me and he walked up and caught me back of the collar. He didn't tell me what he was writing out when he wrote the blank out but he gave me the blank and his fountain pen. I didn't intend to sign it. Naturally I was not going to sign when he said I was not going to get the car back. No use for me paying, he still had the car. He said we would not get it back.

He threatened me by putting his hand back of my collar while I was sitting on the rail. He couldn't have pushed me off the rail if he had wanted to because I still had the use of my hands. I was not scared; I knew I had one before that was overdue and I just paid it on up. At the time Mr. Stembridge handed me this paper, Mr. Terry put his hand back in his pocket and was standing right up on me. Mr. Terry didn't ever take his hands out of his pocket, even when he backed back to the door. Mr. Stembridge didn't have his hand in his hip pocket. I didn't see him put his hand in his belt. I didn't tell you Mr. Stembridge had his left hand in his pocket and had some brass knucks there.

It was not me who told the police about the brass knucks. I said what Emma said, I didn't see them. Emma said he had some brass knucks and she saw them. I didn't grab him. I didn't see the brass knucks. I didn't raise my hand. The only pistol I saw was Mr. Terry's pistol. It was in the right-hand side pocket of his coat.

I am sure he had on a coat. Both of them had on coats, always do wear coats. He had me in the collar with his right hand. He had his left hand in his pocket and he had pulled it up.

Emma could see the brass knucks but by me sitting down on the banister, I couldn't see them. I was not trying to see any knucks. I said Mr. Stembridge walked behind me. Yes, I was sitting on the rail. He came to be behind me because I was sitting there. He came walking on the side of me. Wouldn't that be behind me? He was behind me; he was not in front of me. He was not standing behind the rail. When he caught me in the neck, I didn't attempt to fight. If I had, Mr. Terry was going to shoot. During the 4 or 5 seconds that Mr. Stembridge held me in the collar, I looked in his face, I didn't look at his hands. My mother saw the brass knucks.

Mr. Stembridge asked Emma what the hell she had to do with it and he broke at her, he was running when he said it, he was running at her. I didn't see the brass knucks then. I couldn't run, Mr. Terry was standing on me. I saw Mr. Stembridge after Emma and I saw him when he caught her but I didn't see the knucks. I saw him run after her through the door and I saw him catch her in the first room when she went to go in the second door. I didn't see the brass knucks out then. I didn't see his pistol out then. Mama was already coming up the steps when Emma and Mr. Stembridge ran in the house. I don't know exactly when my mother saw the brass knucks. I didn't say she saw them on the porch. She went in the house behind them. She was not running, she just walked in calmly. They had just gotten through the second door when my mother went in. I was looking in the door and still on the porch. I didn't see it all because I didn't stay on the porch.

I saw him when he caught Emma. I don't know whether he hit her or grabbed her by the head. I was about as far from them as I am from you. I couldn't tell whether he hit her or not. She was hit with something. I saw the place. I was looking straight in from a distance of about twelve or fifteen feet. If he had had his pistol or brass knucks in his hand, I would have seen them but he didn't have his hands behind him. He had his hands in front of him. He was running from me and was going to catch her with his hands.

I went in the other door because I wanted to get out of the way. I told you I went in there after my rifle. That is the truth about it, I did go in after my rifle. As I went in the door, I didn't lock it. If I had locked it, I would not have had the intention to come back there. If I had locked it, I know I couldn't have got back out there. I came back out of the front and I went back through the house to the back.

The shooting lasted about 4 or 5 seconds, it happened all at once like a bunch of firecrackers. I went to get my rifle and came back on the porch but I didn't see anybody then. I came out of the front door and I didn't see Mr. Stembridge or Mr. Terry. If I had seen them, I would have shot but I didn't get back in time and they had gone. From the time I went in my door until I came out, it was at least three minutes.

My rifle was in the second room behind the chest. It was about thirty feet from where I went in. I had put it there; I knew where it was. I didn't go straight to it because my wife asked me what was the matter. She was talking to me and I didn't go straight to it. During those two or three minutes, I went in the drawer to find some 22 cartridges for the rifle. It is a single shot rifle and I didn't have a cartridge in it. I didn't go through my side of the house as soon as the shooting let up and didn't go inside of the other apartment through the back door. I didn't go in there in less than 25 or 15 minutes because I went to the store and come back and got there in the car with the police before I went back in the house.

I don't know that the police came out there that night. I was at the hospital. The police talked to me at the hospital. They asked me about the pistol; they asked us did we have a pistol. They didn't ask me, they asked Mama; they didn't ask me nothing about the pistol. I was right there in the room. As to whether the police asked me if there was a pistol out there because they said Mr. Terry and Mr. Stembridge claimed we had a pistol, I say didn't nobody get a pistol. When the investigating officers said Mr. Terry and Mr. Stembridge said we had a pistol out there and they asked me if I had a pistol out there, I told them we had a gun out there. That was on Monday night. I did not tell the law enforcement officers that I had that pistol, I didn't put my hand on the pistol. As to the policemen getting us all together and asking us was there a pistol out there anywhere in that house, I say that that morning they came out there and got it.

It is right that the police talked to all of us that night after the shooting. They asked did we have a pistol after them. I told them we didn't have one after them. We didn't put it in the newspaper that I didn't have one. The police didn't tell us that day that Mr. Terry and Mr. Stembridge said we had a pistol. The police searched the place but they didn't search my side, only the place where the shooting occurred; they couldn't get in my side; my side is next door and in the same house. Yes, I told the police the next morning that I had my step-father George Harrison's gun in my side of the house. I didn't tell them the first night because they didn't ask where the gun was that night.

They didn't ask if we had one, they asked did we have a pistol after them. They didn't ask if there was a pistol in the house. As to whether the police asked me if I had a rifle in the house; they saw the rifle when they came in. I did not tell the police that night after the shooting that I had a pistol; I hadn't got one; I didn't have one that night; I got George's pistol that Sunday night; the shooting occurred on Monday evening. George kept his pistol under his bed, under the mattress, in the third room back. George is my mother Mary Jane's husband. On Sunday night, they were not in their apartment next door to me and I went in there by myself and got the pistol from right under the bed where he kept it, between the mattresses. It was not under the pillow. It was a 32 automatic and it was loaded all the time.

As to whether or not my mother, Mary Jane Harrison, would be telling the truth if she said George kept his pistol under the pillow, I say I got it from under the mattress. I didn't get it from the pillow. I took it to my side of the house and put it between the mattresses in the second room. It was loaded.

I said I went in there to get my 22 rifle to shoot them because they had shot up my folks and that I came right back after them. I knew that there was more than one pistol shooting. I knew that Emma and my mother couldn't have a pistol in there because I had it in my apartment. Sure Mr. Terry and Mr. Stembridge had two pistols. I thought Mr. Terry had his in his coat pocket. I saw the print of it in his coat pocket because he had his hand on it pointed toward me. I knew they had two guns. I meant to go out there and shoot with them and get them away from there. I had got a 32 automatic pistol the night before and put it in the second room of my house between the mattresses on my bed, fully loaded, and could have reached in there and got it and could have walked out there and it wouldn't not have taken me three minutes but I didn't know how to operate the pistol so I got the 22 rifle.

I know that it didn't have but one shot but I could load one. As to my spending 3 minutes getting a 22 rifle in shape to go out and fight with them with those two fast shooting pistols they had, I say they didn't have any cartridges, they were empty with all that shooting.

I know they had shot them all up. As to my passing by the 32 pistol and going in the next room and getting the 22 rifle and coming back after they had gone, I say that I didn't get the 32 pistol because I didn't know how to operate it. I went and got the pistol and brought it to my side of the house and didn't have any reason to bring it there because nobody was bothering me. I could have gone around there and got anything I wanted and carried it months or years because nobody used that pistol.

That pistol hadn't been shot, I reckon, in 9 or 10 years. I didn't have any reason to bring it to my side of the house. As to my sneaking in the other side just as soon as the shooting died down to get that gun, I didn't have to go get the gun because if it had been there nobody would have moved it. I did not run out the back door of my apartment on my side when the shooting occurred. I didn't go out the back until I went through the front and went and met Mama. I ran to the front door and ran to the back door and found Mama and Emma coming out of the back door. I didn't see Mr. Terry and Mr. Stembridge after the shooting.

I gave the pistol to policeman Ellis about 9:30 the next morning after the shooting. He didn't come and find it because he couldn't get in my side unless he broke all the window glass out. I didn't give it to him that night because they didn't ask about it that night. They didn't search next morning. They came and asked George did he have a 380 automatic, if I am not mistaken, that is what he said. The pistol was actually a 32 automatic. George told them he had one. He didn't tell them where it was. Policeman Ellis asked him to let him see it. He went to go to his bed to get it, I told him it was on my side. George didn't get a chance to look in the bed because I told him where it was. The police didn't come there to search because they had already searched the house. That was the first that George knew the pistol was on my side as he never took it off but left it there under the bed. George didn't tell the police the night of the shooting that he had a gun because they didn't ask him did he have a gun. George did not say anything about my getting his gun and not telling him as I could go in his side and get anything I wanted. I had never got the gun before. No one had been prowling around my house. As to why I got the pistol, I say if I had got it for somebody I would have shot somebody or something of the kind. You can ask anybody around there, I haven't had no words around there with anybody. As to why I got it, I say I just went in and got it. I did not steal it, I can get anything I want from out of there.

It is not true that Mr. Stembridge and Mr. Terry started talking to me when they came up on the porch. It is not true that Mr. Stembridge tried to get me to tell him what I would do about this debt and that I was just as confusing as I am on the witness stand. He said I was going to pay for it. As to my refusal to sign this slip saying "Pay to Marion W. Stembridge the amount of $50.00 and charge to my account (showing slip to witness)" and as to my blowing up, I say that he didn't insist, he didn't hardly raise his voice. I didn't get off that rail and grab him around the neck. I didn't even put my hand on him. Even when he grabbed me in the neck, I kept sitting on the rail.

When my mother went in the room, I didn't even move. I was sitting on the rail right in front of that door and could see all the way through. My mother came exactly when the thing broke out. Emma said look at the brass knucks but she didn't scream and say it. She just said like anybody might have been telling somebody. She was standing no more than about a foot from me – the porch is not more than 4 feet wide.

I didn't try to go in the house because Mr. Terry would shoot me; I saw the print of his gun through his coat; I didn't ever see the gun. Mr. Terry didn't open his mouth the whole time he was out there. He just stood up there with the gun in his coat pointing it at me with his hand on it. He did not stand there pointing the gun at me for more than 2 or 3 seconds. He was pointing the gun at me as my mother walked up the steps. Mr. Terry was on the side of the porch next to the house and not on the side next to the rail. I was still sitting on the rail. My mother did not have to walk right between me and Mr. Terry, she walked by him, he was standing close to me. She walked behind Mr. Terry. As to my having said he was standing next to the house, I said when he came to hand Mr. Stembridge the note, he never did get back.

Mr. Terry was standing right by my feet. As to my saying a while ago he was on the porch next to the house, I said he never did get back. He was between me and the door. The porch is not more than six feet wide. Mr. Terry was not standing in front of me, he was standing kind of back with his hand in his pocket.

When all this happened, my mother was coming up the steps. Mr. Terry was standing covering me when Emma and Mr. Stembridge ran in the house. He was still standing covering me when my mother came up the steps. My mother come all the way around to get by and went in the door. She had 3 feet to walk in back of Mr. Terry. She walked in back of him to go in the door and he did not turn and look at her. He could see her coming up the steps by turning his eyes. He let her walk in back of him and then he backed off of me and backed back to the door. When he backed to the door and turned to go in, he was still facing me and my mother and the others were inside the house. I didn't follow him in. I went in the other door. I hadn't been trying to get in all the time. He had turned his back when I ran in the other door.

Emma lived with my mother; she had been there about 3 months. My mother was working but she had gotten off to come home. Emma had a regular job then. She kept mother's house and washed and ironed there, swept up and kept everything clean and made up the beds. Emma never did make up George's bed, Mama always made up his bed by herself before she went to town. Everything at the house knew where George's pistol was.

MARY JANE HARRISON, Sworn for the State.

Direct Examination by Mr. Baldwin

My name is Mary Jane Harrison. I was not there on March 7, 1949 when Mr. Marion Stembridge and Mr. Terry first came to my house, I went down to Mr. Herbert Chandler's store. On the way back from the store, I stopped at the house next door to me and tried on a dress that Sarah was making for me. I did not hear any kind of racket at my house while I was in that house. The house that I was at was about 30 feet from my house.

When I came out of that house and looked on my porch, Mr. Terry and Mr. Stembridge was standing on the porch. They were standing right opposite of Johnny, that is the way both were standing and I stood there on the porch and looked at them a few minutes. Well afterwards I just saw Mr. Stembridge, he walked right behind Johnny and when he got right behind Johnny he took good pains, he took his right hand and he put it down in Johnny's collar, holding to him. When he was holding to him he still had his left hand in his pocket. I called him, said, "Johnny", I said, "What the matter with you all?" Either one didn't hear me. I come down, I didn't hurry a bit, I walked on over and got near-about to the door step and went up the door step. I said, "Look, Buddy, why don't you get up from there?" He said, "Mama, Mr. Stembridge has got a thing for me to sign." Mr. Stembridge said, "Ma, hell" but neither looked back and when I come up on the porch Mr. Stembridge had those brass knuckles on his left hand and he was holding Johnny with his right hand and Emma got up there, said, "Lord have mercy, look at the man standing up here with brass knuckles on and his hand in little Johnny's collar." He made a rake to hit her and she dodged. Before he hit at her he said, "What in the hell God damn you got to do with it." Those are the words he said. She tore off in the house and he tore off in there behind her like he was tearing down a panel. I come up the steps.

I didn't use any curse words or bad language and Emma Johnekin didn't call him anything. I didn't make any threats and nobody got mad but him. Emma ran in the room. When I entered the door, they were right by the foot of the bed in the second room. They were holding each other and I saw a place on her head where he had hit her with the knucks. He had burst the skin.

Q. What did you do when you went in?

A. When I went on in there I didn't do anything because I couldn't do anything but when I went in, just about the time I got right in the middle door

Q. Middle door of what?

A. Just about the time I got out of the living room, the front room and went in the second room door, got right in the second room door Mr. Sam Terry come right on behind me off the porch and he shot me in the back. A little before I got to Mr. Stembridge and Emma I was shot again right there. I kept right straight by them; I didn't do nothing.

The bullets went in my body. I could feel them and the shock of it. I went right on by Mr. Stembridge and Emma and never did get hold of them. I went on in the kitchen and went to lay on the kitchen table and dropped on my knees and was shot twice. While I was on that table, Emma come out of the room and sit down on the trunk. Mr. Stembridge had shot her in the arm. Yes, she came out of the second bedroom and sit down in the third bedroom, which is a part of the dining room. She sit on the trunk after she was shot in the arm and hit on the head. After she sit down, I know Mr. Stembridge shot her twice, I only know that and he shot 3 times. While I was on the table, Emma said, "Lord have mercy, Mary, he has hit me in my stomach" and I raised up and went to turn around to look at her and just as I went to turn around Mr. Sam had got middle way of the dining room and bedroom and when I went to turn around to look at her, I just twisted because I was paralyzed in the shoulder, he ran out there just a little piece and I was at the table and he just shot me right there and I said, "Come on, Emma" and she got up and me and her went on out the back door. When I went out of the back door I started to the other house and I saw a car parked. I didn't have a gun after them. Emma Johnekin didn't have a pistol. We didn't go in there trying to get a pistol. I have never shot a pistol in my life.

The shooting started about that second door (referring to diagram) in the second room. I was shot 3 times there. There are 2 bullet holes in the wall and one in the door facing. There was a bullet on the top of the bed cover. There is a bullet hole in the dining room right over the trunk where Emma was sitting. They found a bullet behind the stove. Three bullet holes is all that we could find.

"Q. Can you show the jury any of these holes in you – show me where the first one was – can you pull up your dress?

Mr. Ennis: I object to any wounds being shown the jury that are on this particular witness. It is not the deceased and it would not be admissible in this case. If he has any evidence to show as to the nature of the wounds on the deceased, for which this defendant is on trial, that would be admissible but it would not be admissible to show it to this jury here.

BY THE COURT: Well, Mr. Baldwin, I don't think you can make an exhibition of those wounds without subjecting the witness to a rather embarrassing position.

Mr. Baldwin: It won't have to disrobe her. I want to show some of them. All she has to do is to pull up her dress.

Mr. Ennis: I would like further for the record to show that my objection is, it is for the purpose of prejudicing this jury. It is highly prejudicial to the defendant and improper and irrelevant and not germane to the issues involved in the particular case.

BY THE COURT: I will let it in for the present time, if he can show those wounds without undue embarrassment.

Q. Where did the first bullet hit you – right in the middle of the back?

A. Yes, sir.

Q. Where did the next bullet hit you (witness shows on body); hit you right in the side there?

A. Yes, sir.

Q. Where is the next one (witness shows); hit you right in that shoulder?

A. Yes sir.

Q. Where is the next one (witness indicates on body); hit you right in the breast?

A. Yes, sir."

None of us at the house cursed Mr. Stembridge or Mr. Terry. Neither Emma nor I had any kind of a weapon, nor did we try to get any kind of weapon. Emma Johnekin was the first who went into the house, she was running; the second one, right behind her, was Mr. Stembridge; I went in then and Mr. Sam Terry came in behind me. All my little children were right there; they were right there in those bedrooms while the shooting was going on. They came in behind Mr. Terry. All that shooting happened in just half a second; all the shots were fired in a short length of time. After they finished shooting, both of them ran out of the house; when I looked around both of them were just running. Emma and I went on out of the back door and I saw his car parked behind the house.

I don't know how many times Emma Johnekin was shot but I saw 3 holes in her. I don't know how many shots were fired in all. The shooting that killed Emma Johnekin took place in Baldwin County.

Immediately after the shooting, Emma and I walked out to the back and I started around the house but Johnny met us and said, "Don't you all try to walk, you all go inside the house and lay down." We went in Johnny's side from the back. Johnny went over to the next door and told those people to come over there and do something for us while he was going to the store and call the Sheriff, police and the doctor. He went running to Mr. Hardy's.

The police came right immediately, time he called them, looked like they were already coming. I estimate it is about 300 yards to Mr. Hardy's store from the front of the house. When the police got there, I was lying on the bed and he asked me what had happened and I just couldn't tell him nothing. I was in bad condition. They did not look around the house. The police carried me to the hospital right then and also carried Emma. My little girl and three policemen went with me.

We own a pistol. We always kept it around there in the living room-bedroom. In the third room back. It was not there that day. I didn't know where the pistol was, I didn't know it was around there. I was not making for that pistol when I went in the house. I can't shoot a pistol. Emma lived three days, I think after she was shot.

They never got that bullet out of me. I am still carrying it around.

Mr. Ennis: I am very familiar with the rule of law with reference to the admission of testimony for the present time and I want to arise now and address myself to the court and make the objection that I made a moment ago and ask that the court exclude from this jury all evidence on the part of this witness with reference to any wounds that may have been inflicted on her by Sam Terry. The witness testified that Sam Terry shot her. Sam Terry is not on trial. The defendant is not on trial for shooting this woman. They are not joint defendants. There is no evidence of any conspiracy. The state does not contend that in any way whatsoever. He has completed his examination of this witness and I respectfully say that such testimony should be stricken from the record and the jury instructed to disabuse their minds of that evidence, for it is highly prejudicial and most harmful and hurtful to this defendant.

BY THE COURT: Now, Mr. Baldwin, do you desire to be heard on that?

Mr. Baldwin: Yes, sir. We do contend that there is a conspiracy between these two men to do an unlawful act. The unlawful act was to force this boy to sign an assignment of his wages. They were both engaged in that act – force him against his will, had him in the collar. The evidence shows they had brass knucks and were going to make him sign it. Where two people engage in an unlawful enterprise and then that goes into another unlawful act they are still engaged in that unlawful enterprise, backing each other up as they go along. Each one is bound by what the other one does all the way that enterprise. Etc.

Mr. Ennis: I think the highest and best evidence on this particular question is the indictment itself. The Solicitor General has drafted a joint indictment against Marion W. Stembridge and Sam L. Terry. It may have been at one time the state was basing it on conspiracy but the grand jury on this indictment finds a no bill against Mr. Terry, as far as this trial is concerned.

Mr. Baldwin: That doesn't make any difference what the grand jury finds because he can still be indicted by a second grand jury and that does not make any difference anyhow. Mr. Terry is a witness, sworn here. Their contention as they outlined to the jury is that nobody had a pistol but Mr. Stembridge. We have got a right to see if that is true and show the fact that he shot, but I never dreamed of a proposition where you couldn't present wounds in a case, all in one transaction, all part of the res gestae of the case. Certainly you can present the wounds to show, if nothing else, how many shots were fired.

BY THE COURT: Well, I will adhere to my former ruling, Mr. Ennis; I will leave it in for the present time.

Mr. Ennis: In other words, I still have a right to renew my objection at any time before we go to the jury.

BY THE COURT: Yes."

Cross Examination by Mr. Evans

I do not know what caliber automatic pistol my husband owned. He kept it under the pillow in the bedroom next to the kitchen. He never puts his hands on it, it is moved first one place and then the other in making the bed, sometimes it is left on the dresser. Ordinarily, he kept it under the pillow. My son, Johnny Cooper, got the gun Sunday evening, the evening before the shooting occurred the next day. Johnny always goes around there and gets a gun or rifle or something and takes it to his side, but George didn't know he had it around there and, at that time, I didn't even know it. It was customary for him to come and get either one he wanted and to take them in his house. I don't know how many times he had gotten that pistol before. He didn't go hunting with the pistol or target shooting. I don't know what he got it for. When he would get the pistol, he would tell me and not tell George. I would not tell George and George would not know about it. I guess he just wanted to have something on his side for protection. Johnny didn't have a rifle over there that day. The rifle was Harvey's, another one of the boys. The boys were gone hunting with the rifle. They were going to kill, I don't know what, rats or something, left there soon Sunday morning and went in the country with it. The rifle was there Monday. It was not there Sunday. I don't know where the rifle was Monday. I don't know whether the rifle was on Johnny's side. I did not see Johnny with the rifle the day of the shooting. I don't know whether he went to the front door with the rifle. I don't know the reason he had the pistol; he was not mad about anybody and not expecting anything. If the pistol had been in my side of the house under that pillow that day that the shooting occurred, I would say it was in there and it had a right to be in there. If it had been, he would have said it, because the pistol was not in there.

Nobody told the police about George Harrison's gun when they came out there because they didn't ask nothing about it. I don't know when I told the police that we had a pistol out there but it was after they asked me if we had one, it might have been the next day. I didn't tell them Johnny had it, I didn't even know he had it.

I thought the pistol was in my side of the house just like it always was but I did not make any effort to get to that pistol because I didn't know how to use it. I did not see Johnny go in there after the shooting had occurred and pick that pistol up off the floor. He didn't go in the house we went out the back door at the same time Mr. Stembridge and Mr. Terry went out the front door. I turned to the right as I went out the back door. I started to the left side. I didn't start over to Johnny's side. Johnny saw me when he came out of the door. He come out of his door then. We met in the back just as the shooting was over. I did not stay inside the house any length of time before I left out of the back door.

When the trouble started, I was out on the porch of my neighbor Sarah Youngblood's house about 30 feet from my house and saw Mr. Sam Terry and Mr. Stembridge and Johnny and all the children on my porch. Emma was sitting so I couldn't see her. Johnny was sitting on the banister, Mr. Terry standing right close to Johnny and Emma was sitting kind of off in front of them. All of the children were just clustered around. I stood there on the neighbor's porch no more than about a second. I saw Mr. Stembridge walk right behind Johnny. He just stepped over there, he had his hand behind him. He was standing beside him; I don't mean on the ground. He didn't put his arm on him, put his hand down in his collar and held him.

I asked them what was the matter. They never heard me; they were 30 feet away. The folks in the neighbor's house didn't even hear it. Mr. Terry was closer to me than Mr. Stembridge. Mr. Terry didn't look at me. I didn't holler loud. After that I just kept walking to my house. I didn't look back. I saw Mr. Stembridge with his hand in Johnny's collar and I saw that pair of knucks. I didn't see them from the other porch, I saw them when I come up the steps. When I was coming up the steps, I saw his hand half-way out of his coat pocket. As I came across and up the steps, I didn't run or hurry.

When I got on the second door step, I saw him with his hand up that far. During the time I came off of the other porch, down the steps on the other side of the house, walked 30 or 35 feet between the houses, and came up my steps and got on my porch, Mr. Stembridge was just holding Johnny in the neck. Mr. Terry was just standing there with his hand in his pocket. Mr. Stembridge had his left hand half-way out of his coat pocket with brass knucks on it. As I came up the steps, Johnny was between him and the State sanitarium with his back to the South. Mr. Stembridge was facing Johnny and facing me. As to how he had Johnny in the collar by the right arm if he was facing this way, he didn't put his arm around him like that. When he got ready to put his hand down in Johnny's collar, he kind of stepped a little bit around him. I did not say that when I first saw them he had his hand in his collar, I said I looked at him when he put his hand down in there. I did not say that when I first came out on the neighbor's porch that I looked and saw Mr. Stembridge with his hand in Johnny's collar.

The knucks that I saw were black and had brass on them. I don't know where they are and don't know if the police ever found them. All the children saw the knucks but Johnny said he never saw them.

As I came up the steps, I was talking to Johnny but he never did even hear me. When Emma said, "Look at that man with those brass knucks," Mr. Stembridge broke to hit her with those knucks on his left hand and she dodged him. He come out with his hand and fastened her with the knucks and she dodged him and tore off in the house and that man tore off in the house right behind her. Johnny was there when all that happened. Emma was sitting right in front of the door about 4 or 5 feet from them. Mr. Stembridge turned Johnny loose, pulled his left hand out and hit at her out there on the porch. Johnny said he had never seen the brass knucks. I saw the knucks when he sprang at her, but Johnny was so scared he didn't see nothing. Johnny was standing up then. He was still sitting on the rail when I came walking up the steps but when I called him, he heard me and he got up. That was before Mr. Stembridge turned him loose. When Mr. Stembridge made that swing with the knucks, Johnny had got up, I was coming up the steps, Mr. Terry was between Johnny and my door and was about one step away from Johnny with his hand in his coat. Mr. Terry was standing there by the side of the door with his back against the wall when I passed him. Yes, his back was against the wall. I didn't go between Mr. Terry and Johnny. They were back from my side, they were not right in my door, they were more in his door than they were in mine. Mr. Terry was against the wall; he was not close to the rail.

Emma got up, Mr. Stembridge swung at her and she went running in the house, I went in the house behind him. When I started in the door, I saw Mr. Stembridge and Emma. He had fastened her right over here side of the head with the knucks. There was a place in her head about that long and blood running all down. They were in the second bedroom, I didn't see the knucks then, she was holding him around the waist and I don't know what he was doing, he had a pistol. He did not have it out then. She did not have a pistol. I don't know what he had done with the knucks but he ran in the house with his knucks because he hit her side of the head with them. I didn't see the knucks after I looked inside. He hit her on the left side. She was bleeding about as bad as anybody could. I didn't open my mouth, got so excited I couldn't say nothing. When I looked at them, in the second room, they were just standing up there side of the bed, I don't know what Mr. Stembridge was doing. He was doing all he could do, she was just holding him around the waist, holding one of his hands – I don't know, she said she was holding his hands. I saw her holding his hands. He had his other arm loose. I reckon he started to shooting her. I didn't see him shoot her but I know he shot her. I saw him when he shot her on the trunk, when she was sitting on the trunk. I wasn't standing there watching them. They were right straight ahead of me but Mr. Terry had shot me 3 times, I couldn't stand up there.

"Q. Before you ever got to Mr. Stembridge and before he ever got his pistol out you were shot three times from behind?

A. Yes, I was shot three times, every time behind.

Q. Didn't the first one knock you down?

A. No, sir.

Q. Did any of them knock you down?

A. Yes, I fell down.

Q. Did you know you were shot when you were hit the first time?

A. No, I didn't really know I was shot, I didn't know what happened to me.

Q. Did you know you were shot the second time?

A. Yes, I knew it then because I saw Mr. Terry behind me shooting.

Q. You turned and looked and saw him shooting?

A. Yes, sir. I did look back behind me and saw him.

Q. That is when you quit looking at Mr. Stembridge?

A. Mr. Terry, when I went in the door, Mr. Terry come right on in the door right behind me and time I entered in the second door Mr. Terry had shot me but before I got to Mr. Stembridge he had shot me again. He had shot three times before Mr. Stembridge shot a time.

Q. Then you went from there and laid down across the kitchen table?

A. Yes.

Q. Then Mr. Terry shot you again, is that right?

A. Yes, shot me.

Q. Are you sure it was that next shot he made, are you sure he did the other shooting?

A. He shot me every time.

Q. Did you turn and look at him as he shot you the last time?

A. That is why he shot me, I went to turn around and tell Emma to come on.

Q. Mr. Terry shot you the fourth time?

A. Yes, he shot me."

While I was on the table in the kitchen, I heard Mr. Stembridge shoot but I didn't see him shoot and when I looked again I was trying to see about Emma, she kept hollering, I was trying looked like to realize myself and to get her and when I looked she was coming on at the time, face all bloody and right arm all tore up, she was bleeding, and when I looked around then I wanted to say something to Emma but I couldn't speak right then. I saw her when she dropped on the trunk and fell over that way and Mr. Stembridge come right there and stood right inside that door and shot at her twice, stood there on the trunk, on the shoulder and next time he stuck the pistol right there to her stomach. I saw that with my own eyes, and he shot her in the stomach. God knows I am telling the truth.

While this was going on, I reckon Mr. Terry thought I was going to die on the table or it looked like I was going to raise up. He ran in there and decided he would shoot me again. He looked around and saw me fixing to raise up. When I turned around, he hit me, and both of them got right together and sold out the front door and I went out the back door. I told the police officers that Mr. Stembridge shot me when they came in there that morning talking about it.

Q. You told them Mr. Terry shot you?

A. Yes, and he was talking about Mr. Stembridge. I said, "Mr. Stembridge ain't shot me, Mr. Sam Terry shot me." That was several days after the shooting. They had told the police that Mr. Sam Terry shot me. All the children told them and Johnny told them. Johnny did not see it. He knew Mr. Terry walked off the porch and time he walked off, the pistol fired. I don't know who told the officers that Mr. Terry shot me right after it happened, I know I told them. Yes, it was a couple of days before I told them. I don't know whether the police officers took a bunch of warrants for Mr. Stembridge or not. I don't know whether they didn't take any for Mr. Terry or not. I haven't ever taken a warrant for Mr. Terry. I am not just accusing Mr. Terry because I don't want the jury to believe what Mr. Terry says in Mr. Stembridge's defense. I would not say Mr. Terry shot me if he didn't shoot me. If the ballistics report from Mr. Stembridge's gun shows that those bullets that came out of me were shot from Mr. Stembridge's gun, I say Mr. Stembridge didn't shoot me.

Mr. Stembridge couldn't shoot me coming to him. I was going to Mr. Stembridge and he couldn't shoot me in the back coming to him. He was obliged to shoot me in the face, in the front somewhere. I couldn't tell how many times Mr. Terry shot.

(Referring to diagram) I looked at this bullet hole in the door facing yesterday but I don't know who shot that bullet. Yesterday, when I talked with you at my house, I told you I didn't know who shot the bullet but they said that the bullet came straight and I said if the bullet came straight, Mr. Terry must have shot it. As to whether I told you positively yesterday that Mr. Terry shot it, I say he could have shot it. Yes, I said Mr. Terry shot it because he was shooting straight. I said he could have shot it because he was shooting straight.

It is not true that I was up there on the porch when Mr. Stembridge and Mr. Terry came up and was there all the time this thing happened. It is not true that I was there with Emma and Johnny and that while Mr. Stembridge was insisting that he do something about his bill that Johnny came off that rail and Emma cursed Mr. Stembridge and broke in there to get that gun.

Redirect Examination by Solicitor Baldwin
My children, Louvenia, age 11, Martha, age 9, and Will, age 13, were around the house during the shooting.

GEORGE HARRISON, Sworn for the State.
Direct examination by Solicitor Baldwin
I am George Harrison, husband of Mary Jane. We have been married about 4 years. The first I knew about the shooting was when I came home from work that night and my wife and Emma were in the hospital. I went back to the house the next morning and the children and I picked up hulls and cartridges and turned them over to Chief of Police Ellis. I also turned the bullets over to Mr. Ellis. We looked carefully in the house.

Cross Examination by Mr. Evans

I had done some business with Mr. Stembridge before all this occurred and I never had any trouble with him or Mr. Terry. I was not in the automobile deal. Mr. Stembridge talked to me about it after trouble about the payments on it. He first asked me where were the boys and what they were doing and told me to tell them to come to see him and I would tell them just what he said. I don't remember them going to see him.

When this shooting occurred, I owned a pistol and it stayed in my house in the dresser drawer, or in between the mattress, or under the pillow. I never did have a special place to keep it. The last time I saw it, it was either between the mattresses or under the pillow. The police did not talk to me the night of the shooting.

Chief Ellis and another man came out to my house to make a search the next morning.

Chief Ellis asked me for that pistol. He didn't ask me where it was. He didn't look for it as I told him that I would let him see it. When I started to get the pistol, it was not there. I didn't ask Johnny if he had it. I don't know whether Johnny was there when I went to look for the pistol or not but Johnny brought the pistol in there and I gave it to the Chief.

When the Chief of Police and I went to look for the pistol, we went to the bed first, where it was supposed to have been, and I looked first under the pillow, looked under the tick, then in the dresser drawer. Johnny has had that pistol on his side before. It is a 32 Savage automatic pistol. It shoots 9 times. When I got it back, we inspected it and it had not been shot. I don't know when was the last time it was shot. I don't know when was the last time I saw it. I have been down here over three years and it hadn't been shot in a long time before I left. All the cartridges I had for the pistol were in it and I don't think it was full. I did not have any extra cartridges around the house and the Chief did not search for any extra cartridges. The police didn't search my house. They didn't search the closet in back of the front room. They didn't make any search in the house at all. Yes, there is a closet in back of the front room door about 4 feet deep with a curtain in front of it. They did not search that closet. I got one bullet out of the facing of the door and turned it over to the Chief and there is some in the wall that have not been got out. I didn't get them out of the wall because I didn't want to tear up the wall. I haven't seen where they come out. I saw 2 holes in the wall. I didn't get one out of the wall in the second room because that would tear up the house. I told the police officers about the bullets I thought were out there, they saw the holes. I don't remember what the police said about it.

Redirect Examination by Solicitor Baldwin

The first and second rooms are bedrooms; the third room is a dining room with a bed in it. Right inside the third room there was a trunk at the time of the shooting and there is a bullet hole that goes in the wall about 30 inches from the floor up the wall right there. I saw you measure it with a yard stick about two days ago. Yes, the bullet is still in there somewhere. That wall has got great big sheets of sheet rock on both sides. The house belongs to Mr. Goldstein. The reason I didn't go in there was because I didn't want to tear up all that expensive wall. Mr. Frank Evans, Mr. Stembridge's attorney, has been out there and has seen that hole. He did not go in there and get it. He and Mr. Ellis, Mr. Lingold and none of you went in there to get that bullet. If Mr. Evans makes arrangements with Mr. Goldstein to pay the damages, he is at perfect liberty to get it.

Mr. Stembridge told me to tell the boys to come to see him and better do it pretty quick or there would be some trouble about it and be some serious trouble and said for them to come and make payments on the automobile, "what they owed me, don't there would be some serious trouble" and he did tell me that Johnny owed him some insurance some way or other and told me to tell him he was going to collect that money or beat him to death. He said, "Of course we have never attempted to do anything to anybody here in the office, but" says "We will come out there and do that," says, "We will come out and beat him to death or collect that money." That is what he told me.

Recross Examination by Mr. Evans

Mr. Stembridge said he was going to whip on the boys if they didn't pay off. That was along about Christmas. This didn't occur until March. When I told them Mr. Stembridge said he was going to whip on them I don't know really just what they said about it. I remember might good what Mr. Stembridge said because he said more than they said, if they said anything; they didn't answer; they didn't say he couldn't whip on them. They didn't say they would be ready for him. They didn't say that they had had folks to whip on them before. They didn't say they were used to folks whipping on them. I know they didn't make any threats at all.

The boys did not go down and pay Mr. Stembridge his money. They kept his car for a while. Someone else tore the car up while it was in their possession. I do not know how worried they were about Mr. Stembridge's attitude. None of them tried to do anything about it as I know of. I did not do any business with him after he said he would whip on the boys. I told the grand jury about the whipping business and some others. It is not wholly correct that after they had been whipped before like they were in Putnam County that I still did business there.

I told the boys if they thought they could go Mr. Stembridge's way on the automobile to go ahead on or let him know they were not going to do it or couldn't do it. While I was telling them that, I told Mr. Stembridge I was telling the boys what he said. I didn't tell Mr. Stembridge I was trying to make the boys pay him. I told him I would tell them what he said. I told Mr. Stembridge finally those boys were grown, I couldn't make them go. I did not tell him that they were hot-headed and they had had trouble with other automobiles in a good many other places.

EUGENE ELLIS, Sworn for the State.

Direct Examination by Solicitor Baldwin

I am Chief of Police of Milledgeville. I found out about 35 or 40 minutes after the shooting that it had occurred and helped make the arrest of Mr. Stembridge. When Mr. Stembridge was arrested, he had this 380 automatic Colt loaded and in his belt. It had a clip in it at that time. The clip holds 7 bullets and 1 in the barrel. These are the bullets that were in the clip and the barrel at that time. One side of the pistol was rusty and the other side was blue steel.

George Harrison turned 6 hulls over to me. They were the same caliber as the Stembridge pistol. There are all the hulls and I couldn't find any more. George Harrison turned over 3 bullets to me at the same time. They are here and they are the same caliber as the Stembridge pistol. I got two more bullets in connection with that shooting. This one was removed from Emma Johnekin's body and this one was given to me by Dr. Woods and was taken from her arm. The one that was taken from her body was in her stomach and the undertaker took it out after she was dead.

I kept in touch with Emma Johnekin every day while she was in the hospital until she died. Emma was wounded in the arm, in the shoulder and in the abdomen. There were 4 marks on her. That night, I saw on her body where a bullet went in her stomach and later on that bullet was taken out of her pelvic bone. In my opinion, from my examination of what I saw, I believe that that bullet that went in the abdomen caused her death.

I made a careful examination of the house where the shooting occurred. There was a trunk sitting here with a bullet hole in the wall just above the trunk. There was one in the wall there in that second room, it was in the door right next to the wall. I do not remember any other bullet holes. I don't remember whether or not a bullet went in either door facing.

Cross Examination by Mr. Evans

I do not know where the 3 bullets were found in the house that were delivered to me. They did not attempt to tell me where they came from. Two bullets came out of the negro

Emma. I got 5 bullets in all and all of them were of the same caliber as the Stembridge gun.

The G.B.I. agent took the 5 bullets for a ballistic report to Dr. Jones in Atlanta. He has this ballistics report, I don't have it.

I got 5 bullets and 6 hulls and I looked at the walls, the floor and ceiling to see if there was evidence of bullets there and so far as I know, these 5 account for all the bullets. I do not know whether or not there is still a bullet in Mary Jane Harrison. If there is a bullet in Mary Jane Harrison, that would be 6 bullets and 6 hulls.

The Stembridge pistol is in the same condition now with the same degree of rust as it was when I got it. I don't know of my own knowledge whether these bullets or hulls were fired from the Stembridge pistol. I don't know of my own knowledge what caused the death of Emma Johnekin.

Redirect Examination by Solicitor Baldwin
My opinion is that one of these bullets killed Emma Johnekin. She is dead.

J. E. JONES, Sworn for the State.

Direct Examination by Solicitor Baldwin
My name is J. E. Jones. I am an operator with the Georgia Bureau of Investigation and my duty is to assist the Sheriffs and municipal governing authorities and superior court judges in the investigation of any criminal case in which we are invited. I was called on this case on March 7th, the night it happened, and I went around to the hospital that night and talked to Emma Johnekin and while I was there, I noticed three wounds on her. There could have been more. There was one in the right arm; there was another one in the abdomen and there was another burned mark on the back on the left side. There was a bullet hole in the shoulder but I couldn't swear which side of the body it was on. It seemed as if the burned mark on her back had been caused

PAGE 31 MISSING FROM ORIGINAL TRANSCRIPT

The hospital or Mr. Beckum had already been to the hospital, one or the other and that they were in a critical condition and they wanted me to go up and talk with them. I found Emma –

Mr. Ennis: I object to this statement of the witness.

BY THE COURT: I sustain the objection as to that but on the other you may go ahead.

Mr. Ennis: May I call the court's attention to the 16th Ga. App. 172?

BY THE COURT: You may go ahead, Mr. Baldwin. I will instruct the jury in my charge.

Q. Did she make a statement to you as to the cause of her being shot?

A. Yes, she did.

Q. As to who shot her?

A. Yes.

Mr. Ennis: We understand the record shows your honor overruled my objection?

BY THE COURT: Yes, I overruled the objection.

Q. Did you write down what she said?

A. Yes.

Q. Write it down in long hand?

A. Yes.

Q. What did she say?

A. May I read it?

Yes. (Witness reads)

When Mr. Stembridge and Terry came there all of us were on the porch. He asked about Richard and Johnny told him Richard was not here. "Where is Richard?" "He is working." And Johnny changed the subject, Johnny said "I will pay you, Mr. Stembridge, for what I owe you. I went to work at the State." "Haven't you been working there all the time?" "No, sir." Then he asked Johnny, "Will you sign a paper for Richard?" "No, it doesn't seem right." And she spoke up, "Lord have mercy," said, "He has got on brass knucks" and turned to Mr. Stembridge and said, "Haven't you?"

Mr. Ennis: I object to anything he is reading in that statement that Johnny is saying. He is giving a dying declaration, supposed to be a statement of the deceased and there are statements purported to be made by Johnny that the deceased is saying not in the presence of this defendant.

BY THE COURT: The statement that Johnny made a request of the defendant – go ahead.

(Witness continues reading) "He has got on brass knucks – haven't you?" He turned to go in the house. "God damn it, what is it to you?" And he grabbed me and hit me with his knucks. He hit me on the head. Mary ran where I was and pulled him loose from me. He shot me in the hand and he shot at Mary. I went on inside the house and sat on the trunk. He came to the door and shot me in the shoulder and in the stomach. I didn't have a gun, neither a knife and Mary had neither gun nor knife. I swear this information is true. When he hit me I grabbed him and Mary pulled us apart. He had a gun and started firing. Signed, Emma Johnekin. This was signed in my presence and signed in the presence of deputy sheriff Buford Lingold and Louvenia Harrison and Johnny Cooper, the latter two being relatives of the deceased." I saw Mary Jane Harrison that night. She seemed to be in the same condition as Emma. She had been shot also. I talked to her that night.

Cross Examination by Mr. Evans

I had 2 years of pre-med at Mercer University. I have not had medical training. Emma Johnekin had a hole in her elbow. She had an abrasive wound on the right side of her head. I am positive the one I saw was on the right and if there was one on the left I didn't see it. I couldn't swear who her doctor was. I was new in this town at that time, he was introduced to me, I don't remember his name. As to my consulting with her doctor as I was going to take this so-called dying declaration, the doctor was in the room and I asked him in her presence her condition and that was when he put a 12- or 14-inch-long probe into her stomach. He never did answer one way or the other. As to whether he didn't answer as to her dying condition, I say he didn't answer my question. He came in while I was taking the statement. I don't remember the name of the doctor. As to whether I could anticipate that, as an investigating officer, I should know that the identity of the doctor would come up on the trial of this case, I say I know who the witnesses are that were there during the entire time, the doctor came in when I was about half way through with the statement and left before it was finished. I couldn't swear to the name of the doctor. As to my knowing the attending physician when I take a dying declaration as an investigating officer, I say I can't always get a doctor. Even though the doctor was available, I didn't think it was necessary. I didn't turn to the doctor and tell the doctor to tell her she was fixing to die because at the time I was in there, the doctor was making an examination and when I was taking this statement, talking to her about this, the doctor left immediately to go to see the other woman. I have been in cases before where dying declarations were involved. The doctor was in the room. I asked him the question. I had been told what he had said, he or some other doctor, as I have told you before, being a stranger in town, I didn't know which doctor had made the statement to Mr. Ellis. He simply told me they were in a critical condition and desired me to go up there. I wrote down the names of those present during the entire time.

It is not necessary that it should only be through a doctor that she would be conscious of a dying condition. There were other people in the room that heard her make the same groans and when I asked her the question did she realize the seriousness of her wounds and she said yes and when I asked her if she knew she would probably not live through it and she said yes and when I asked her to be very careful and not to leave out anything at all, I explained to her, I even told her I was sure she didn't want to go on to her reward and have the blood of some innocent person on her because she failed to make some statement and she said yes and then she began to talk and I began writing and during that time the doctor came in and he put the probe into her abdomen about 14 inches down into her abdomen and as soon as he took it out I asked him what was her condition. He did not answer my question one way or the other, he went on out to the other room.

I did not go and talk to the doctor when he was there available and ask if she was in a dying condition because the Chief of Police had told me that the doctor had made the statement to him. It is true that I had heard that the other negro woman was in a dying condition too. She didn't die but she made a statement to me, though, as if she had. I believe that the other negro woman thought that she was going to die. I turned that statement over to the Chief of Police. My only copy is in Atlanta. I couldn't swear the exact words of the statement but it said virtually the same thing. I took it down. I don't remember every word she said.

She said she was next door at the time Mr. Stembridge came up and she saw them on the porch and came over. When she arrived there on the porch there was a scuffle. She heard Emma say that Mr. Stembridge had on brass knucks. I asked her if she saw the brass knucks; she said she did. She said she heard Mr. Stembridge make a statement to her, "What business is it of yours?" She said she saw Emma go into the house, Mr. Stembridge followed her and she came in behind. She told me she was shot in the back by Mr. Terry. She put all of that into what she thought was her dying statement the night that I talked to her, the same night she was shot. She said she tried to get to them, to the people that were fighting, and was shot again. She said she went out to the back door and saw a car.

If there was that big a conflict between the two witnesses in their so-called dying statements where one said that "I got in a tussle in there and Mary came through and pulled the fellow off me with the gun and he then shot me in the hand and turned and shot at her," and if the other made the statement, "No, I walked in there and was shot in the back and was shot again in the back and didn't go around them and went and lay down on the back table," as to this question whether or not I would notice that, as an investigating officer, I say that the other witness is here, you may question her as to what her statement is. I have the statement from her.

I do not know whether Emma was under morphine or not at the time she made her statement. I did not ask the doctor whether she was under morphine, I was told by the nurse that nothing had been done to her. She was not a special nurse assigned to Emma, she was a general nurse. As to my seeing that a person is not doped up when I take a dying declaration from them, I say she was talking to me as any person that knew what they were saying. I have not said I had any medical experience. I was in a hurry to get into the room.

I went to the house where the shooting occurred and investigated it. I didn't get the bullets. When I arrived there, the door was locked, the house was closed, I had to come back to town. That was the night of the shooting. I went back the next day and found 2 bullet holes in the wall, one in the second room on the right wall and one in the third room on the right wall and those 2 bullets are still in the wall as I did not get them. As to whether the jury is entitled to that evidence in this case, I think it would be the place of the court or the city police or someone else to recommend that I go out and tear down that wall to get those bullets. It is a solid wall; you would have to cut through to get inside. It would be expensive. As to whether the State and the people who investigate a crime are under a duty to produce these bullets in the trial of this case, I say it would be the place of the Sheriff or the police or the court to rule on that and go and remove them out of the wall in as much as I don't feel responsible for the expense of tearing down somebody else's wall. It is beside the point how much I think it would cost. As to my having had a ballistics report made and as to my duty to get the two bullets which went in the wall, I say I was not the only one investigating. That would be for the court or the city or the county to decide, not for me. Yes, I also saw what looked like a bullet hole in the door facing. The bullet had been removed.

It is possible that all 3 of the bullets could have been removed. However, I did not see any marks on the wall. I went to the other side and looked to see if they came through. I am sure that there were still 2 bullets out there. The other investigating officers know that they are there. I couldn't answer whether they attached any consequence to those 2 bullets or not, they might or might not help convict or clear a man, as far as I am concerned. They might or might not have any bearing in this case, if it could be proven what gun they were shot from.

I had a ballistics report made on all the bullets that were found. I have not provided you with any knowledge about what that ballistics report contains. I don't know that you have any knowledge as to what kind of gun these bullets came out of. There were 6 hulls that I sent in from out there.

I haven't read the ballistics report; that report is to be mailed or has been mailed to the Chief of Police in Milledgeville. I took it to Dr. (Herman) Jones' laboratory and requested them to mail the answer to the Chief of Police in Milledgeville. I was told by him what it contained but would that be permissible? All I know about is that it was to be mailed to Baldwin County.

I have never read the ballistic report. I have not seen it since I have been in Milledgeville. As to my being the chief investigator in this case and never having seen the ballistic report, I ask why do you say I am the chief investigator in this case?

Redirect Examination by Solicitor Baldwin

Mr. Evans must have been in this house too; he drew this picture out there. I don't have any objection to him taking those bullets out. If the County will pay for it, I will be glad to take out the bullets. There is a bullet now that has not been cut out of the wall back in the third bedroom. That was right over the trunk where Emma Johnekin was sitting when she was shot.

Recross Examination by Mr. Evans

As to whether or not when I have a ballistic report favorable to the State, I generally bring it into court, I say it is generally mailed to me and, as a general rule, they bring it down themselves, if they are to come.

If the ballistic report showed the bullets were fired, for instance, from Mr. Terry's gun, the report would be here as evidence, if it had not been mailed. As to the ballistic report being available and as to the ability of the State to bring it in here, if they want to I am sure they can, if they get the report from Dr. Herman Jones.

(Recess until the following morning)

Mr. Jones on the stand

I have been with the Georgia Bureau of Investigation since September of last year. Previously, I was with the Department of Labor, State Department of Labor, as a claims investigator; prior to that with the Retail Credit Company as an insurance investigator. During the war and before my entrance into the service, I was with the Macon Police Department as auxiliary police.

I was in Milledgeville when this case occurred, was called on the case and immediately went into my duties in the investigation of the case. My duty is to assist Sheriffs, municipal governing authorities and superior court judges. I didn't hear anyone placed directly in charge of obtaining the evidence. All of us who were working on the case secured what evidence we could. All of us were working together. I take my orders from the Sheriff or Chief of Police in any case I am working on. If it was any lead in this case, it would be the Chief of Police. He was the directing officer. I was answerable to him. He assigned me the duty of assisting him in the investigation. He asked that I secure statements from the two women in the hospital. He asked that I have the gun and the projectiles and the shells analyzed, which I did.

The ballistic reports, in order for them to be carried to the Fulton County Laboratory, some arrangement for payment must be made. Mr. Marion Ennis was contacted as county attorney. I told the Fulton County Laboratory to direct the bill to Mr. Marion Ennis. So far as I know, the original copy was sent to him also. I did not receive the original copy; I did not wait there until it was completed.

As to my saying yesterday that the ballistic report would be sent to the Chief of Police, the Chief of Police told me he has not received it and I said so far as I know, it might have gone with the bill. I have not seen it. I didn't make any effort prior to yesterday to determine that the ballistic report was available.

I had a copy of the ballistic report that was sent to me, as I told you yesterday, that I haven't read. I don't have that copy with me. I can secure it in a few minutes. (Witness goes out of courtroom and gets ballistic report).

I have not read this report. I testified yesterday that I knew what the substance of the report was. This report is the same in substance as I knew.

This report is dated July 12, 1949, about a week and one day ago. I received the report 5 days ago. As to my having the report available yesterday, I told you yesterday I didn't have the original and I hadn't read a copy. As to my having received this report 3 days ago and knowing I would be a witness in this trial and failing to read my copy, I say I was under the impression that the original would be in the courtroom. I requested that it be sent here and I have not seen it. That is a carbon copy as you can see. As to whether it is customary for the laboratory to send one to the Chief investigating officer, one to the man who requests it and one the county authorities responsible for payment, I would say that the original usually goes with the man from the laboratory if he comes to the trial. It is true that when the Fulton Laboratory makes a ballistic report for another county, they send the original report to the investigating officer and, if requested, to the investigating man who brought the materials in.

I requested a copy of the ballistic report in this case. Yes, I got it. As to anybody being disturbed about not finding the original for this prosecution, I did not hear anyone mention it.

As to my duty to have the ballistic report, since the State was trying this case under the theory that Sam Terry fired 4 of these shots, I say I mean this, I mean I received my report about 3 days ago in Madison. Milledgeville is a little further than Madison. I assumed someone here in Milledgeville, Baldwin County, has the original copy. I haven't been able to find it and I still haven't been able to find it. I delivered the materials for the ballistic report to the laboratory. (The defense introduced the witness's copy of the ballistic report into evidence).

The ballistic report is headed, "Laboratory report on Marion W. Stembridge, white male," then "Emma Johnekin, black, female, deceased, Mary Jane Harrison, black female, wounded, officer Jimmy Jones, Georgia Bureau of Investigation, Milledgeville, Baldwin County, Georgia. On July 8, 1949, we received in the laboratory in person from Mr. Jimmy Jones, Georgia Bureau", etc.

I asked the laboratory to make an analysis and asked them to send the report to the Chief of Police, in Milledgeville. I asked the Chief if he had received his report, the day after I received mine. I don't remember asking him the next day. I asked him again yesterday afternoon after court and he said he had not received it.

The theory of this case is that Mr. Sam Terry shot some of the times. That is what one of the witnesses would say. Yes, some more of the witnesses will say that.

In other words that is what I have got this case based on. I didn't think it was my duty to bring the carbon copy of the ballistic report into court yesterday. I would have disclosed that I had the carbon copy if I had been asked. You asked me if I had read the report and I told you no. I knew the contents according to what they told me. As to my being the man to see that the Chief of Police got the report and as to my duty to do something to see that he got it, I assumed that surely he would have it by Monday. I found out next day he didn't have it. I assumed he would have it. I received mine in the evening mail; I asked him next morning and he didn't have it. I went about my work, I was not concerned with it, I thought he would receive it that afternoon. I didn't say night before last that I talked with him about it. I said yesterday afternoon after court he told me that he had not received it. As to whether this report was important enough to the State's theory in this case for me to have been on the alert and to have asked him, I say I have seven counties in this territory and didn't return here from time to time. I asked him about it until court time yesterday and told him I had received a carbon copy and I assumed that it would be here or that he would find out about it. I don't come into Baldwin County every day.

I consider it material to this case whether all these bullets were fired from Marion Stembridge's gun or whether some were fired from Sam Terry's gun or some other gun.

If all the bullets were fired from Marion Stembridge's gun inside that house, then some of the witnesses would be lying when they say that some were fired from Terry's gun.

As to whose duty it is to determine whether or not all those bullets were fired from the same gun, I say all of the bullets cannot be secured. There are 2 bullets still in the wall. According to an X-ray that I saw, there is one in the body of Mary Jane Harrison. That makes three. If there is another one in the body of Mary Jane Harrison, I don't know it, there may be. I say there is three.

There is no evidence that the 2 bullets have been taken out of the wall. This would be the duty of some investigating officer.

I am an investigating officer. It is true that the theory of this case is that Sam Terry did part of this shooting and I would say that the first thing which I should do would be to find the bullets that didn't have the ballistics that identified them with the pistol of Marion Stembridge and they would probably be the bullets we were looking for. So with this in view, I sent for this report.

I did not find any bullets except that were shot by the Stembridge gun.

I didn't think it was worthwhile to go further and get one out of the wall because time after time they have said that Marion Stembridge put his pistol right down there and that is where he shot right through the wall. I think we have sufficient evidence to show which gun fired that projectile. It was the Stembridge gun so I really didn't see any use to take it out of the wall. If that projectile had gone into the inside of the wall and struck a knot, it might be in the ceiling or under the ground or most any place and one might remove the entire house and never find the projectile. I didn't attempt to remove the plaster board to look in. As to whether I am indicting a man without taking the trouble to look through a little plaster wall that would cost may be a dollar to do, I say I didn't know how much it would cost to remove the wall and perhaps the entire section of the wall. I couldn't positively say that it would be lying just beyond that wall. I would say it would cost a considerable amount to defend a murder case. It is not my duty to remove a person's wall. It would be for the city or county to request it. It would be somebody's duty on the investigating force. It has not been done.

The ballistic report reads as follows:

"On July 8, 1949, we received in the laboratory in person from Mr. Jimmy Jones, Georgia Bureau of Investigation, one 380 caliber Colt automatic pistol 110946 with seven loaded cartridges in the clip and one in the barrel. Pistol said to have been taken from Marion W. Stembridge, white male. One green glass bottle labeled 'Six empty cartridges, found in the Harrison residence, Oconee Heights 3-8-49; containing six 380 Remington U.M.C. fired shells, initialed inside shoulder of shell E.A.E.' 'One green glass bottle labeled 'three bullets found in the Harrison residence in Oconee Heights, 3-9-49, Stembridge case, containing three fired 380 projectiles, initialed on the base E.E.' 'One green glass bottle labeled, 'From Emma Johnekin's right arm, Richard Binion clinic, Dr. Woods, 3-9-49. Stembridge case' containing one fired 380 projectile, initialed E.E. on the base. One green glass bottle labeled, 'One bullet removed from Emma Johnekin's pelvic bone, 3-11-49, Stembridge case' containing one 380 fired projectile, initials on base E.E. Service requested: To compare Colt automatic "A" with "B" shells, "C" projectiles, "D" projectile and "E" projectile."

I requested the service of the laboratory to determine if all these bullets and all these hulls came out of the Stembridge gun.

The results of the ballistics report are as follows:

"Results: Tests were fired from evidence Colt "A" into recovery box, using 380 Remington automatic ammunition. Test shells were placed under comparison microscope with evidence shells "B" and an examination was made. Upon completion of our examination we find that all six evidence shells did match with the test shell. It is therefore our opinion that this evidence pistol "A" did fire all evidence shells "B". Test projectile was placed under comparison microscope with evidence projectiles "C", "D" and "E" and examinations were made. Upon completion of these examinations we find that "C", "D" and "E" projectiles did match with test projectile. It is therefore our opinion that evidence "A" automatic pistol did fire all evidence projectiles "C", "D" and "E".

This ballistic report is as accurate as finger printing. I knew the results yesterday. As to whether I knew it at the time I went to the grand jury, I didn't go into the grand jury room, I was not called.

At the time the grand jury met, I knew the results of the ballistic report of my own knowledge. I passed this information on to the people in the prosecution and it was known to them when the case went into the grand jury room. I have a feeling for the citizens of Georgia and a duty toward them who are accused of crime when I discover there is no reasonable basis for prosecution.

From the amount of evidence in the ballistic report, I do not think Sam Terry ought to be indicted but the feelings of the people who have been shot must also be taken into consideration. No, the feelings of the people who have been shot do not justify the prosecution of an innocent man. According to that report, if all of the evidence that could be found were based entirely on that report, then certainly he should not be indicted for attempt to murder. That report does not contain all of the projectiles, neither does it have all of the shells. As to whose duty it was to get them, I couldn't get the projectile out of the body of a person. The doctor refused to remove the projectile. I suppose the doctor is available for testimony.

I can't answer whether I have ever been in a case where a lawyer has tried any harder to get the State to bring in evidence than you are having to do in this case.

When I said that you had to make some allowance for the feeling of the people who were shot, I mean that there are people who are willing to swear that they were shot by a certain person and, of course, their sworn statements must be considered also.

We don't have the bullet that went into her body.

I was not in here when she said 4 of the bullets went into her. Yes, she did tell me that. I investigated and got her statement to that effect. I didn't produce her statement here yesterday. Yes, I knew the contents.

She told me that Sam Terry shot her 4 times. If I knew I had the other 3 bullets that were shot into her, I would not be handicapped by the one bullet that is still in her. I don't know that I have the 3 bullets. I don't know that they were in those green laboratory bottles.

All of the cartridge hulls are from Mr. Stembridge's gun. I didn't feel it was my duty unless I was requested to get the bullets out of the wall.

Chief Ellis reported the shooting to me at about 7 or 8 o'clock that night and I immediately went to the hospital and went to the room of Emma Johnekin and got her statement. I then went into the x-ray room where Mary Jane Harrison was and got a statement from her and then went to type those statements. As to whether I should have taken the time to type those statements when they gave me clues or direct evidence to the fact that I could go to the house and find the bullets shot by both of these guns, I say I went out to the house first but I couldn't get in the house. As to my asking for a key to the house, there was no one at home. They were on the way to the hospital. As to whether they were on the way or at the hospital, I say they were not all at the hospital when I left, if they were, I didn't see them. As to who I asked for the key to the house, I was told when I left that George was at the house and I went out there with the intention of seeing him there; when I arrived George was not at the house. I went back to town. No, I didn't see George at that time. I looked for George. I didn't find him that evening. As to where George was that evening, there were also about six other persons working on the case at the same time and I didn't take charge of the case. As to who was supposed to investigate the house, I didn't hear anyone assigned to the house. I didn't take charge because I work for the persons who call me to assist them and not direct them. The house was checked. I don't know whether it was that night or next morning. As to my inability to find George and knowledge that the house should be checked, I thought that someone else was looking for him or would locate him.

I checked with the people who had been shot, checked the house and couldn't find George, the house was locked and I didn't feel like it was important enough to force the door or pull the window so I came back to town looking for George and I couldn't find him, then I went to the City Hall and Mr. Stembridge was in jail there and I wanted to hear his side of the story. He told me he would like to make a statement. I went over to the County jail with him. He asked me to stay with him and I rode with him from the City Hall to the County jail. I didn't hear him say that he desired me to take it down; I did make notes and took it down.

Mr. Stembridge, of his own volition, told me his side. He said they had a gun. He said he did all the shooting. That immediately pointed to a bad conflict of the evidence. I went to see Mr. Terry after I left him.

I talked with Mr. Terry but did not get a signed statement. He said he did not do any of the shooting. It occurred to me then that somebody ought to go out there and get hold of those bullets. As to what I did, the bullets were being looked into by Mr. Ellis or Mr. Beckum I believe was on at the time.

I don't know whether Mr. Beckum went out there that night or not, by the time I left those two people, I had another appointment in another County and when I came back early the next morning, the police had the bullets.

As to my duty to keep down tampering with the bullets as evidence, I don't see how the shells or bullets that were given me later could have been tampered with. It could have been possible to have made some substitutions. It is true that the longer the bullets were left out there after the crime was committed, the more chance there would be of tampering with them. If I were in charge, I would think the investigating officers had a duty to throw a mantle of protection around anybody accused of crime, particularly murder, by seeing that those things that reasonably could have been done were done. If I had been in charge and couldn't have found George, I probably would have got in the house. It is almost impossible to say "I would have got in" in as much as I didn't. I can only say I probably would have gone in if I had had to saw the door down if I had been in charge.

I have Mr. Stembridge's statement in long hand. This is the statement that he gave to me. He did not ever make any other statement to me. His written statement is substantially what he said all the way through. There has been no change in his position since the last time I talked with him.

Redirect Examination by Solicitor Baldwin

No, I am not trying to hold anything back in this case. Yes, I offered to tell them this ballistics report yesterday evening. Yes, they refused to let me tell it. There was no secret that I had gotten the ballistic report. The county authorities told us to make it and pay for it, Mr. Marion Ennis did. That was before he was employed in this case but he was county attorney and it was necessary for us to ask him. The County always pays these experts to make these examinations.

I was in there when the doctor probed the wound in Emma Johnekin's stomach. She was the girl that died within 2 days. The doctor had a round piece of wood about the size of a pencil lead or perhaps a little larger and a swab of cotton on the end and he dipped that in some solution and showed us the path of the bullet. He put it into her stomach through the bullet hole and ran it out. There were 3 openings in her abdomen. He followed the stick during its entire length, beginning here, looping through a roll of fat and then back into the abdomen for the entire length of the probe. The probe was at least 12 or 14 inches long. It ran down in that direction to that bullet wound 14 inches on down. It went diagonally right through her stomach. It went 14 inches and I couldn't say whether it had even reached the bottom then. She was dead a short time after that. From having seen that done and my examination of her, it is my opinion that the bullet in her abdomen caused her death. I am fully aware that Mr. Evans knows about those 2 bullets in that wall and that he knew about it yesterday. He made this picture some time ago and he knew about it then because he put them on the picture and nobody was holding him back from getting them out of the wall.

State rests.

T. A. MADDOX, Sworn for Defendant.

Direct examination by Mr. Ennis

My name is T. A. Maddox; I live in Eatonton, Putnam County; I am in the dairy business and have lived in Putnam County all my life. I know Mary Jane Harrison. She was Mary Jane Cooper before she married George Harrison. I know her general character in the community to be mighty bad. I would not believe her on oath.

No Cross Examination

W. J. ROBERTS, Sworn for defendant

Direct Examination by Mr. Ennis

My name is W. J. Roberts, I was raised and lived in Putnam County. I know Mary Jane Harrison; she was a Cooper before she married. I know a little something about her reputation in the community in which she lived. I do not know her general character. I know the reputation that she bore in the community in which she lived was pretty bad. I would not believe her on oath.

Cross Examination by Solicitor Baldwin

She had not had any kind of case in court in Eatonton that I know of.

SAM L. TERRY, Sworn for defendant.

Direct examination by Mr. Evans

I am Sam Terry. I am coroner of this County. I am employed by Mr. Marion Stembridge. It was late in the afternoon of March 7th I accompanied Mr. Stembridge out to Oconee Heights to talk with Mary Jane Harrison. Her two sons, Richard Lee and Johnny Cooper, had a long past due account, one of which they neglected to attend to, one that they persistently stayed away from, refused to discuss it one way or the other. When we got to the house we found two women, two negro women, and one negro man. The man happened to be Johnny Cooper as I later learned, the two women Mary Jane Harrison and the woman that is dead. We got there, we both, Mr. Stembridge greeted them very nicely and walked up on the porch and I accompanied him. I stopped at the top of the steps. Mr. Stembridge went around, Johnny was facing south, there was a banister there, with his right leg up on the banister. That threw Mr. Stembridge facing me. He talked to him about his account and asked him why he was reluctant, not only him but his other brother and his mother, to come in and discuss it. Saying at the same time, "We have never put a hardship on you, we have carried you when we couldn't carry others, we have actually fed you. I can't understand to save my life why you don't come in, some of you, and talk this matter over. I am still willing to play ball with you, let you pay it out in your own way. Now, what do you say about it?"

They talked on, everything was all right, by the tone of the conversation it looked as if we would not be there but a minute or two. Finally he turned to me and said, "Sam, I had a card there, order on Johnny's salary."

I took a small card, this is the card right here, this is what I wrote, Gentlemen, wrote it out very hurriedly. I don't remember what is on there, walked over and handed it to Johnny with my fountain pen, it was right there, stepped back to the top of the steps, Johnny went to write it. He was sitting on the rail all the time. He went to sign his name on it.

When I walked up there and carried this card there were two negro women muttering to themselves, one to the other. I don't know what they were saying, didn't make any difference to me. As soon as I handed him that I came back to the top of the steps, I guess the distance possibly to Mr. Baldwin, not over that far, Mr. Baldwin and myself, and when he was about to sign it the negro woman on the south side or the right entrance of the house, says, "Don't sign that thing, Boy" and immediately the one this side said, "No, you don't, don't you sign nothing."

Well, he hesitated for a moment, he didn't sign. She told him again, "Don't you sign nothing." Well, he told Mr. Stembridge, he said, "I am not going to sign it, no, sir, I am not going to sign it. I am going to let the rest of them pay it." Mr. Stembridge said, "Johnny don't you think that you owe that to me after I have been so kind to you and your family, not only you but your family, when you jumped from one job to another and you couldn't keep it long enough and the chances were it was about something like this, that you owed somebody, don't you think it would be better for you to sign that? If you don't, I am going to have to take you into court and when I do that you know what that means. It will be that much more on you and big court costs and you couldn't stand that. Won't you sign it?"

Says, "No, I am not going to sign, no, I am not going to sign it" and when he said that he come off and his arm went up to Mr. Stembridge, and when he did that – I would like to have that diagram (diagram of house is handed witness who holds for all to see), he was just about this distance right here from this door here. When he come off there and grabbed Mr. Stembridge, that threw them at a 45-degree angle with the center of this division here in his former position. They stood there for just a moment, when this woman right here in this door says, "Look at that white man with his hands on my boy" and she immediately turned, she said, "You white son of a bitch, I will shoot your damn heart out" and she kept that up until she disappeared in the back.

Looked as if Mr. Stembridge was frozen there for just a moment and also the negro man. You can imagine how I felt too. Mr. Stembridge got up; I mean he pushed the negro back to the railing. Mr. Stembridge looked as if he was trying to make up his mind – he ran to the door and caught the latch up, this is the entrance of it – it looked as if he was trying to make up his mind whether to run for it or whether to go down and go in there and catch her before she could shoot him, as she had already made that remark that she would do.

I didn't know what to do. I kind of turned as if to go as if to follow him or get ahead of him. I certainly would have got ahead of him if he had come my way, but he didn't, he shot in the room. As soon as he did that I stepped up within approximately two feet of that door and stopped, expecting the negro out any moment, to make a dive for it and which he did immediately. When he did that I was standing there with my hands in my pocket, thinking what am I going to do, what I can do. You can imagine what a position I was in.

A few minutes ago when I said Mr. Stembridge stopped at the door jamb and then shot into the room, I mean he ran into the room, I don't mean he actually made a shot.

When he went into the room, Johnny was still on the porch and Johnny attempted to go into that same room. The woman standing between the two doors followed Mr. Stembridge in that room. The boy attempted to follow her in but I jumped up between him and the door. I did not have a pistol. I don't know whether he had one or not. He didn't show it.

I stood there for I reckon a second or two, and I told him, "You can't come in here, don't you try to come in here." He kept making his way, he stepped back until he got even with the other door. Then he made a dive for it and slammed the door to and locked it.

He didn't go through over me because he figured possibly I had a gun, I had my hand in my pocket and stuck my finger out, he couldn't tell whether I had a gun or not and he backed up. He went in the door to the apartment on the South. That is not the one the shooting took place in and I did not see him anymore.

After he went in the South apartment door, for a second I kept my eye on that door. I didn't know whether he was coming back out there or not, I didn't know what he was coming out with. I had given up; I knew that they had the advantage of me but he didn't come out and I turned around and as soon as I heard him going back towards the back of the house I turned around and when I turned around I observed Mr. Stembridge holding a negro woman's hand up. Which one it was I don't know. And she had a gun in her hand. They were weaving from room to the door, the middle door leading into the back, and about that time I hollered out, I said, "Look out, Marion, look out, he is coming around the other way." I saw them stop, and about that time they started shooting. I didn't know who was doing the shooting, whether Mr. Stembridge was doing the shooting or whether the negro was doing the shooting or who was getting shot. I was tied up by the door, I couldn't leave there because there were two other negroes supposed to have been there, her husband and her other son, which I knew were very bad, mean negroes.

The shooting was done so fast until I couldn't keep up with them, in fact, it excited me, I didn't know how many shots it was, couldn't tell you to save my life. Immediately, I saw one of these women go down as if she had stepped off into the back, as if she had stepped on an uneven step, from one room to another. Marion came bouncing out then and before he got there he hollered to me at the front door, said, "Go on, Sam, go ahead." I didn't move. He got almost to the door and said, "Go ahead, Sam, there is going to be more shooting." Well, I left there then in a big hurry. We came on down to the car as quick as we could possibly get there.

I put Mr. Stembridge out at his place of business, came down and stopped in front of Culver and Kidd's, rushed over to the corner, I saw Parker, the policeman, said, "Where is Ellis?" He said, "He is not here but Beckum is here." I said, "Let me see him right quick." Beckum was in charge, I observed at the same time that the phone was ringing and one of the policemen was answering and he had put the receiver down and ran down to the cafe and here come Beckum. I told Parker to start with, "I want to see him, Parker, I want to talk to him and tell him about the shooting we were in out at Oconee Heights." He said, "All right, here comes Beckum." I hollered to Beckum three times, I know. I know of three times I hollered at him. It was before he got to the phone. When he got away from it, when he hung up the receiver, he said, "All right, Boys, come on, there has been a shooting at Oconee Heights, let's go" and off they went.

Cross Examination by Solicitor Baldwin
I work for Mr. Stembridge. I do not make any loans myself. I do appraisals and collections. I am not familiar with all the books. I do not have the ledger sheet on these negroes' account. I couldn't get it, Mr. Stembridge could possibly get it. I don't know whether Mr. Stembridge produced it as evidence on the bond hearing or not. We looked at it. I don't have the least idea how much the automobile was sold to the negroes for. Mr. Stembridge looked after the automobile part of the business. I don't remember telling you what it sold for on the bond hearing. I might have told you when I saw the sheet. I don't remember what it was. I don't look after that part of it and it is not familiar in my mind. I don't remember the amount of the note. I think Mr. Stembridge took it; I am not sure. If I took it, I took it on his word. This paper was here before, I don't see any reason why it should not be here now. I can't get it, Mr. Stembridge will have to get it, he keeps those papers.

I didn't ever make any collections on this automobile on the outside, only in the office. I think I made some in the office. We didn't have to put credits on the note, we give them credit on the ledger page and when the note is paid, we return it to them marked paid. It is not necessary to credit a note on the back, they got a receipt written by whoever receives the money. As to my knowing that I am supposed to enter a credit on a note every time a payment is made, I do know when you get a receipt that is prima facie evidence of it being on the back of the note. If I make a payment on a note, sometimes the bank credits it on the back.

This is the note. This note is for $1027.00. I witnessed it as a notary public. I didn't take the note, I witnessed it as notary public. There is a big difference in a notary witnessing a paper and in accepting it through the process of dealing with them. It is possible that I accepted some payments on this note.

I imagine I had been out to this negro house about 3 times before this shooting occurred. I did not carry a pistol out there. I did not on one previous occasion get out and go to the door and then go back and get my pistol and put it in my pocket. I certainly didn't. I don't carry a gun with me at all. I have never carried a gun at all. I have never carried a gun on my collection trips. I told the jury that I had my finger in my pocket sticking out like a pistol. It is true that I told the court on the bond hearing that I had a paper bradding machine in my pocket sticking out like a pistol. I had both of them. I didn't have a pistol, I had the clip, a small stapling machine, because I had been out on an inquest and Mr. Stembridge caught me as I was going back to the office. I don't know whether I used that as a pistol or my finger; I had my hand on it.

When I got to the house, I didn't know Mary Jane Harrison, I couldn't pick them out of that crowd right there to save my life. I didn't know which one was the mother of the boy Johnny. Both of the women were there when we got there. Mr. Stembridge directed me to write an order for that negro to sign. It is true this order doesn't say how much he was to pay a week. He discussed that with him. Mr. Stembridge told him, "Your amount is $50. I will put down here in my handwriting whatever you say you can pay and how little, just so we get it started and when you get it started you will pay out before you know it." It doesn't say when it was to be paid, it just says he was to pay Mr. Stembridge $50 and it isn't directed to anybody.

I did not say on the bond hearing that Mr. Stembridge grabbed him back of the neck and said "You will sign it." No, I didn't say that. I don't think my lawyer opened his case by saying Mr. Stembridge said "You will sign it;" I don't remember that. I know he didn't grab him back of the neck. He didn't grab him anywhere; the negro grabbed him. Mr. Stembridge grabbed that negro too. I am not holding anything back. The woman said "Look at that white man got his hand on that boy" and when she turned and went into the room, she started to cursing him, called him a son of a bitch and said, "You white son of a bitch, I will get my gun and shoot your damn heart."

It is true that these negroes knew I was coroner. It is true that these negroes knew my father was sheriff of this county for a long time. It is right that they knew Mr. Stembridge as a prominent man. As to these negroes jumping and cursing Mr. Stembridge and I, I say that they did, that you know it and there is the record before you. They called Mr. Stembridge a white son of a bitch. She said "Take your hands off that boy you white son of a bitch." She might have said "my boy," I don't deny that. Then she went in the house. The woman that said that was in the door next to me. It was the one on the porch towards Milledgeville that said that. Both of the women looked black to me. Mary Jane looked black. I am talking about the one that went into the house first, the one next to me. I think she said "my boy;" I know she said "that boy." After she made the statement that "I will shoot your heart out you son of a bitch," Mr. Stembridge went in there behind her. As to her saying anything about "white", she may have said that. Anyway, she said "I am going to shoot your heart out you son of a bitch." As to my leaving out the word "white" in my statement, I will say it now. I will put the "white" in there. I don't know whether she went back and got the pistol or not. I was not in position to see in there. She was the first one that went in and she said that she was after the pistol. Mr. Stembridge went in there after her. He hesitated for just a second. It looked like he was trying to make up his mind whether he wanted to go in or leave out in a hurry. He went in. The other woman on the lower side went in next. Didn't anyone go in next. I never did get off the porch. After the first woman went in there, everything happened and the shooting was over in just a matter of seconds. To tell the truth, I don't know how many shots I heard. Couldn't say whether it was 2 or 8, 9 or 10.

I have a personal pistol, a 38 S. & W. revolver that was my father's. I don't have and don't need an office pistol. I have never pulled a pistol on a negro in the office. Nothing ever comes up that would necessitate my pulling one there.

I don't know which room it actually took place in; all the scuffling going on was in the door it looked like between the front room and the next one, if there is a next one. I don't know how many rooms in there. The only thing I saw was peeping in the first one there. I didn't go in there to find out.

I never did see Mr. Stembridge carrying a pistol. I never saw him with a gun on him in my life and I worked right there with him. He evidently had a pistol with him that day but I did not see it until we got back to the office and I asked him, questioned him about it, asked him what he was shooting. I said it sounded like a popgun to me. He showed it to me and I had never seen it before. I have been working for Mr. Stembridge about a year and a half.

I was looking in the direction of the shooting when it took place. It was kind of dark in there and I couldn't tell what room it took place in but I could tell that it was in the door.

I saw the negro woman's pistol when I turned around to tell him to "Look out he is coming around the other way" and I saw her arm when she was trying to get it down. I could tell that because they were in the door where the light shown through. He did not get shot anywhere or get any wounds on him. I don't know what kind of pistol the negro woman had. It was dark and looked like an automatic to me, I couldn't tell. It is right that I couldn't say what room they were in but I could tell that was a dark pistol and looked like an automatic that the woman had. I don't know whether Mr. Stembridge shot all his bullets or not. I don't know whether it was 2 shots or 10 shots or what. I asked him how many times he shot. He said 7 times and that the gun held 8. He said he hit the two of them. He said he didn't shoot all the bullets out. As to whether when he put 4 shots in each one of those negroes they dropped their pistol, I say when this woman went down in the back, I heard something hit the floor and I suppose that it was the pistol, I don't know.

As to whether I am highly intelligent, I hope so. I don't think it would have been a fine thing for us to have picked up that pistol lying on the floor and brought it with us. I didn't get shot. No one put their hands on me. Mr. Stembridge was not hurt except for some scratches he said he got. I don't know that these women were well shot up, I didn't go that far into it. I know that one of the women died right after that.

After the shooting was over, we came right on to town as fast as we could. You are right, we ran away from there. We didn't leave 2 women in there and a little fellow. That little fellow is a great big man, big heavy-set fellow. I wouldn't say how much he weighed. He looked to me like he was about 22 years old, large enough for that anyway. I couldn't say whether he weighed about 135 or 140 pounds. I weigh 215 pounds. When we ran away from that place, I was making toward the car as quick as I could get there.

Johnny Cooper went in the door and slammed it and locked it. I made a statement to Mr. Jim Jones right after this thing happened. He was very nice and considerate. I certainly did not tell him the woman had a nickel-plated pistol. I am absolutely sure that I did not tell him she had a nickel-plated pistol. I stand on the statement that she called him a white son of a bitch rather than a plain son of a bitch.

DEFENDANT'S STATEMENT

Sometime ago George Harrison started to doing business with my grocery store down on Wayne Street. The first thing I knew he was buying $15 or $20 a week from us and paying up his account all right. They owned two automobiles in the family. George owned one and Richard Lee owned one. They were old automobiles and they were always in the shop and the first thing I knew I was lending from $10 to $50 at a time and at times they owed me as much as $250, that is, just repair bills. In the end George paid his account out all right and his account was satisfactory with me.

But the first of May last year the finance company that had financed Richard Lee's car took it away from him, Richard Lee's and the family car as I understand it. George owned a car and Richard Lee and Mary Jane Harrison and Johnny Cooper owned another automobile. When they took away the car owned by Johnny and Mary Jane and Richard Lee, the family, who were still in debt to me and who had up to that time handled the account fairly satisfactorily, began working on me to finance, to buy them another automobile, and I was not in the automobile business.

I had no automobile to sell and no automobile at all except the one that I used and no interest in any automobile business. They kept raising the amount that they promised to pay until about, well it was the 18th of June, I believe, about the middle of June anyway, they found a 1941 Chevrolet down at Mr. Clarence Hodges for sale and I consented to loan them $850 to buy this automobile; in fact, I bought the automobile from Mr. Hodges myself.

The way the transaction happened they gave me a note for the amount of this transaction plus the balance already owed to me by them, by the three who were on this note. The note is in evidence, was signed by Richard Lee Cooper, was signed by Mary Jane Harrison and signed by Johnny Cooper. And when they brought Johnny Cooper in there to sign they told me he was more than 21 years of age.

We did not do business with minors. We know of course that a married woman cannot endorse for her son except for meat and bread, something like that.

After I had bought this car for them, including all of their back transactions in this one note, Richard Lee was to pay $17.50 a week, Mary Jane had some money coming in from some source, I don't know, she was to pay $10 on the 4th day of every month, Johnny Cooper was out of a job at the time, I believe, and he was to pay $5 a month. They kept up – along about the first of August this car was run into from the back by a lumber truck by someone who we later found was able to pay the damage. The state patrol came along right after the wreck, investigated it, found that the other man was to blame, arrested him, prepared to come here to the trial of the case. We went into it and got from the state patrol a map of the whole transaction and a statement of what they would come here and swear to, in our attempt to collect the damage, which amounted to about $350, out of the party who had run into Richard Lee Cooper, who was driving the car at the time and when we financed this car we added only 6% interest, and at their express request they would pay $17.50 a week, and they didn't want the car insured and I didn't insure the automobile.

The automobile was not insured. It was not insured by their express request because that would have cost $150 more and I required them to about pay it out in a year. They couldn't have gotten up enough money a month to pay out the insurance transaction. They went on and made payments on this automobile for a month or six weeks after it was hit. They made their last payment on the 13th day of September, 1948.

In the meantime, I was trying to get them to sign a claim against the man. I told them we had already engaged an attorney, we had investigated and found that the man was worth the money, all we had to do was to sue them and get the money out of them for the damage to this automobile. At first they were quite agreeable but after a while they seemed to get the idea maybe we would have to pay it anyway, "get me another car" or something like that. As I say they made their last payment on the 13th day of September.

George Harrison was still doing business with us. I think we continued to do business with George Harrison from now on so far as I know. George Harrison was still doing business with us. We were still advancing some other members of his family and selling them groceries and stuff like that on credit. Every time I would see George Harrison, or every time or two, he was in twice a week, every two or three weeks or something like that, after I found they were not paying on the account I talked with him about it and he would tell me, "Now, Mr. Stembridge, those are young boys and they are hot headed and they don't know. You just leave it to me. I am going to get them in line. They owe you and they ought to pay you and I know it and they know it but they are not my boys but I will get them, you leave that to me, I will get them in." I sent George Harrison out along about the first of November to bring Richard Lee Cooper. He hadn't been in since September.

Mr. Terry had already gone out two or three times to talk to him at the house about it and they had given him evasive answers and made numerous promises about coming up on such and such a date and hadn't done so. George Harrison went and got Richard Lee Cooper off the street and brought him in and I talked with him about it and Richard Lee Cooper's attitude was challenging and bordering on the insolent. It was not something that I had to take up and I didn't take it up at the time. I didn't do anything about it. A few days later I sent for Richard Lee Cooper and told him he would have to return that automobile.

He had been driving it all the time, from August until, well, say November 15th. I sent him word to bring in the car and when he came in I told him he would have to leave it with me. We would put it in the garage and keep it locked up until he got money enough to catch up back payments. He could then take the car out, use it or have it fixed or do anything else he wanted to do about it. He turned the car over, he said, "All right, I will do that" and made new promises, "Yes, I am going to pay you" and specified certain amounts and certain dates. He took the car at my direction down to Mr. C. D. Hodges' garage on South Wayne Street, and I had called Mr.

Hodges and he turned the key over to Mr. Hodges. Mr. Hodges locked up the car completely, locked the key up in his desk inside his place of business, and then in two or three weeks I had reports that Richard Lee Cooper was driving this car again. One of the officers told me he saw him driving it again. I investigated it, called up and checked on it and I found sure enough he was driving it again. I took the matter up with Mr. Hodges and Mr. Hodges said, "Yes, that car was moved away from here one night." They had gone and stolen it. The car was hit from the back and the body part was badly damaged but it would still run. They had stolen this car away from Hodges' garage and had it out running around town. The next time I sent Mr. Terry to bring the automobile to Mr. Hodges' garage. I kept it until after this transaction we are now talking about, foreclosed on it in the superior court, got an order from Judge Carpenter to sell it and sold it. Because it was so badly battered up, I had to buy it myself. That is what became of the automobile. When I sent for this car about, I will say December 1st, there still was a large amount of money, an important amount of money, the balance due on this car, after al payments, was about $859, and in the meantime I had lent Richard Lee Cooper money, which was to repair the automobile, and the balance now due is about $859, I mean the balance due when I foreclose on this automobile. But George was telling me all the time, he would come back once a week, whenever I would see him, "Mr. Stembridge, some of these boys been out of a job, let me handle them." Sometime in December, Richard Lee Cooper called by the office and told me he was going north and don't fool around with him anymore. Along in January, I found he had not gone north and he was working, and found out where he was working. So I got a report after then they were working at the State Hospital.

I intended to go out, February 10th was pay day at the State Hospital, and talk with him about it but I got busy and didn't go out. March 7th, just before pay day, - just before pay day March 10th, at the State Hospital, in the afternoon of March 7th, I told Sam, Mr. Terry, "Come on, I want you to go with me on a little trip." He did not know whether he was going on an appraisal trip to appraise an automobile or appraise a piece of property, he did not know where he was going. Because of the fact that Richard Lee Cooper showed that attitude when I tried to get him to sign this claim against these people and the fact that by this time I was getting reports that I was dealing with a situation and I couldn't get anything too much specific about it, but I was dealing with these folks who were not just what I thought they were, I put my gun in my pocket. I don't carry a pistol. It is the first time I ever carried one on a collecting trip I feel certain; I don't remember ever having carried one before. This pistol I bought 30 odd years ago and it has laid in the right-hand desk drawer since that time except occasionally when I take a trip for a week or two in an automobile I put it in the glove compartment. I had it with me that afternoon in my hip picket.

We went out as close to the house as we could get. The roads were muddy and couldn't get close to the house. As Sam and I got up close to the porch, we saw this woman, whom I had never seen before and who must have been more than 21 or 22 years old anyway she was no girl. She was not quite as tall as Mary Jane but she was stout. I had never seen her before. This woman and Mary Jane were standing on their front porch and Johnny Cooper was leaning against the railing with his hand above an upright post, the first upright post after you get on the porch, right near the door leading into the rooms on this side – by the way, the same family occupies both sides of the house. As we walked up on the porch, this woman disappeared into the first room, Emma Johnekin I found out. Mary Jane Harrison went into the second room. I spoke to all of them as I got up on the porch. I began asking Johnny about his account; it had run for about six months, what was the matter? Well, he had not had a job. "Well you had a job part of the time." "Yes, I haven't had a job much of the time." I said,

He said, "Yes, sir, I have a job now. I just got a job out at the State Hospital." I said, "When do you get paid off?"

He said, "I get paid off the 10th" – Thursday or Friday, whatever it was. I said, "All right, how much money you got coming at that time?" He told me. I said, "You owe me \$20," as he admitted yesterday, "on another account. You owe me \$5 a month for six months on this account. Suppose you give me an order to your employer to pay the \$50 to me and will catch you up to date and pay the balance at the rate of \$5 a month like you had promised to pay it." "All right, sir, I will do that." Mr. Terry had stopped at the steps about 10 or 12 feet away, and I said, "Sam, write out an order, please" and I was talking with Johnny about where Richard Lee was working, what had been the trouble and I was telling him, "You don't have to pay it all, I know you can't. The object in a situation like this is to get it started and the first thing you know you have got the thing done and the account has disappeared."

It was perfectly and completely friendly. Sam brought the card up and gave it to me. I am rather certain that Sam handed the card to Johnny and handed the fountain pen to Johnny and Johnny took it and started to sign it. About that time I heard some mumbling and grumbling back of me. It started about that time and all at once one of them said, "He is not going to sign that thing" and the other one said, who was right directly back of me in the first door, Mary Jane said, "Johnny don't you sign that thing" or words to that general effect. The one in the second room had evidently come out on the porch. Emma said, "He is not going to sign that thing." I said, "Well, he is going to sign it, he has already signed it" and Mary Jane said, "Well, he is not going to sign it" and about that time Johnny jumped or got down off that porch and slapped his arm around my neck. I began pushing him around pushing him off of me and Emma who was standing in the door says, "You take your hands off that man, you son of a bitch", you white son of a bitch or son of a bitch.

To tell you the truth it was so fast and so unexpected and Mary Jane was cursing too at the same time, said, "I will get my gun and shoot your heart out." And I pushed Johnny off me and turned around to face them. Say this is the door leading into the first room. I turned around to face that door. She ran in there. The room is only nine by nine I found out, ran in there and grabbed her hands under the pillow, turned around and started towards the door. I got back of this door jamb until she got in about a foot and a half, and it occurred to me that she was fooling with that pistol and she was not shooting it. I didn't want to kill her; I didn't have any business killing people. It then occurred to me maybe if I could knock her down it would settle the whole matter. I had the door jamb on her, I reached in over-handed and hit her on the right side of the head with the back end of that pistol. But I didn't hit her hard enough. She staggered, threw out her hand against the wall and began to close her eyes and first thing you know that pistol dropped on the floor all at once.

She took a deep breath and reached down to get that pistol and I shot at her. I think I hit her, I hit her somewhere. I shot at her shoulder. I had her right there, I could have shot her in the heart the first time, the second time killed her sure enough, standing right there in two feet of her. I didn't want to kill her even then. What I wanted to do was to get out of it and not get hurt. When I shot her this gun dropped on the floor and about that time Mary Jane came in through the front door and slammed against me and tried to get her hands around my neck and push me over against the bed inside the room. The room was full of furniture, the bed about five feet wide maybe and some opening between the furniture. Mary Jane jammed me over against this bed, I looked up. She was trying to get her arms around my neck. I looked up all at once she was hitting me with one hand and part of the time trying to grab me around the neck. I looked up and Emma had recovered, was not hurt much evidently. She had this pistol in her hand, had got it up from the floor some way. I grabbed her arm and held her hand up like that and about that time Mary Jane caught me around the neck like this and I began to black out and I began to shoot. I shot three or four or five times then, I don't know how many times I shot. I jerked my head down under and got my head out and about that time they began to release their hold on me and Mary Jane says, "I am shot" and started to run through the back door.

It happened right there in the front room, about a foot inside the front room from the door, I would say. Mary Jane ran towards the back and I didn't see her any more. Just as Mary Jane turned me loose I saw Johnny Cooper running through this door of the front room at the back end, grab up this pistol off the floor and he got it up about a foot high before I saw it. I squared off to shoot him, he jumped back of this door jamb into the second room. I found out later it is a closet but just like I told Mr. Jones in my statement that night I said it was a door jamb. It was a place back there two or three feet he could jump back there. He jumped back there with that pistol, he never got it more than a foot high, when he saw I was fixing to shoot he dived back of that door jamb. I didn't see him anymore but I knew he had that pistol. All at once Emma recovered and lunged at me again and I shot her again and she staggered down to the floor. I looked around and there was Sam standing in the door facing us.

I said, "Come on, Sam, let's go. There is apt to be some more shooting here, that boy has got a gun." I went by Sam and we went on out to the porch. He said we ran. We moved hurriedly but I kept looking back. I didn't know I had shot the woman three or four times, that is the truth. I have taken some time to tell you exactly what happened but the whole thing happened in less than 30 seconds, everything was over and we were out in the car. We came back to town. I asked Sam to go and notify the police what had happened. I didn't go out there to shoot those people. As I said before, we are not in the business of shooting people. We are in the business of serving them, what we try to do. We expect to get paid for it, get a living out of it. I didn't want to shoot them, I had nothing against them to tell you the truth and to tell you the honest truth I don't know. I didn't want to get shot, that was my situation. I didn't want them to kill me and that is the reason I shot them and that is the only reason I shot them. I shot them in defense of my life.

Defendant rests.

Testimony in Rebuttal for the State

C. S. BALDWIN, JR., Solicitor General, Sworn for the State.

Direct examination by Solicitor Baldwin

(By Mr. Baldwin) I wish to state that there was no effort to conceal this ballistic report from the grand jury, that they had the information that all these bullets and these hulls were fired out of Stembridge's pistol. I told them that myself. I also wish to state that on the bond hearing I was cross examining Mr. Terry and asked him to produce his records on the ledger that they had in this case, their records in this case. Finally Mr. Stembridge jumped up and pulled out the ledger sheet, threw it down and said "Here it is."

Mr. Evans, his lawyer was there, and he did not agree to that. The Judge ruled if he produced it voluntarily, I could look at it and I looked at it and wanted to make a copy of all the transactions but they would not allow me to take it out of the court room. Mr. Evans objected to me taking it out.

Mr. Evans: If you feel like we are unfair, while we have rested we have still got time to do it. I am going to ask for a little recess and let Mr. Stembridge bring the ledger sheet up and put it in evidence.

Mr. Baldwin: All right, do that. That will relieve me from testifying.

Mr. Evans: He has to go to the office.

Mr. Baldwin: I am willing.

(It is agreed that Mr. Baldwin may state what he remembers of the ledger sheet.)

(Witness continues) The item of June 18th when he said he sold the automobile, up to that date he had the family owing him – all of the family was on one ledger sheet of those negroes, the Cooper negroes, he had a balance that day of $71.66 up to that date on the automobile and then he had an entry of $850 and right opposite that he had a balance they owed him, was $1093.66 or $1098, I took it to be 93 but it might have been 98.

(By Mr. Evans) Do you need the ledger papers?

A. I don't need it unless you do.

LOUVENIA COOPER, Sworn for the State.

Direct Examination by Solicitor Baldwin
My name is Louvenia Cooper.

Examination by the Court as to Competency
My name is Louvenia Cooper. I have been in school and I am 11 years old. I was sworn as a witness in this case and the purpose for which I held up my right hand was to tell the truth. If I fail to tell the truth, the devil will get me. I know that I will be punished by law if I did not tell the truth. My understanding of the oath that I took yesterday when I raised my right hand was that I was to tell the truth. I realize I will be punished if I do not tell the truth.

Examination as to Competency by Mr. Evans, Defendant's Counsel
I swore as a witness yesterday. When I swore I raised my right hand. Some others were raising their right hands too. My mother raised her right hand. I do not know what an oath is. I know what swearing is. I have never been in court before and have never been here when other folks swore before. I never did swear before. Mr. Baldwin didn't tell me what swearing was. My mother told me. It has not been long ago that she told me. When she told me, Mr. Lingold and Mr. Shepard Baldwin and the G. B. I. and Mr. Sergeant Ellis were there. The other little girl was there too. They told her what swearing meant. They told me if I swore and told a story that

the bad man would get me. I already knew that. Up until that time, I didn't know that if I told a story up here in the court house that they would make a charge against me. If I told a story up here, they would send me to jail. Mama told me that. I think that somebody shot my Mama. If somebody shot my Mama, I think I would have a right to come up here in court. I do not think I would have a right to tell something that was not exactly true to help convict the person that shot my Mama. I think I would have to tell the strict truth, tell exactly what I saw.

Direct Examination by Solicitor Baldwin

I was at home when Emma and Mary Jane got shot. When Mr. Terry and Mr. Stembridge first came up, Johnny and Emma and me and Martha and we got a little baby and Josephine, Johnny's wife, were all there and Will, he was up under the house. Will is my little brother. Mary Jane was not there when they first came, she had gone to the store. When Mr. Stembridge and Mr. Terry walked up on the porch, Johnny was already on the porch; he was not doing nothing but sitting down on the banister of the porch. They said nothing but "Where is Richard?" And Johnny said, "Richard is working" and Johnny said, "Ain't that where he is Emma?" and she said, "Yes, that is where he is working." He said, "What are you going to do about his car?" Johnny said, "Nothing."

Then Mr. Stembridge said "nothing" and Mr. Stembridge told Mr. Sam to write out an order. Mr. Sam went over there by the wall and wrote something or another and read it and handed it to Mr. Stembridge, Mr. Stembridge read it and handed it to Johnny. He took the note and Mama was coming out of the next door and Johnny asked, "Mama, must I sign this paper?" and Mr. Stembridge said, "Mama, hell." He said, "You going to sign this paper." Then Mr. Stembridge went around there and caught Johnny in his collar. Johnny did not catch him.

Mr. Stembridge had some brass knucks and Emma said, "Look at that man got brass knucks" and when she said that he turned Johnny loose and she ran in the house and he ran in the house after her. He caught her. Emma went in the house and he went in behind here. He was real close behind her and both were running. Mama went in the house after Mr. Stembridge. Neither Emma or Mary Jane cursed; neither one said anything about a son of a bitch. Mary Jane went in behind Mr. Stembridge. Mr. Terry come in behind Mama.

No one went in behind Mr. Terry. When Mr. Terry backed off Johnny, Johnny ran in the door on his side. When Mr. Terry went in, me and my little sister, Martha, went on in behind him in there. When Mr. Terry went in, he shot Mama right there in the back. I saw him when he shot her. I was right behind him. Mama was in the first room when he shot her the first time. We walked on through. When she jumped out where Mr. Stembridge was, he shot again. Mr. Stembridge and Emma were tied up and Mama did not go between them, she went on around them. She did not grab hold of any of them. She went on in her room, which was the third room. She went in there and he shot again and she got in the kitchen and laid on the table. As she went to straighten up and said, "Come on, Pete", as she went to say that he shot again.

In the meantime, Emma had Mr. Stembridge's arm, trying to hold it to keep him from getting his pistol. When he got his pistol he shot her in the arm and she come up and then shot her twice in the shoulder and shot her in the stomach. She just went to sit down on the trunk like this and he was standing right over her and he just shot her in the arm and in her shoulder. He shot her in the stomach while she was on that trunk. Mama and Emma did not have a pistol. After the shooting, Mr. Stembridge and Mr. Terry both ran out of the house. They didn't say anything when they left, they both went running. When I come out of the door, I saw them go around the house running, fanning their coats. Yes, sir, I am telling the truth.

Cross Examination by Mr. Evans

I had gone to school that day and got back at 3:30. When I got to the house at 3:30, Mama, Emma, Louise, my sister, my brother's wife's sister, Josephine, the baby, and Johnny were all at the house. My mother was working but she got off from work and had come back at 3:30. After I came in from school, I studied my lessons for about thirty minutes then all of us went out on the porch and sit down. Mama was there too. She didn't do anything but sit on the porch. She was not there when Mr. Stembridge and Mr. Terry came up. She had gone to the store. She told me she was going to the store and I told her to bring us some ice cream back and she brought it. It was Chocolate fudge ice cream. I am sure that she brought Martha and me ice cream. When I met her the ice cream was not melting. I met her on the porch. She was going next door to try on a dress.

She was going next door to try on the dress and she gave me the paper sack and told me to give Martha one of them. I met her up the road and got the ice cream and she went in and tried on a flowered green and white dress that Miss Sarah May Youngblood, who lives next door, was making for her. She didn't stay in there more than about a second. She did not stay in there 15 or 20 minutes.

As to how long my mother told me to say she stayed in there, she ain't told me nothing. When my mother came up on our porch, Martha and I were sitting on the end toward Milledgeville, sitting on a bench together or on the swing. It was not a swing on the porch, it is a long rocking chair. It was on the side toward Milledgeville. It was up against the house opposite the window. It was not at the head of the steps; it was on the porch. The steps lead up on to the porch. They go right up to where we were sitting. We were not on the end of the porch. I was sitting on the arm of the chair. I was not sitting on the arm of the chair towards Milledgeville, I was sitting on the other end of the bench. I was on the end of the porch toward Milledgeville but we were not right at the steps, the bench is not right at the end of the porch. I don't know whether we were about 8 feet from the steps or not. We were sitting right in front of the door leading into our side. The chair was right in front of the door. My sister was sitting in the same rocking chair. It was a long chair made like a rocking chair and two other chairs that go with it on the porch. One of the chairs was in front of the door leading into our side of the house. There were no chairs between our door and the steps leading down off the porch. There was a big 5 gallon can of kerosene sitting down there.

While we were sitting on the chair, Emma was on the other side and Mr. Stembridge and Johnny. I reckon my mother had gone to Mr. Young- blood's. I got the ice cream from her just before she went in the house. When I went back there, Mr. Stembridge and Mr. Terry were still there, when I got there, I was to meet Mama. They were not there when I left. Mama had gone in the house. I saw Mama 3 houses away. She stopped and gave me my ice cream.

We walked by one house together and she went in the Youngblood house. I went and put the packages up and came back on the porch and just as I got back on the porch, Mr. Stembridge and Mr. Terry were on the first door step. I didn't see them coming in back of me when I went to put the packages up. I didn't see them walking up at all until they got on the foot of the door steps, Johnny said he didn't even see them. I went on eating my ice cream. When they came up, I was sitting on the arm of the rocking chair in front of the door to my side of the house. Emma was in front of the other door leaning up there and she came around and sit down in the chair. My sister was sitting next to me. Johnny was sitting on the banister and was just sitting up there looking back at Emma.

The first thing they said when they came up those steps was Mr. Stembridge said, "Where is Richard?" Mr. Terry didn't ever say nothing. He stood there all that time and never said a word. He didn't open his mouth. As to whether that is the same thing my Mama said, I don't know what she said. As to whether Mama and Johnny said he never opened his mouth, I don't know what they said. I saw this all myself. After Mr. Stembridge said, "Is Richard here?" he said "What you all going to do about his car?" He was talking to Johnny. As to whether he said "What you going to do, Johnny?", I say he said "What you all going to do about this car?" Johnny answered, "Nothing." Then Mr. Stembridge told Mr. Terry to write that order and he went over there and wrote the order and read it and handed it back to Mr. Stembridge and Mr. Stembridge read it and handed it to Johnny.

Johnny didn't do nothing, he asked Mama, Johnny said, "Mama must I sign this paper?" and Mr. Stembridge said, "Mama, hell." I am sure those are the exact words they used. I know he said "Mama, hell" about something. Some others remember that besides me. I guess all of them remember it, they all heard it.

When my mother started up the steps, she heard Mr. Stembridge say "Ma, hell." She said, "Why don't you tell the man to take his hand out of your collar?" Mr. Stembridge had Johnny by the collar and he had his brass knucks most of the way out. I didn't see him work his arm up and down. I think he had his knucks in his left hand. They were brass and black. I saw them. I saw them when Emma said, "Look at the man got on brass knucks" and I come around there. I walked around and looked at them. While I was looking at them, he did not pull them out of his pocket, he kept them in there. I did not go up there and look in his pocket. He had them about almost out of his pocket. Just enough for me to see them. I went around there and looked in his pocket.

When Emma said that, he ran in the house behind her and hit at her. When she went to run, he struck at her but he couldn't hit her then. She ran and he ran behind her and struck at her. She was not sitting down when this started, she was standing up and she was leaning beside the door and went and stood in the door. I saw him when he struck at her. I saw the knucks on his hand. He turned Johnny loose and struck at Emma. He had knucks on his left hand. He had something in his right hand. He had a pistol in his right hand and he struck with his knucks. They went in the house then. Johnny stood out there on the porch.

Mr. Stembridge had hold of Johnny. Johnny didn't have hold of him. Just before Mr. Stembridge struck with those knucks, he and Johnny were not standing up there holding to each other. Johnny was not looking over at Emma. I don't know where he was looking, he was not looking at Emma. He was sitting up there and Mr. Stembridge had his right hand in Johnny's collar, turned him loose and struck at Emma with his left hand with his knucks. Johnny was looking at that. I don't know whether Johnny saw the knucks or not. I saw them. Johnny was standing right there. I didn't hear Johnny say whether he saw the knucks or not. Yes, we all got together and talked about it. Mr. Stembridge had brass knucks on. He had a pistol in his other hand. He did not point the pistol at Emma as he went in the door. He didn't ever take it out until he got in the house because she was holding his hand when they were tied up.

As to whether I just told you that he had a pistol in his right hand when he struck with his knucks with his left hand, I say but he didn't have it in his pocket. Mr. Stembridge didn't have his hand in his back pocket. He had Johnny with his fight hand and knucks on his left hand. As to whether after Mr. Stembridge turned Johnny loose, I said he struck with his left hand, I now say he didn't take it out until he got in the house. No sir, he didn't have it in his right hand. The pistol was in his right-hand side coat pocket. I saw his pocket sticking out there. I never did see the gun in his pocket. I did not see him when he pulled it out of his pocket, I was in the house when he pulled it out of his pocket. Emma and him was tied up and I was in there where Mama was when he pulled it out of his pocket. I saw him and Emma tied up. When Emma turned him loose, I reckon he got it, when she turned loose his hand, I reckon then he got his pistol and shot her in the arm. I walked by them when they were tied up. They were in the second room.

Mr. Terry had done shot Mama when I walked by them. I was right behind Mr. Terry. Mr. Terry walked by Emma and Mr. Stembridge. After Mr. Terry went by Emma and Mr. Stembridge, I walked back of Mr. Terry and walked by them too.

I was right behind Mr. Terry when he shot all 4 times, I don't recon Mr. Terry shot any more than 4 times. I didn't count the shots. I couldn't see around Mr. Terry. I didn't say nothing to him.

When I passed Mr. Stembridge and Emma, Mr. Stembridge had not started to shooting Emma, she was holding his hand then. That put me in the back of the house, in the kitchen. I never turned around. I didn't go out the back door, when he shot Emma in the arm, she come up and went to sit on the trunk and then he shot her in the stomach. I had already passed by where Emma and Mr. Stembridge were before Mr. Stembridge ever shot. After I passed Emma and Mr. Stembridge, I did not go out the back door and I did not go to my mother who was on the table, I stood still there. Mr. Terry was standing up there shooting Mama, he was almost opposite the bed. We were in the third room.

As to whether I said Mr. Terry went all the way through the house and Mama lay on the table looking back to see if Emma was going to be shot and that Mr. Terry was still shooting, I say he didn't go any further than the third room, he didn't go in the kitchen. I did not go any further than the third room.

I went along back of Mr. Terry and after Mr. Terry had shot my mother 4 times and after Mr. Stembridge shot, I stayed right there and both of them ran out of the house. The first time Mr. Terry shot my mother, she was in the first room. The second time Mr. Terry shot her, she had gone by Mr. Stembridge in the second room. The third time Mr. Terry shot her was in the third room and the fourth time Mr. Terry shot her was when she went and laid on the table in the fourth room. I was about as far from her as I am from you and I was right in back of him. I was right by the side of them, by them. Right in back of Mr. Terry.

When I passed Emma and Mr. Stembridge, neither one of them was shot as I passed. I passed right by them. They were standing right in the door and I walked right through.

Emma and Mr. Stembridge were standing right in the door and the first to walk through was my mother and the next to walk through was Mr. Terry and I was the next to walk through. Nobody else walked through. My little sister was standing there in the front room door. She never did come in there at all.

I had followed Mr. Terry right back into the kitchen and when he got as far from me to you, he shot my mother the fourth time. I know his gun was black but I don't know what kind it was. He shot 4 times. Emma was shot 3 times or 4 times. There were some bullets that I don't know whether they hit anybody or not but I know 2 are in the wall. Yes, they are still in the wall, nobody has gone in there to take them out. I have been there all the while and I have not seen anybody take them out. I was not there when the bullet was taken out of the bed. No, sir, I didn't have the hulls picked up. That morning when I came to the house, I picked up a piece of lead by the stove.

I didn't see Mr. Stembridge when he shot Emma in the arm but I saw him when he shot her in her shoulder and in her stomach, I was in the third room. Mr. Stembridge was standing beside the door and she was sitting on the trunk. I was on Mama's bed and Emma was sitting at the foot on the trunk. He shot her three times while she was sitting on the trunk. He just come to the door and shot her. He was standing close to her, close as I am to you. Mr. Terry was still there. About the time Mr. Terry got there, Mr. Stembridge and him came on out together. I did not go out the back door with my mother. I came out the front door and the last time I saw Mr. Terry and Mr. Stembridge, they were going by the last house in the car. I didn't go back and say nothing to my mother, I came out of the front door. I did not see Johnny come out the front door, he had gone back in the house.

ROSS JOINER, Sworn for the State.

Direct Examination by Solicitor Baldwin
My name is Ross Joiner. I have and run a business here in Milledgeville known as Joiner's Market. I have known Mary Jane Harrison about two years. I think I know her general character and reputation in the community in which she lives. She works in my home and has been working there just a little over a year. I would think her general character and reputation in this community was the very best. From my knowledge of her character and reputation, I would believe her under oath.

No Cross Examination

EUGENE A. ELLIS, Recalled for the State.

Direct Examination by Solicitor Baldwin
Q. Mr. Ellis, did you take any photographs or pictures of the body of Emma Johnekin, the deceased, in this case?

A. Yes, I did.

Q. Have you got those pictures with you?

A. Yes

Mr. Ennis: I object to pictures of the body of the deceased being exhibited to this jury. It is prejudicial to this jury, improper and I move that this witness not be allowed to exhibit to this jury pictures of the deceased woman.

BY THE COURT: Mr. Baldwin, do you intend to offer the pictures in evidence?

Mr. Baldwin: Yes, they show the blows and bullet wounds on the body.

BY THE COURT: You may go ahead.

Q. Did you take this picture?

A. Yes, I did.

Q. Did you take this one yourself?

A. Yes.

Q. Where was the woman when you took these two pictures – was she dead then?

A. Yes.

Q. Do you see this one made by Mr. Stancil?

A. Yes.

Q. Where was her body then?

A. In the undertaking establishment in Eatonton.

Q. Come down here – I will ask you whether or not this spot is the bullet wound in the back of her shoulder?

A. Yes.

Q. Did you see this before she was dead, those holes?

A. Yes.

Q. On her back in this picture, I will ask you whether or not that is a burned place where the bullet evidently crossed her back?

A. Yes, I would say so.

Q. This cut open place here on her body is what?

A. That is where they cut it open to get the bullet out of her pelvis.

Q. This picture here of her abdomen, you see three holes there?

A. Yes.

Q. What are they?

A. This one here goes right into the abdomen and this one just goes in and comes back out and goes back in.

Q. It went in and came out and then went back in?

A. Yes.

Q. Like it went through a wrinkle in her stomach?

Mr. Ennis: I would like for my brother not to continue to lead this
        witness.

BY THE COURT: I sustain the objection to the question as leading.

Q. Explain that wound on her to the jury?
A. The bullet went in here and came out and went back in there.

Cross Examination by Mr. Evans

I didn't probe that wound. I just made that statement from by observation of the
bullet holes. I believe Dr. Woods was the physician in charge of this patient. I
believe he would know exactly what the bullet did. It was my belief it went in and
came out. What I testified was as to my belief. (The court ruled out the witness's
previous testimony as to where the bullet traveled so far as it was based on the
witness's belief).

Redirect Examination by Solicitor Baldwin

I looked carefully at this wound on her myself. I looked at the wounds while she
was alive and also while she was dead. In my opinion, the bullet went into the skin
and came out and went back in again.

Recross Examination by Mr. Evans

I do not know whether Dr. Woods is available. I believe he is in town.

Redirect Examination by Solicitor Baldwin

Dr. Woods is available to the defense too.
Mr. Baldwin: We offer in evidence these pictures.
   Mr. Ennis: I would like to renew my objection to the admission in
evidence of the three pictures he has offered and especially do I direct my
remarks to the picture that was made after the body had been mutilated and the
change in the character of the body when they were getting this bullet out. I think
that would not be admissible; it was not as it was when she died but had been
changed by the operation of the doctors.

BY THE COURT: I will overrule it.

State Rests

Testimony in Rebuttal for the Defendant.

SAM L. TERRY, Recalled for the Defendant.

Direct Examination by Mr. Evans

When Mr. Stembridge and I went up on the porch the afternoon of the shooting, I didn't see any children on the porch or in the house or in the yard, I didn't see anybody but those three people, not at any time. I didn't see a little girl about 11 years old on the porch, I didn't see anybody but those three people. As to whether a little girl 11 years old followed me around, no, sir, she didn't have to follow me around because I didn't move very much. There weren't any children in the yard that I could tell.

Cross Examination by Solicitor Baldwin

As to my moving when I was leaving there, I sure did.

Mr. Ennis: I wish to renew objections to the testimony of Mary Jane Harrison with reference to being shot by Sam Terry and likewise renew objection to the testimony of Mary Jane Harrison in exhibiting wounds to the jury. The grounds of objection are that the defendant is not on trial for committing any offense against the witness Mary Jane Harrison, that he is not on trial for shooting Mary Jane Harrison. The witness Mary Jane Harrison stated that the defendant did not shoot her. The evidence is wholly prejudicial and harmful to the defendant and is designed to prejudice the jury and on those

grounds. I renew the objection.

BY THE COURT: I will adhere to my former ruling.

Mr. Ennis: Your former ruling was that you left it in for the present time and is it overruled now?

BY THE COURT: I overrule your renewed motion to strike it.

Defendant Closes

AGREEMENT OF COUNSEL AS TO BRIEF OF EVIDENCE

We agree that the foregoing 77 pages is a true and correct brief of the evidence adduced in the trial of the case of The State v. Marion W. Stembridge therein referred to.   This 3rd day of   Nov , 1949.

C. S. BALDWIN, JR   (signature)
Solicitor General, Ocmulgee Circuit.

Frank O. Evans, Marion Ennis and James M. Watts, Jr.,
 Attorneys for Defendant.
(signature)   Frank O. Evans

APPROVAL OF BRIEF OF EVIDENCE

The State   Trial for Murder in
                                                 Baldwin Superior Court

        v.

                                                 July Term, 1949

Marion W. Stembridge

The foregoing 77 pages, constituting the brief of evidence in this case,
 is hereby approved as a true and correct brief of evidence produced
upon the trial of the above state case. Let the same be filed as part of the record therein.

        This 3 day of   Nov   , 1949.

George S. Carpenter (signature)
Judge, Superior Courts,
Ocmulgee Circuit.

APPENDIX 3

BILL OF EXCEPTION

Docket No................File...............Ocmulgee Circuit.

Court of Appeals of Georgia

MARCH
OCTOBER Term, 19...........

Marion W. Stembridge

....

VS.   Plaintiff in error.

The State of Georgia

.

Defendant in error.

ORIGINAL BILL OF EXCEPTION

Filed in office..........December 27,..........19 49

.............J C Cooper..............
Clerk Superior Court, Baldwin County, Georgia.

Filed in office...19.........

....
Clerk Court of Appeals of the State of Georgia.

Frank O. Evans,
Marion Ennis/ and
James F. Watts, Jr.,
Counsel for plaintiff in error.
P.O.   Milledgeville, Georgia.

G. S. Baldwin, Jr.,
Solicitor General,
Ocmulgee Circuit
Counsel for defendant in error.
P.O.   Milledgeville, Georgia.

GEORGIA, BALDWIN COUNTY

Be it remembered that on the 19th day of July, 1949, at the regular July term, 1949, of the superior Curt of Baldwin County, before Honorable George S. Carpenter, Judge, then and there presiding, there came on for trial the case of the State of Georgia against Marion W. Stembridge; the same being an indictment wherein the said Marion W. Stembridge was charged with the offense of murder.

Be it further remembered that after evidence had been introduced and both sides closed, the jury returned a verdict finding the said Marion W. Stembridge guilty of voluntary manslaughter.

Be it further remembered, that said defendant in regular course and within the time prescribed by law, duly filed his motion for new trial, filed his brief of evidence in said case and his amended motion, all of which were approved and certified by the judge, and the said motion for new trial was duly and regularly continued for hearing until December 1, 1949, said judge overruled said motion for new trial as amended to which judgment of the court overruling said motion for new trial as amended, plaintiff in error then and there excepted, now excepts and assigns the same as error.

Marion Stembridge names himself as plaintiff in error herein and the State of Georgia as defendant in error.

And now comes plaintiff in error on the 19th day of December 1949, and within the time prescribed by law and presents to the Honorable George S. Carpenter, judge of said court who presided in said case, this, his bill of exception, and asks that the same may be signed and certified in order that the said case may be carried to the Court of Appeals of Georgia, so that the errors herein alleged to have been committed, may be considered and corrected.

Plaintiff in error specifies as material to a clear understanding of the errors complained of, the following portions of the record, to wit:

1. The indictment together with all entries thereon, together with the plea of not guilty and the verdict of the jury entered thereon.
2. The motion for new rial, together with amendment thereto, and order overruling said motion for new trial as amended.
3. The brief of evidence, agreement of counsel thereon, and approval of said brief by said Honorable George S. Carpenter.
4. The charge of the court together with all entries thereon.
5. The sentence of the court.

Plaintiff in error most respectfully submits this his bill of exception.

Frank O. Evans
Marion Ennis and
James M. Watts, Jr.,
ATTORNEYS FOR PLAINTIFF IN ERROR
By: Frank O. Evans

JUDGE'S CERTIFICATE

I do certify that the foregoing bill of exceptions is true and contains all of the evidence sand specifies all of the record material to a clear understanding of the errors complained of, and the clerk of the Superior Court of Baldwin County s hereby directed to make out a complete copy of such portions of the record as are in this bill of exceptions specified, and certify them as such, and cause them to be transmitted to the next terms of the Court of Appeals, in order that the errors alleged to have been committed may be considered and corrected.

This 19th day of December, 1949.
George S. Carpenter
Judge, Superior Courts
Ocmulgee Circuit

WAIVER OF NOTICE REQUIRED BEFORE CERTIFICATON

I hereby approve the within bill of exceptions as being correct and complete as to the averments of fact therein and hereby waive the requirement of notice as provided for by Title 6, Section 908.1 of the Code of Georgia.

This 17th day of December, 1949
C. S. Baldwin, Jr.
Solicitor General,
Ocmulgee Circuit
Attorney for Defendant in Error

ACKNOWLEDGEMENT OF SERVICE

Due and legal service of the within bill of exceptions and the judge's signed certificate thereon is hereby acknowledged and all other and further service is hereby waived.

This 20th day of December, 1949

APPENDIX 4

COURT OF APPEALS DECISION

33573
Court of Appeals of Georgia

Stembridge v. State

84 Ga. App. 413
(Ga. Ct. App. 951) 65 S.E.2d 819
Decided Jun 5, 1951

DECIDED JUNE 5, 1951.

REHEARING DENIED JULY 17, 1951.

Manslaughter; from Baldwin Superior Court —
  Judge Carpenter. March 1, 1951

James M. Watts Jr., for plaintiff in error.
Marion W. Stembridge, pro se.

C. S. Baldwin Jr., Solicitor-General, contra.

(*a*) Newly discovered evidence which is only impeaching in character will not authorize the grant of a new trial.

(*b*) The Court of Appeals is a court for the correction of errors of law only and is not vested with discretionary power as to issues of fact. *Blanchard* v. *Savannah River Lumber Co.,* 40 Ga. App. 416, 419 (149 S.E. 793).

DECIDED JUNE 5, 1951. REHEARING DENIED JULY 17, 1951.

This case first appeared before this court after the plaintiff in error had been convicted in the Superior Court of Baldwin County for the offense of voluntary manslaughter. See *Stembridge* v. *State,* 82 Ga. App. 214 (60 S.E.2d 491). During the trial of that case a witness for the State, Mary Jane Harrison, testified that the victim, Emma Johnekin, after having been struck and shot by the defendant, entered the third room of the apartment, which consisted of four rooms located one directly behind the other with doorways opening in a straight line; that the victim after entering the third room seated herself on a trunk located therein, and that the defendant followed her into this room and shot her twice more while she was seated on the trunk. After the judgment of this court became final, the defendant filed in the trial court an extraordinary motion for a new trial on the ground of newly discovered evidence. Attached to the extraordinary motion for a new trial and made a part thereof is a statement made by the witness Mary Jane Harrison shortly after the shooting and while she lay in a wounded condition in the hospital, she having also been shot on the occasion on which Emma Johnekin was killed. This statement was made as a dying declaration but the witness recovered and testified at the trial. A part of the statement set up in the extraordinary motion for a new trial and alleged to be material thereto is as follows: "We did not mention a gun. There is one in the house, but it was in the back bed room [third room] near the kitchen and neither of us had got that far — shot at least one time, and Emma never got out of the front bed room until the men had already gone."

The extraordinary motion for a new trial is also supported by the affidavit of J. E. Jones, an investigator connected with the Georgia Bureau of Investigation, to the effect that he turned the statement of Mary Jane Harrison over to the defense attorneys in September, 1950, some months after the conviction, and that he had not known that she had sworn contrary to this statement on the trial or he would have called the matter to their attention at that time. Also in support of the motion were affidavits of the defense attorneys which stated in substance that they did not know until the trial of the case that such a statement had been made, although they made every possible effort to uncover all pertinent evidence. Also attached to the motion were the affidavits of ten of the jurors who convicted the defendant for the offense of voluntary manslaughter on the trial, all of the jurors stating that had the newly discovered evidence consisting of the statement of Mary Jane Harrison which contradicts material portions of her testimony been introduced in evidence on the trial, they would never have agreed to any verdict except one of not guilty.

The extraordinary motion for a new trial was overruled by the trial judge and the exception is to this judgment. (*i.e., the Bill of Exceptions*)

TOWNSEND, J. (After stating the foregoing facts.)

Code § 70-204 states in part as follows: "A new trial may be granted in all cases when any material evidence, not merely cumulative or impeaching in its character, but relating to new and material facts, shall be discovered by the applicant after the rendition of a verdict against him." Extraordinary motions for a new trial based on newly discovered evidence are provided for in Code § 70-303. From the affidavits attached to the motion it appears that the defendant's attorneys could not, in the exercise of all diligence, have discovered prior to the trial that the chief witness for the State had made prior contradictory statements which might have cast serious doubt on her credibility as a witness. It further appears that evidence that the defendant and the deceased did not leave the first room would have been material, since on the trial of the case the defendant contended that he shot the Harrison woman in an effort to protect himself against an assault by her, whereas it was the State's contention that as she fled from him to the back of the house he deliberately followed with the intention of killing her. Under Code § 38- 1803, one method of impeaching a witness is by proving contradictory statements previously made by her as to matters relevant to her testimony and to the case. When this is done, the effect of the evidence and the credibility of the witness is entirely a matter for the jury to determine. See *Reed* v. *State,* 163 Ga. 206 (135 S.E. 748). It is thus evident that the newly discovered evidence is no more than impeaching in character, for which reason it falls under the inhibition of Code § 70-204, although in every other respect it meets the requirements of this Code section dealing with the circumstances under which a new trial may be granted on the ground of newly discovered evidence. See *Taylor* v. *State,* 77 Ga. App. 532 (48 S.E.2d 711); *Burke* v. *State,* 205 Ga. 656 (54 S.E.2d 350).

(b) It has been frequently held that the ultimate criterion by which the merit of newly discovered evidence should be measured is the probability of a different result. See *McDaniel* v. *State,* 74 Ga. App. 5 (38 S.E.2d 697); *Harper* v. *State,* 50 Ga.

App. 298 (177 S.E. 886); *Todd* v. *Jackson,* 24 Ga.

App. 519 (101 S.E. 192); *Carson* v. *State,* 20 Ga.

App. 82 (92 S.E. 549); *Paden* v. *State,* 17 Ga.

App. 112 (86 S.E. 287); *Nolan* v. *State,* 14 Ga.

App. 824 (82 S.E. 377); *Deason* v. *State,* 11 Ga.

App. 759 (76 S.E. 73); *Fehn* v. *State,* 11 Ga.

App. 328 (75 S.E. 208); *Moore* v. *State,* 11 Ga.

App. 259 (74 S.E. 1102).

These cases must be distinguished from the one at bar because the newly discovered evidence was of a character whose probative value might be assessed by the courts in that it proved a new and different state of facts rather than merely attacking the credibility of the witness, in which latter case its value is within the exclusive determination of the jury. We know of no better way to show such value than by the affidavits of the ten jurors that they would have voted for a verdict of not guilty had this evidence been presented to them. This was matter for the consideration of the trial court, in whose discretion the grant or refusal of an extraordinary motion for a new trial largely rests. See *Rogers* v. *State,* 129 Ga. 589 (4) (59 S.E. 288); *Brown* v. *State,* 141Ga. 783 (1)

(82 S.E. 238); *Towler* v. *State,* 24 Ga. App. 362 (100 S.E. 787).

The Court of Appeals, however, is a court for the correction of errors of law only and is vested with no such discretion. It can pass only upon the question of whether the action of the trial court in overruling the extraordinary motion for a new trial was error as a matter of law. The matter being discretionary with him, the judgment was not erroneous.

However, the excellent showing made might constitute a compelling reason for a tribunal invested with discretionary powers such as the Pardon and Parole Board of this State, to take affirmative action which is beyond the purview of this court.

The trial court did not err in overruling the motion for a new trial.

Judgment affirmed. MacIntyre, P. J., and Gardner, J., concur.

APPENDIX 5

U.S. SUPREME COURT DECISION

U.S. Supreme Court
Stembridge v. Georgia, 343 U.S. 541 (1952)
Stembridge v. Georgia
No. 474
Argued April 22, 1952
Decided May 26, 1952
343 U.S. 541

Syllabus

Having been convicted in a Georgia state court of involuntary manslaughter and his conviction having been affirmed by the Court of Appeals of Georgia, petitioner moved in the trial court for a new trial on the ground of newly discovered evidence. Denial of this motion by the trial court was affirmed by the Court of Appeals on adequate state ground. Petitioner then moved in the Court of Appeals for a rehearing on that decision and, for the first time, attempted to claim a violation of his federal constitutional rights. This motion was denied by the Court of Appeals without opinion, and the Supreme Court of Georgia denied certiorari without opinion. Thereafter, petitioner obtained from the Court of Appeals an amendment of the record purporting to show that, on the motion for rehearing, it had considered the federal constitutional question and decided it adversely to petitioner. Without seeking a review of this amending order in the Supreme Court of Georgia, petitioner applied to this Court for certiorari, which was granted.

Held: it now appearing that the decision of the Supreme Court of Georgia might have rested on an adequate state ground, the writ of certiorari was improvidently granted, and the case is dismissed. Pp. 343 U. S. 542-548.

1. Since the Supreme Court of Georgia, which was the highest state court in which a decision could be had in this case, was not asked to pass upon and did not pass upon the amending order of the Court of Appeals, this Court has no occasion to consider its effect. P. 343 U. S. 546.

2. Since the Supreme Court of Georgia's earlier denial of certiorari without opinion might have rested on an adequate state ground, this Court will not take jurisdiction to review that judgment. Pp. 343 U. S. 546-547.

3. The amending order of the Georgia Court of Appeals does not change the posture of this case, since it does not remove the strong possibility, in the light of Georgia law, that the Supreme Court of Georgia might have rested its order denying certiorari on a nonfederal ground. P. 343 U. S. 547.

Case dismissed.

Page 343 U. S. 542

A writ of certiorari having been improvidently granted in this case, 342 U.S. 940, the case is *dismissed,* p. 343 U. S. 548.

APPENDIX 6

JUDGE ROWLAND'S OLE TIMEY SOUTHERN JUSTICE

Documents relating to the final release of Marion Stembridge from his guilty verdict in the death of Emma Johnekin were provided by the Johnson County Clerk of Court.

GEORGIA, JOHNSON COUNTY

TO THE HONORABLE J. ROY ROWLAND JUDGE OF THE SUPERIOR COURT, DUBLIN CIRCUIT.

The petition of Marion W. Stembridge shows the following facts:

1.

Petitioner is illegally detained and restrained of his liberty and is held in illegal custody by B. H. Webb, a resident of said county, and petitioner is now confined in said County.

2.

The cause or pretense of said illegal detention and restraint is under and by virtue of a certain void and illegal conviction and sentence imposed by the Judge of 8and made a part of this petition as Exhibit A.

3.

Petitioner shows that his conviction is void for the reason that said conviction was obtained by the knowing use of perjured testimony and by the suppression and withholding from the trail court and from the trail jury of evidence that would have shown that petitioner was not guilty and that would have resulted in a verdict of not guilty. Petitioner shows that this knowing use of perjured testimony or this suppression of evidence that would have shown petitioner to be not guilty are each a violation of the due process clause of the Fourteenth Amendment to the Constitution of the United States, and, as such, void the judgment of the trial court in this case.

4.

Petitioner attaches as a part of this petition for habeas corpus a transcript of the record of an extraordinary motion for new trail made in Baldwin Superior Court, designated as Exhibit B.

5.

Petitioner shows that the verdict of the jury convicting him of voluntary manslaughter was based on the testimony of Mary Jane Harrison, witness for the state as set out on pagers 51 to 79.

6,

Petitioner shows that at the time the evidence of the witness Mary Jane Harrison was introduced by the state in his trail, which trial resulted in a conviction of voluntary manslaughter, J. E. Jones, an officer of the State of Georgia , and Eugene A. Ellis, Chief of Police of the City of Milledgeville, a subdivision of the State of Georgia, both of which said officials were then and there acting as representatives of the State, which representatives were actively engaged in assisting the Solicitor General in the prosecution, and said officials representing the State of Georgia had in their possession at the time of petitioner's trial the statement in writing set out on pages 178 to 180 inclusive, which was signed by the witness Mary Jane Harrison when she thought she was in article of death and which was made by her as a dying declaration, which statement, if it had been shown to the jury or if the statements made in this written declaration had been made known to the jury, would have resulted in petitioner's acquittal.

7.

The Solicitor General prosecuting petitioner's case for the State of Georgia either had actual possession of a copy of this signed statement or had notice of its contents and knew that such dying declaration had been made and the statements made therein, and such written statement made by Mary Jane Harrison as a dying declaration was in possession of these officers acting for the State of Georgia, who were actively engaged in an effort to obtain a conviction.

8.

The testimony of the witness Mary Jane Harrison given upon petitioner's trial under oath by her was perjured and false and the State of Georgia acting through its representatives knew of or had reason to believe the falsity of said testimony when it was introduced upon petitioner's trial which resulted in his conviction.

9.

Petitioner was ignorant of the contents of the statements made by Mary Jane Harrison in this dying declaration and did not learn of its contents until more than a year after petitioner's trial and conviction and the fact that this witness had made a dying declaration entirely at variance with her sworn testimony on petitioner's trial was not discovered by petitioner until more than a year after his trial and conviction, and the statements made by Mary Jane Harrison in her dying declaration were not disclosed upon the trial or divulged to petitioner or his counsel, although the State's Representatives were obliged to know or had conclusive reason to believe that her testimony delivered on his trial was false and perjured.

10.

Even had petitioner known that the State's Representatives were in possession of the dying declaration which would show that her testimony on his trial was perjured, petitioner would have had no remedy at law to force the State's Counsel or its representatives to deliver such dying declaration to petitioner to be used on his trial.

11.

Petitioner alleges that he was not given a fair and impartial trial and was convicted without due process of law because under the laws of Georgia any witness testifying under oath is presumed to speak the truth. The laws of the State of Georgia do not permit a defendant in a criminal case to be sworn in his own defense or permit his unsworn statement to be accepted as sworn testimony and there is no presumption provided by the Georgia laws that the unsworn statement of the defendant is true. The Solicitor General knew or had reason to believe that defendant had no witness other than himself to controvert and disprove the sworn testimony of the State's witness, and knew that under the ruling of Freeman V. State, 122 Ga. 48, a witness cannot be impeached by the unsworn statement of the accused, and the State of Georgia acting through its officers denied to petitioner a fair trial when it concealed and withheld from petitioner the contents of the statement made as a dying declaration of the State's witness.

12.

Petitioner alleges that the conduct and acts of the State of Georgia, its counsel, and its representatives as set out in this petition, have denied to petitioner due process of law and the equal protection of the law as guaranteed by the Fourteenth Amendment to the Constitution of the United States, which is follows:

"All persons born or naturalized in the United States, and subject to the jurisdiction thereof, are citizens of the United States and of the State wherein they reside. No State shall make or enforce any law which shall abridge the privileges or immunities of citizens of the United States; nor shall any state deprive any person of life, liberty, or property, without due process of law; nor deny to any person within its jurisdiction the equal protection of due process of law; nor deny to any person within its jurisdiction the equal protection of the laws. "

13.

Petitioner alleges that the conduct and acts of the representatives of the State of Georgia in obtaining and permitting petitioner's conviction on the perjured testimony of Mary Jane Harrison is in violation of the Fourteenth Amendment just quoted and also violates Article 1, Paragraph 2 of the Constitution of Georgia, which provides as follows:

Protection to person and property is the paramount duty of Government, and shall be impartial and complete.

Such conduct and acts on the part of the State of Georgia, its counsel, and its representatives likewise violates Article 1, Paragraph 3 of the Constitution of the State of Georgia, which provides as follows:

"No person shall be deprived of life, liberty, or property, except by due process of law."

14.

Due process of law was denied petitioner in his trial and he was deprived of his liberty without due process of law because the State of Georgia acting through its legal representatives caused petitioner to be convicted by the introduction of sworn testimony of Mary Jane Harrison which was known to be false and his conviction obtained on such false and perjured testimony is void because in violation of the Fourteenth Amendment of the Constitution of the United States and Paragraph 3 of Article 1 of the Constitution of the State of Georgia.

15.

Petitioner at the time of his trial and his conviction was a natural born citizen of the United States and a resident of the State of Georgia and was entitled to the protection afforded him by the Constitution of the State of Georgia, and the acts committed by the legal representatives of the State of Georgia in procuring his conviction on perjured testimony, which was known to be false, violated petitioner's rights guaranteed him by the Fourteenth Amendment to the Constitution of the United States and violated Paragraph 3 of Article 1 of the Constitution of the State of Georgia in that petitioner was denied due process of law.

16.

Petitioner shows that because of the acts of the State as set forth in this petition and the denial of his constitutional rights, the trial court lost jurisdiction of the case and his trial was rendered void and the verdict of the jury based on such false testimony is void and the sentence imposed upon

him is likewise void because the conviction of petitioner procured by perjured testimony, which testimony was known by the State's Representatives to be false at the time it was introduced, denied petitioner due process of law as guaranteed by the Fourteenth Amendment to the Constitution of the United States and this conduct on the part of the State of Georgia and its representatives renders the whole proceeding of the trial, the verdict, and the sentence void.

17.

Petitioner alleges that the authorities legally representing the State of Georgia in the trial of petitioner's case deliberately suppressed evidence which would have impeached the State's witness Mary Jane Harrison and refuted the truth of her testimony delivered on the trial of petitioner's case which caused his conviction, and petitioner was thereby denied due process of law and not afforded a fair and impartial trial. Briefly summarized, Mary Jane Harrison testified on the trial which resulted in petitioner's conviction that the victim, Emma Johnekin, entered the third room of the apartment, which consisted of four rooms located one directly behind the other with doorways opening in a straight line; that the victim, after entering the third room seated herself on a trunk located therein and that the defendant (present petition) followed her into this room and shot her twice while she was seated on the trunk.

At the time the State's Counsel and the State Officers prosecuting petitioner's case knew that the witness Mary Jane Harrison had made a statement as a dying declaration and material parts of such statement so made as a dying declaration being as follows:

"We did not mention a gun. There is one near the kitchen, and neither of us had got that far…shot at least one time, and Emma never got out of the front bedroom until the man had already gone."

18.

The said Solicitor General knew that under the law as expressed by a decision of the highest court of Georgia, a declaration made as this one was made in *articulo mortis*, and "the sanction under which these declarations are made, in view of the impending death and judgment, when the last hope of life is extinct, and when the retributions of eternity are at hand, is of equal solemnity as that of statements made on oath."

19.

The said Solicitor General knew further that the appellate courts of Georgia have held that such statements usually carry much weight with juries, and the Solicitor General knew or had reason to believe that if this written statement of Mary Jane Harrison was shown to the jury it would probably result in no conviction of the accused.

20.

The said officer had reason to believe that if he withheld the said written statement of Mary Jane Harrison from said jury the said jury would probably convict accused.

21.

The State, through its prosecuting officers, knew or had reason to believe that under the evidence in all probability the court would charge the jury the principle of law governing the determination of the credibility of witnesses established by the laws of Georgia, in substance, if not in the exact words, which it did, as follows:

"You are made by law, Gentlemen, the exclusive judge as to the credibility of witnesses. In Passing upon their credibility you may consider all the facts and circumstances in the case. …"

As to the credibility of the witness, Mary Jane Harrison, the State knew that the jury was entitled to have the State submit the suppressed statement made in what she believed herself to be in the article of death, and knew that in all good conscience the jury could not fairly determine her credibility without the suppressed writing. The withholding by the State of this writing from the jury prevented the jury from considering material facts and circumstances as to the credibility of the testimony of Mary Jane Harrison, upon whose testimony the jury found the accused guilty and resulted in his conviction.

22.

The Solicitor General argued to the jury that it was their duty to convict the accused on that part of the testimony of the witness Mary Jane Harrison, in which she swore that the accused followed the deceased into the third room and there shot her, and stated to the jury that the accused had offered no evidence to contradict that part of the testimony of said witness, saying in substance:

"If there is evidence here of a certain happening with no evidence to   contradict it, the jury must believe the only evidence on the subject."

And the state vigorously contended to the court and jury that the shooting of Emma Johnekin in the third and last room of the house while she was seated on a trunk, was cold-blooded murder.

23.

Petitioner shows that each and all of the foregoing acts of prosecuting officers constituted a fraud upon the court and jury and denied him his constitutional rights as herein alleged to the extent that the court and jury lost jurisdiction of the case and the verdict and sentence was void.

24.

The petitioner shows that ten of the jurors who tried petitioner and who convicted him gave affidavits in support of an extraordinary motion for new trial to the effect that if they had been advised of this previous statement made by Mary Jane Harrison, which would have necessarily refuted her testimony delivered on the trial and successfully impeached her and would have shown that her testimony on the trial was perjured, that they would never have agreed to convict petitioner but would have acquitted him. And so it is that the deliberate suppression of this evidence which would have successfully refuted the truth of the testimony of the State's witness on the trial, and the introduction of this false testimony on the trial, deprived petitioner of a fair and impartial trial and denied him due process of law guaranteed by the Federal Constitution.

25.

Petitioner alleges that the State of Georgia provides no adequate corrective process to determine and declare petitioner's conviction void unless this writ of habeas corpus is granted and petitioner released from custody, his conviction being absolutely void because of the facts hereinbefore alleged showing the knowing and intentional use of perjured testimony in order to obtain his conviction.

26.

Petitioner alleges that he has reason to apprehend that the defendant, the respondent herein who is illegally restraining petitioner of his liberty, will remove him beyond the limits of the County.

27.

The petitioner further shows that the case in which he was convicted is that of voluntary manslaughter and that the minimum sentence imposed upon him is only one year, and that unless he is admitted to bail and allowed his liberty under bond, the probability is that he will be compelled to serve all or a great part of the void sentence before any final judgment is rendered in this proceeding.

28.

Petitioner is able to give reasonable bail and hereby offers and tenders bail in any reasonable amount which may be fixed by the Court.

WHEREFORE, Petitioner prays that your Honor issue the State's writ of habeas corpus directed to the said B. H. Webb, requiring him to bring your petitioner before the court at the time and place specified in the writ for the purpose of examination into the cause of petitioner's detention.

Petitioner further prays that the court issue its precept directed to the Sheriff or other officers as provided by Section 50-109 of the Code requiring said officers to search for and arrest petitioner's body and bring him before the Court to be disposed of as may be directed by the Court.

Further, petitioner prays that the Court fix a reasonable bond and allow petitioner to be at liberty under bail, such bond to be in an amount fixed by the Court to be approved by the Sheriff of this County, conditioned that petitioner shall personally appear at the time and place fixed for the hearing of this habeas corpus and that petitioner shall personally appear whenever required by order of the court to abide the final order and judgment of this Court in said case.

Victor Davidson
T. Arnold Jacobs
Jackson and Jackson
ATTORNEYS FOR PETTIONER

Exhibit A

STATE OF GEORGIA, BALDWIN COUNTY.
INDICTMENT IN THE SUPERIOR COURT

THE STATE

NO. 2847 MINUTES T FOLIO 486

vs.

MARION W. STEMBRIDGE: FOR MURDER

Tried at July Term, 1949, and verdict of guilty of voluntary manslaughter.
WHEREUPON IT IS ADJUDGED BY THE COURT,

That the Defendant, Marion W. Stembridge be remanded to the common jail of Baldwin County, and there safely kept until a sufficient guard shall be sent from the State Board of Corrections of Georgia, and then delivered, and shall be by said guard taken to the State Penitentiary or such other place as the State Board of Corrections of Georgia may direct, where he, the said Marion W. Stembridge be confined at labor for the full term of not less than one year and not more than three years.

Witness my official signature in open court, on this 21st day of July, 1949.

George S. Carpenter
Judge, Ocmulgee Circuit

****

GEORGIA, JOHNSON COUNTY.

Personally came before the undersigned attesting officer authorized to administer oaths, Marion W. Stembridge, who being first duly sworn deposes and states on oath that the allegations in this petition for habeas corpus are true.

Marion W. Stembridge

Sworn to and subscribed before me,
This 17 day of July, 1952.
J. Roy Rowland
Judge Superior Court, Dublin Circuit , Georgia

****

GEORGIA, JOHNSON COUNTY.

To B. H, Webb

You are hereby commanded to produce the body of M. W. Stembridge alleged to be illegally detained by you, together with the cause of the detention, before me on the 27 day of August, 1952, at 10 o'clock A.M., at Wrightsville, Georgia, then and there to be disposed of as the law prescribed.

Ordered further that said hearing be had on affidavits, documentary and other evidence and/or Oral testimony and that each party serve the other with copies of any pleadings or affidavits 10 days before said date.

Given under my hand and official seal, this 17th day of July, 1952.

J. Roy Rowland
Judge, Superior Court, Dublin Circuit.

****

GEORGIA, JOHNSON COUNTY

TO THE SHERIFF, DEPUTY SHERIFF, CORONER, ALL AND SINGULAR THE LAWFUL CONSTABLES OF THIS COUNTY.

Marion W. Stembridge, the applicant for the foregoing writ of habeas corpus having filed, along with his petition therefore his affidavit that he has reason to apprehend that B. H. Webb, the person alleged to be illegally restraining him of his liberty will remove him beyond limits of the County, you are hereby commanded to search for and arrest the body of M. W. Stembridge alleged to be illegally detained and bring him before me to be disposed of as I may direct.

HEREIN FAIL NOT.

WITNESS MY HAND AND OFFICIAL SIGNATURE, THIS 17TH DAY OF July, 1952,

J. Roy Rowland, Judge
Superior Court, Dublin Circuit

Marion W. Stembridge, petitioner in the foregoing writ of habeas corpus, having been arrested and brought before me;

And it appearing that the said M. W. Stembridge stands convicted of voluntary manslaughter with a sentence of not less than one nor more than three years, said offense being one in which bail is properly granted under law; and the said M. W. Stembridge requesting the Court to admit him to bail pending a final hearing and determination of this petition for habeas corpus;

And the Court being of the opinion that bail should properly be allowed in this case;

And it is therefore ordered by the Court that Marion W. Stembridge, the petitioner, be allowed to remain at liberty and be admitted to bail upon his entering in the bond with good security to be approved by the Sheriff of this County in the sum of $Five Thousand Dollars, conditioned that Marion W. Stembridge shall personally appear whenever required by order of this Court and shall personally be present and appear whenever required by order of the Court and shall personally be present and appear to abide the final order and judgment of this Court in this case.

SO ORDERED, this 17 day of July, 1952.

> J. Roy Rowland
> Judge, Superior Court
> Dublin Circuit.

Filed in office, this 18 day of July, 1952.

> C. B. Harrison
> Clerk

****

GEORGIA, JOHNSON COUNTY:

I have this day served the defendant B. H. Webb personally with a true copy of the within petition and process.

This the 17 day of July, 1952

> J. D. Alexander
> Deputy Sheriff.

MARION W. STEMBRIDGE   No. _____
     Petitioner
       vs.

B. H. WEBB, WARDEN
Johnson County Public Works Camp   HABEAS CORPUS
     Respondent

The within and foregoing petition and Habeas Corpus and the writ of habeas corpus issued on said petitioner be and with the approval of the court is hereby dismissed, this 20 day of August, 1952.

> Victor Davison, Jackson and Jackson, T. Arnold Jacobs
> Attorneys for Marion W. Stembridge,

The foregoing petition is hereby dismissed by me, this 20 day of August, 1952.

Marion W. Stembridge

Marion   W.   Stembridge,

Petitioner.

In the name and behalf of the citizens of Georgia , charge and accuse Marion W. Stembridge and Sam L. Terry, of the County and State aforesaid with the offense of Murder for that the said accused on 7 day of March, in the year of our Lord Nineteen hundred and forty nine in the assault in and upon one Emma Johnekin in the peace of God and said State then and there being, then and there unlawfully, feloniously, willfully and of his malice aforethought, did kill and murder, by shooting the said Emma Johnekin with a certain pistol which the said accused then and there held, and giving to the said Emma Johnekin then and there a mortal wound, of which mortal wound the said Emma Johnekin died.

And so the Jurors aforesaid, upon their oath aforesaid, do say that the said Marion W. Stembridge and Sam L. Terry the said Emma Johnekin in manner and form aforesaid, unlawfully, feloniously, willfully and of his malice aforethought, did kill and murder, contrary to the laws of said State the good order, peace and dignity thereof.

Baldwin Superior Court
July Term, 1949

Mattie Smith
Prosecutor

C. S. Baldwin, Jr.
Solicitor General

WITNESS FOR THE STATE
Eugene Ellis
J. E. Jones
B.T. Lingold
Richard Lee Cooper
Johnnie Cooper
George Harrison
Mary Jane Harrison
Louvenia Harrison
Martha Cooper
Will Cooper

The defendant waives copy of indictment and list of witnesses, also waives being formally arraigned and pleads not guilty.

C. S. Baldwin, Jr.
Solicitor General

Frank O. Evans
Marion Ennis
James M. Watts, Jr.

Defendant's Attorney

******

July 19, 1949
Number 3839
Baldwin Superior Court

July term 1949

THE STATE

VS

MARION W. STEMBRIDGE AND
SAM L. TERRY

MURDER

True Bill on Marion W. Stembridge
No Bill on Sam L. Terry

Ralph Simmerson
Foreman
Mattie Smith, Prosecutor

C. S. Baldwin, Jr.
Solicitor General

We, the Jury, find the defendant Marion W. Stembridge guilty of voluntary manslaughter with penalty of 1 to 3 years.

This the 21st day of July 1949.

T. E. Owen, Foreman

Exhibit   2. The sentence of the court.
STATE OF GEORGIA. BALDWIN COUNTY

Indictment in the Superior
Court
No. 3847 Minutes T Folio 486

THE STATE

vs

MARION W. STEMBRIDGE   FOR MURDER

Tried at July Term, 1949, and VERDICT of guilty of voluntary manslaughter.
WHEREUPON IT IS ADJUDGED BY THE COURT,

That the defendant, Marion W. Stembridge be remanded to the common jail of Baldwin County, and there safely kept until a sufficient guard shall be sent from the State Board of Corrections of Georgia, and be then delivered, and be by said guard taken to the State Penitentiary or such other place as the State Board of Corrections of Georgia may direct, where he, the said Marion W. Stembridge be confined at labor for the full term of not less than one year and not more than three years.

Witness my official signature in open court, on this 21 day of July 1949.

George S. Carpenter
Judge, Ocmulgee Circuit

Exhibit 3. JUDGMENT and remittitur of Court of Appeals   33573

Court of Appeals of the State of Georgia

ATLANTA, June 5, 1951

The Honorable Court of Appeals met pursuant to adjournment.   The following judgment was rendered:

M. W. Stembridge v. The State

This case came before this court upon a writ of error from the Superior Court of Baldwin County; and, after argument had, it is considered and adjudged that the judgment of the court below be affirmed. MacIntyre, Gardner and Townsend, JJ., Concur.

BILL OF COSTS, $15.00

Court of Appeals of the State of Georgia

The petitioner having voluntarily dismissed his petition for habeas corpus and the writ of habeas corpus, said dismissal is hereby authorized, allowed, and approved by the Court and it is ordered that the petition be and the same is hereby dismissed, this 20 day of August, 1952.

J. Roy Rowland

J. Roy Rowland, Judge Superior Court,
Dublin Circuit.
GEORGIA, JOHNSON COUNTY,
Filed in office Aug. 20, 1952.
C. B. Harrison, Clerk

CLERK'S OFFICE, ATLANTA, JUL 16 1952

I certify that the above is a true extract from the minutes of the Court of Appeals of Georgia, and that M. W. Stembridge paid the above bill of costs.

Witness my signature and the seal of said court hereto affixed the day and year last above written.

Morgan Thomas, Deputy Clerk,
(Official seal impression)

****

In the Superior Court of Baldwin County, Georgia, July Term 1952.

It is considered, ordered and adjudged that the within remittitur and judgment of the Court of Appeals of Georgia, be, and the same is hereby made the judgment of the Superior Court of Baldwin County, Ga. Let said remitter and this order be entered upon the minutes of this court. In open Court. This the 17th of July, 1952.

J. C. Cooper   Clerk   George S. Carpenter
                                         Judge Superior Courts
                                         Ocmulgee Circuit.

****

Georgia, Johnson County
Filed in office Aug. 27, 1952

C. B. Harrison
Clerk

MARION W. STEMBRIDGE	JOHNSON SUPERIOR COURT
Petitioner	
vs.	No._____
B. H. WEBB, Warden Johnson	
County Public Works Camp	HABEAS CORPUS
Respondent.	

MOTION TO QUASH THE WRIT OF HABEAS CORPUS

NOW COMES B. H. Webb, Warden Johnson County Public Works Camp, respondent named in the above-entitled action, and before responding to the writ of habeas corpus hereinbefore issued, moves this Honorable Court to quash the writ, and for reason thereof shows:

1.

That this Honorable Court is without jurisdiction to inquire into the legality of the detention of the petitioner because the petitioner is not in the actual physical custody of your respondent. Petitioner is not in the custody of your respondent by reason of the fact that this Honorable Court admitted petitioner to bail in July 17, 1952 and set him at liberty on bond, rendering it impossible for your respondent to produce the body of Marion W. Stembridge as commanded by the writ.

2.

That this Honorable Court is without jurisdiction for the further reason that the writ of habeas corpus was made returnable more than twenty days from the issuance of the writ and that this Court has no power to entertain the matter when the writ is returnable in more that twenty days.

3.

That this Honorable Court in admitting petitioner to bail acted beyond the jurisdiction of this court.

4.

That it is not made to appear by the petition, or otherwise, that Marion W. Stembridge, the petitioner, has stated any cause of shown any reason why he should be entitled to be discharged from the judgment and sentence under which he was detained on July 17, 1952 in the custody of your respondent,

WHEREFORE, the respondent prays that the writ by quashed.

Eugene Cook, Attorney General

M. H. Blackshear, Jr., Deputy Assistant Attorney General
Lamar W. Sizemore, Assistant Attorney General

CERTIFICATE OF SERVICE

Pursuant to order contained in the writ of habeas corpus that the respondent serve copies of any pleading 10 days before return day, I, Lamar W. Sizemore, Assistant Attorney General, of counsel for B. H. Webb, respondent, do hereby certify that I have this day served copies of the foregoing motion to quash upon counsel for Marion W. Stembridge, petitioner, by mailing same to Victor Davidson, Esq., Irwinton, Georgia, T. Arnold Jacobs, Esq., Macon, Georgia, and Jackson and Jackson, Gray, Georgia.

This 16 day of August, 1952.

Lamar W. Sizemore, Assistant Attorney General

GEORGIA, JOHNSON COUNTY
Filed in office Aug 27, 1952
C. B. Harrison, Clerk

Motion to quash this writ is overruled and denied.
This Sept. 6, 1952.

J. Roy Rowland
Judge S. C. D. C.

****

MARION W. STEMBRIDGE   JOHNSON SUPERIOR COURT
Petitioner   HABEAS CORPUS

vs.   No.   4

B. H. WEBB, WARDEN

Johnson County Works Camp,
          Respondent.   *

ORDER OF COURT

Upon hearing evidence in the above-stated case and both parties having closed on August 27, 1952   and this court having taken said case under advisement and reserved its decision until September 6, 1952, it is therefore considered, ordered and adjudged, that this writ of habeas corpus is granted and sustained, and it is the order of this court that petitioner, Marion W. Stembridge, is hereby discharged and freed from custody as prayed in his petition: and the said B. H. Webb, respondent, is hereby ordered and directed to release petitioner from custody.

It is further ordered that the costs of these proceedings be paid by Respondent. This 6th day of September, 1952.

                              J. Roy Rowland
Judge Superior Court, Johnson County, Ga.

****

MARION W. STEMBRIDGE,   JOHNSON SUPERIOR COURT
          Petitioner,
          vs   No._____
B. H. WEBB, Warden Johnson
County Public Works Camp,   HABEAS CORPUS
          Respondent,
          RESPONSE TO THE WRIT OF HABEAS CORPUS

NOW COMES B. H. WEBB, Warden of the Johnson County Public Works Camp and without waiving his motion to quash heretofore filed, and in response to the writ of habeas corpus hereinbefore issued, states that he is unable to produce the body of Marion W. Stembridge at the time and place specified in said writ for the reason that the said Marion W. Stembridge is not presently in the custody of the respondent, and by way of response to the writ and the petition upon which it is based, respondent respectfully shows:

1.

Respondent is unable to produce the body of petitioner Marion W. Stembridge because the petitioner is not presently in the custody of the respondent by reason of the fact that this Honorable Court by ex parte order, entered July 17, 1952, admitted said petitioner to bail and ordered him set at liberty on bond.

2.

Marion W. Stembridge was last in the custody of your respondent of July 17, 1952 and upon order of this court was admitted to bail and set at liberty on that date. Further, respondent says that on July 17, 1952 when Marion W. Stembridge was in the lawful custody of respondent that that custody was pursuant to the judgment of conviction and sentence imposed upon him by the Superior Court of Baldwin County, Georgia, a court of general jurisdiction having jurisdiction of both the subject matter and the person of the petitioner. Respondent herewith attaches and files with this Honorable Court a copy of the indictment rendered by the Grand Jury of Baldwin County against Marion W. Stembridge, the defendant's plea to such indictment, the verdict of the jury thereon, the sentence of the Court entered July 21, 1949, pursuant to the verdict of the jury, and the judgment of the Court entered July 17, 1952 making the judgment of affirmance by the Court of Appeals the judgment of that Court.

3.

Respondent further says that he has no personal knowledge of any of the alleged facts and things complained of and that his knowledge is limited to what appears of record in the trial Court and the direct appeals therefrom and, therefore, for want of information your respondent can neither admit nor deny the allegations of petitioner's application for the writ, but demands strict proof of all allegations.

WHEREFORE, having fully responded, the respondent prays that the body of Marion W. Stembridge by remanded to his custody.

Eugene Cook
Attorney General
M. H. Blackshear, Jr.
Deputy Assistant Attorney General
Lamar W. Sizemore
Assistant Attorney General

****

AFFIDAVIT
GEORGIA, JOHNSON COUNTY.
Personally came before me the undersigned attesting officer authorized to administer oaths, B. H. Webb, Warden Johnson County Public Works Camp,

respondent in the above entitled action, who on oath says that the statements contained in the foregoing response to the writ of Habeas corpus are true.

B. H. Webb

Sworn to and subscribed before me
This 27 day of Aug., 1952
C. B. Harrison
Clerk Superior Court
Johnson County Georgia

CERTIFICATE OF SERVICE

Pursuant to order contained in the writ of habeas corpus that the respondent serve copies of any pleading 10 days before return day, I, Lamar W. Sizemore, Assistant Attorney General, of counsel for B. H. Webb, respondent, do hereby certify that I have this day served copies of the foregoing response upon counsel for Marion W. Stembridge petitioner, by mailing same to Victor Davidson, Esq., Irwinton, Georgia, T. Arnold Jacobs, Esq., Macon, Georgia, and Jackson and Jackson, Gray, Georgia.

This 16 day of August, 1952

Lamar W. Sizemore
Assistant Attorney General

EXHIBIT   1. The indictment together with all entries thereon, together with the plea of not guilty and the verdict of the jurors entered thereon.

GEORGIA, BALDWIN COUNTY
IN the Superior Court of said County
The grand jurors selected, chosen and sworn for the county to wit:

1 Ralph Simmerson, Foreman
2 Grady Moore, 3 George Ross, Sr., 4 G. J. Adams, 5 Longino Little, 6 Geo Powers, 7 Floyd Veal, 8 E. B. Keel, 9 Branson Chandler, 10 Carl Nelson, 11 Guy Roberts, 12 Will Ivey, 13 Bob Watson, 14 Tom Hollis, 15 Grady Villyard, 16 Sam Moore, 17 Noah Jackson , 18 G. C. May, 19 Stewart Barnes, 20. J. A. King, 21 Will Brown

APPENDIX 7

"JUDGE STANDS FIRM ON COURT RECORD"

NEWS REPORT

Former Judge J. Roy Roland today stood firm on the court record and an order he signed last September 6 freeing Marion W. Stembridge from a one-to-three years voluntary manslaughter conviction

Rowland faced defeat for re-election in the Democratic primary before Stembridge's habeas corpus petition was filed in his Jonson County Superior Court last July 17. Rowland said it would be improper to discuss and try to explain his official court action and the record and order should speak for themselves.

Robert E. Warren, Director of Corrections, dug into the circumstances that permitted Stembridge to go free without a single day in jail or prison on the sentence. He commented that the proceedings had some unusual angles.

"But if there was any collusion," he said, it certainly was not with any intentional co-operation on our part.

Warden Ben Hill Webb of the Johnson County prison camp and Dewey F. Hall, who was sheriff at the time, said Stembridge came to Wrightsville with papers in his pocket from the State Department of Corrections assigning him to the Johnson prison. Webb was called to the sheriff's office where Stembridge himself handed over the papers to the warden.

Immediately after that the sheriff served Webb with the habeas corpus petition filed by Stembridge that same day, July 17, 1952, and the sheriff took control of Stembridge, who a few minutes later was released under bond approved by Judge Rowland pending a hearing on the habeas corpus writ.

* * *

Stembridge was sentenced to prison in July 1949 by Judge George S. Carpenter after his murder trial in Baldwin Superior Court resulted in a voluntary manslaughter conviction. He was accused in an indictment of murdering Emma Johnekin, a Negro woman, in March 1949.

Stembridge was also under indictment for perjury for false swearing in connection with a mortgage foreclosure and was convicted in U. S. District Court in Macon last week of offering $10,000 bribes to two federal income tax agents. He was to have ben sentences in that case on Monday. Judge A. B. Conger signed an order Tuesday, closing the case because of Stembridge's death.

The Department of Corrections assignment of Stembridge to the Johnson prison camp was dated July 17, 1952, the same day the Baldwin County Clerk of Court certified Stembridge's conviction to the Department after the Georgia and the Unites States Supreme Courts turned down appeals for a new trial. Records show the habeas corpus petition also was filed on that date and Judge Rowland released Stembridge under bond on July 17, 1952, pending a hearing.

Personal comment: *How did all of these events occur on the same day, when the certification from Baldwin to Atlanta was mailed in Milledgeville on July 17?*

A Milledgeville source informed the newspaper that a lawyer for Stembridge obtained a copy of the certification papers on the morning of July 17, as soon as the clerk received a remittitur in the case from the higher courts, and the clerk mailed the original certificate to the Department of Corrections in Atlanta on the same date.

The mailed copy could to have reached Atlanta until the next day at the earliest.

Warren (Superintendent of Corrections) said he cannot understand how all these events happened as they did. He said the copy of the final order of the Baldwin County court undoubtedly was delivered by messenger to the directions department, but he and others in the department denied flatly that the papers were delivered by a lawyer.

Warren also stated his records show the department's commitment of Stembridge to Johnson County was issued on July 17 and mailed to Warden Webb.

Warren said, "We don't give those orders to anybody. We never have and never will.

... He might have had a copy of the court order or something, but I just can't believe he could have had that commitment order."

Asked how Stembridge could have known he was being sent to Johnson County, Warren said the information could have been obtained from his office readily enough.

Both Warren and his assistant J. B. Hatchett denied they had received any request for a particular assignment for Stembridge. They insisted his assignment to Johnson County was purely routine.

The court record in Wrightsville shows the habeas corpus petition filed July 17 was withdrawn and dismissed by Judge Rowland on August 29 after the State, through the Attorney General's office had moved to quash it on the grounds it set a hearing more than 20 days after the date of filing.

A complete new set of papers was filed on August 20, 1952; these were largely duplicates of the first set. Stembridge was again freed under a bond order by Rowland.

Bond was signed as principal by Roy Hodges, approved by Judge Rowland and Sheriff Dewey F. Hall. Sheriff Hall had also been defeated in his bid for reelection and, like Judge Rowland, would leave office on January 1, 1953.

The Attorney General's motion to quash this writ failed, and Judge Rowland's acts freed Stembridge from all charges related to the death of Emma Johnekin.

Stembridge's petition for release said he was convicted on perjured testimony of Mary Jane Harrison. It claimed she made a dying declaration when she thought she was dying from her injuries, but her statements during the trial conflicted with that "dying declaration." Stembridge said he was unaware of her first statement until long after the trial, but it was in possession of the officers who assisted the State in prosecuting him.

This claim of perjured testimony became the basis of his appeals to State and U. S. Courts for a new trial.

APPENDIX 8

COOK DEFENDS STAFF

Attorney General Cook and his staff were discombobulated about the circumstances that freed Stembridge. This article was published two days after the Sesquicentennial murders.

NEWS ITEM:

COOK DEFENDS STAFF IN STEMBRIDGE CASE

Attorney General Eugene Cook said "the ablest attorney on my staff did everything humanly and legally possible" to appeal an order of Judge J. Roy Rowland freeing Marion Stembridge from a manslaughter sentence last September 6.

M. H. Blackshear, Jr., the assistant attorney general who handled the case, said the planned appeal was held up by "prohibitive conditions imposed by Judge Rowland and that he thought it was impossible to appeal the case after Rowland stepped down from the bench January 1, 1953."

Personal comment: *Rowland DID NOT RESIGN; he was voted out of office in the primaries but held office until January 1. In that position, he had nothing to lose by juking the situation and freeing Stembridge, but what if anything did he gain?*

(This article gave similar details as given in Appendix 7 re Rowland defending his actions.)

Cook earlier said he was "profoundly surprised" when the judge freed Stembridge under bond pending a decision on his plea for freedom in the habeas corpus proceeding. Blackshear thought the judge was wrong in granting bail in the case, but said it was a smoot point when the judge signed an order releasing Stembridge on September 6.

Blackshear, who recently resigned from the attorney general staff, said he waited for some time after the order was filed for the record of the hearing on the habeas corpus proceeding to be completed by the court reporter. But the court reporter failed to get the record ready in the time in which it should have been presented. Therefore, under the agreement with a lawyer for Stembridge, Blackshear said he undertook to draw up a bill of exceptions from memory and presented it to the judge. He had thought it could be corrected by amendments at a later date. A bill of exceptions is the basis of an appeal in such a case.

Rowland, however, refused to sign the bill of exceptions unless certain corrections were made. The conditions set by Judge Rowland included a requirement that the entire 300-page records of proceedings in Stembridge's case before the U. S. Supreme court would have to be inserted into the habeas corpus records "not once, but twice," Blackshear said. Blackshear said the cost would be prohibitive and the people to do the work were not available in the time remaining.

......repeat of the July 17 events...

The remittitur in the case (reporting the outcome of the appeal) arrived in the Baldwin County Clerk of Court's office by mail at 9 a.m. July 17, from the Georgia Court of Appeals where it had been signed the day before. A few minutes later, Attorney Victor Davidson of Irwinton (*one of the team of attorneys representing Stembridge*) arrived at the Clerk's office (Cleve Cooper). Cleve Cooper and Victor Davison went to Judge George Carpenter's office and he signed an order making the ruling of the High Courts the judgment of Baldwin County Superior Court.

Cooper and Davidson returned to the clerk's office, where Cooper gave Davidson a certified copy of Stembridge's sentence. Davidson left. Later that day, Cooper made another copy of the sentence, a copy of the judge's order, a prisoner's history of Stanbridge and other required papers and *(typographical errors in news report; best guess) put them in the mail* about 7 p.m. *(July 17.* These papers could not have arrived in Atlanta until the next day *(July 18)*.

(HOWEVER) Department of Corrections records indicate the papers were received (from Cooper) on July 17, the same day Corrections assigned Stembridge the Johnson County Work Camp, and the same day Stembridge surrendered himself (briefly) to the warden, Ben Hill Webb.

Corrections Director Warren said he did not believe Stembridge actually had his commitment papers, but Warden Webb and also Johnson County Sheriff Dewey Hall insisted he did.

Stembridge's sentence stated he should "be remanded to the common jail of Baldwin County and there safely kept until a sufficient guard shall be sent from the State Board of Corrections of Georgia, and then delivered, and shall be by said guard taken to the state penitentiary or such other place as the state Board of Corrections of Georgia may direct..."

This is a routine form of sentence throughout Georgia.

Stembridge, however, did not surrender to the sheriff in Baldwin County (when all appeals were denied). Instead, he took himself and Roy Roland's "pass jail and go free" papers to Wrightsville—and home free. News reporters kept the issue alive.

Unusual Circumstances Studied

State Plans Investigation Of Stembridge Prison Case

ATLANTA (U) — Circumstances under which Marion W. Stembridge was committed to a Johnson County prison camp and released before he ever entered prison are being investigated by the Department of Corrections.

Th matter was brought to light by The Macon News which has been investigating the case for the past two weeks.

Records in the department's office here show that the final court order sentencing the late Milledgeville banker to 1 to 3 years for involuntary manslaughter was received on July 17, 1952. On the same day, the records show, a commitment order assigning Stembridge to the Johnson County camp and directing that he be taken into custody was mailed to Warden Ben Hill Webb at Wrightsville, the Johnson County seat.

However, Webb told R. E. Warren, corrections director, by telephone today he never received the commitment papers by mail. Instead, Warren quoted him as saying in the telephone conversation, he was called to the sheriff's office at Wrightsville where Stembridge personally handed him the commitment papers.

* * *

Warren said that Webb did not remember the exact date of the incident but the warden said he also was served with habeas corpus papers "before he could get out of the courthouse with Stembridge."

Warren directed Webb to send him all papers bearing on the case so that they may be studied closely. Warren and his assistant, J. B. Hatchett, indicated that an agent might be sent to Johnson County in an effort to determine how the papers came into Stembridge's possession.

Both Warren and Hatchett said that no request had been received for Stembridge to be sent to Johnson County and his assignment to that camp was routine.

"Baldwin County, where Stembridge was convicted, does not use white prisoners," Warren said.

"Johnson is an adjoining county and almost every camp in the state wants a mature white man who has some knowledge of record-keping."

* * *

Stembridge received the manslaughter sentence in 1949 for the shooting of a Negro woman Emma Jonnekin. at Milledgeville and exhausted all appeals before his assignment to the county work camp.

In a violent climax to his career he shot to death two prominent attorneys at Milledgeville Saturday and then killed himself by blowing the top of his head off with a pistol.

At the time, he was under an indictment for perjury and a federal court conviction of attempting to bribe two income tax agents. He was under bond awaiting sentence on the latter count.

APPENDIX 9

JUDGE CONGER'S CHARGE TO THE JURY
in
MARION STEMBRIDGE'S BRIBERY TRIAL

CHARGE OF THE COURT

Gentlemen of the jury, the Defendant Marion W. Stembridge is on charge before you under an indictment returned by the February convening of the Grand Jury in which he is charged with a violation of two offenses, as set forth in detail in Counts 1 and 2. You have heard so much about this case from the evidence I expect you could almost recite this indictment by heart; but in order to be perfectly certain about it, I will read to you what the indictment says. It is very short.

It say that "On January 6, 1953, Marion W. Stembridge did promise and offer a thing of value, to wit, money, in the amount of $10,000 to Yancey Edwards, who was an employee of and acting on behalf of the Bureau of Internal Revenue, Treasury Department of the United States in an official function and under the authority of the said Treasury Department, with the intent to influence the actions and decisions of the said Yancey Edwards in a matter and cause which was then pending before the said Yancey Edwards and which might be brought before him thereafter, to wit, the tax liability of Stembridge & Company, Inc., and Marion W. Stembridge, and the Defendant knowingly and willfully committed said act in violation of 18 USC 201."

The same offense of attempted bribery is charged in Count 2 with respect to a Government employee Julian Odom, Julian R. Odom. It may be that you might have the idea, which is a logical and reasonable one, that since both of these counts grow out of the identical same fact, relating to the same identical issue, repeated at the same time and to both parties, that you would either have to convict both or none or acquit both or none; but that isn't true, as I will get to a little bit later.

Gentlemen of the jury, the fact that this indictment was returned by a grand jury is no evidence at all of the guilt of this Defendant. It is simply the means and method of bringing into Court for trial a person accused of crime and of putting him on knowledge of the facts with which he is charged, so it does not raise any presumption of guilt whatsoever. On the contrary, the Defendant in this case, as in all criminal cases under our system, enters upon the trial of his case presumed to be innocent and that presumption remained with and shielded him throughout the trial and until overcome by evidence that leads you to believe beyond every reasonable doubt of the guilt of the accused.

That word and phrase "reasonable doubt" is one that you probably have heard many times before in this Court or in state courts where you have served as jurors. It is an important phrase in the legal procedure under our system. It means simply what it says. It means a doubt for which you can give a reason, a doubt growing out of the evidence or a doubt generated by the lack of the evidence or some other reasonable doubt.

It isn't a doubt generated in the minds of the jury for the purpose of acquitting at all; but if and when you go to your room and you have given deliberate and conscientious consideration to this case, as you certainly will, and after you bring to mind, the argument of counsel, and the charge of the Court, then there rests in your mind an uncertainty, a wavering, a doubt, if you can shut your eyes deliberately in your jury room, when you are concealed from everyone except yourselves, and say now, I doubt whether this man is guilty or not, that is the sort of doubt the law has in mind. If you should entertain such a doubt with respect to his guilt, it would be the duty of the jury, under out law, to give the Defendant the benefit of the doubt and acquit him.

Gentlemen of the jury, in a case of this length and in most cases there probably has or may have arisen some conflicts in the evidence. If there have arisen conflicts in the evidence, it is for you first to reconcile, if you can consistently do so, so as to make all witnesses speak the truth.

Simply because two witnesses who had equal opportunity do not tell identically the same story with respect to what they saw or heard is not evidence that they are deliberately trying to deceive anyone. If an incident were to occur in this Courtroom before you twelve men and you were asked thereafter to detail what you saw and heard and understood, it is highly likely that you would have twelve different versions of what occurred.

So first try to reconcile the evidence to make all the witnesses speak the truth. If you cannot, it is for you and you alone to say what witness or witnesses were mistaken or what witness or witnesses you will believe.

It is also within the sole province of the jury to determine what credibility you will give to the witnesses. In giving credibility to the witnesses, there are a number of practical matters and things that you can take into consideration. One is the interest of the witness. What interest does he have in the case? It is the experience of humanity throughout the ages that a person with interest more likely will be colored than one without. You can also take into consideration the appearance of the witness on the stand. It is difficult, if not impossible, for any witness to deceive many men, let alone twelve impartial jurors who have no interest in the case, so you looked at the men in the face, all of you, and it is for you to determine what credibility you will give what witnesses in this case. You would also take into consideration, if you wish, the means of knowing the facts to which they testified, as one of the elements.

Gentlemen of the jury, notwithstanding the fact that a great deal has been said here about taxes, tax deficiencies, tax returns, of owing or not owing taxes, fortunately for you and me, we are not trying that tax case. It has indirectly and on the outer rim gotten into this case, but it is not a controlling question at all. As a matter of fact, I don't know to what extent, if any, we are interested in the Defendant's taxes. Anyway that is not our case. Our case doesn't involve the question of whether or not Marion W. Stembridge did in the year 1949 or in any other year under investigation or did not owe any taxes.

We are also, gentlemen of the jury, not interested in the Defendant's previous troubles. There has been some intimation, which I sought to eliminate as far as I could, that Mr. Stembridge has had some troubles of one kind and another; but so far as relates to your duty, we are not interested in that. The only interest we could possibly have in that is that the Government intimates and made statements to the effect that there might have been some sort of delaying action with respect to the tax investigation and the Defendant explains or seeks to explain that by saying that he was involved in personal matters to which he felt obliged to give his undivided attention. That is the only reason it is in this case at all.

There have also been admitted in evidence certain financial statements which this Defendant furnished to someone, I presume to a bank--I don't know to whom, to be exact--but they were obtained from the Citizens & Southern Bank under a subpoena. They were not delivered voluntarily here. The financial statements were subpoenaed, and they were admitted in evidence.

I told you one time that they were admitted in evidence for the one and sole purpose if it would aid you in determining to what witnesses you would give credibility, it being a contention on the part of one that the business was small, it being the contention on the part of the other that the business was rather substantial. It was thought that these statements might indicate who was right and wrong there, but I think also they might be relevant and were admitted on the further ground that they might tend to show the state of mind of the Defendant at the time the crucial conversation in this case took place, his intention, his purpose, his subconscious activities.

There has been a good deal said about a recording device. I don't see where the recording device has any predominant interest to us. It is like the others. It has gotten into the case on the fringes, on the outer issues, not the primary and dominant issues at all. It is contended by the Defendant that the fact that he was taking the conversation carried on between him and these Government agents, the Government agents became irritated and that that might have influenced their statements and their attitude towards him; but that isn't the prime case at all. It might have been of interest to have known what they said and I think it would have been, but an explanation with respect to which there has been no dispute has been given to you regarding the machine and the record that was presumably being played at the time.

Gentlemen of the jury, the taking down of the conversation might irritate a person. I am inclined to think probably it would me, if I were to go in to discuss a matter with a man and he was taking down all I said and I didn't know anything about it; but that is not material in this case at all.

There is just one matter which I will get to in a moment, not whether these men were irritated. It is let in for the purpose of showing you the humanities of the case. Is this case colored in the evidence and mind of these witnesses because their evidence was being taken down? That is the reason.

The real and dominating and controlling issue in this case is one: What did Stembridge say? There are different versions of what he said. You will recall the evidence. My recollection is, briefly--and I am not covering the field and you are not bound by what I say--but my recollection is that the Government contended that Stembridge told these agents that by knowing me, you will be $10,000 better off; that he further told them that I have enemies that will pay you $10,000 to annoy me. They further contend that Stembridge told them that he had leads and knowledge and acquaintances with people in Chicago and elsewhere that they could check and that they would be 10 or 20 thousand dollars better off by having done so. That is not what they said maybe, but that is more or less the substance of the Government's contention. You will know what they said. Twelve of you will come much more nearly remembering it than I do, and I am not trying to bind you down to that at all.

The Defendant says that he told these two men if you want to make some money out of this case, I'll tell you how you can do it. I've got enemies here that will pay you and I've got leads and acquaintances elsewhere that will pay you, and you can come here and you can pick up $500 a week yourselves. He said I might have mentioned the 10 or 20 thousand dollars, I do not recall.

The first thing I would do, if I were on the jury, would be to try to satisfy myself what did this man say? The second thing, and equally as vital to my mind, is what did the Defendant mean and intend by saying what he did?

The statute--let me read it to you now--is very clear and plain. The statute under which this Defendant was indicted and is being tried reads as follows: "Whomsoever promises, offers, or gives"--and there is no evidence about any giving here--"any money or thing of value, or makes or tenders any check, order, contract, undertaking, obligation, gratuity, or security for the payment of money or for the delivery or conveyance of anything of value, to any officer or employee or person acting for or on behalf of the United States, or any department or agency thereof, in any official function, under or by authority of any such department or agency or to any officer of person acting for or on behalf of either House of Congress, or of any committee of either House, or both Houses thereof, with the intent to influence his decision or action on any question, matter, cause, or proceeding which may at any time be pending, or which may by law be brought before him in his official capacity, or in his place of trust or profit, or with intent to influence him to commit or aid in committing, or to collude in, or allow, any fraud, or make opportunity for the commission of any fraud, on the United States, or to induce him to do or omit to do any act in violation of his lawful duty," shall be guilty.

The elements in there or the elements that go to make up the offense are clear. First, did the Defendant make an offer to these two men? Did what he said constitute an offer? Secondly, was it given with the, if an offer--of course, if no offer was made, the investigation would cease. If you find that an offer was made, if you believe that the statement made by the Defendant constituted an offer--and that is for you and nobody else--then it will be necessary for you to believe that it was made for the purpose and intent of influencing these two tax agents favorable to this Defendant. All crimes are composed of act and intent.

I charge you the purpose of the statute under which this indictment was rendered is to protect the public from the evil consequences of corruption in public service. Thus the gravamen of the offense described in this indictment is the offering, procuring of a bribe for the purpose of influencing official conduct. An essential element of the crime is that the Defendant offer or promise a bribe with the corrupt and criminal intent to gain some advantage thereby. Attempting to gain an advantage by this means and with corrupt intent is the evil charge the statute is designed to prevent.

I charge you, therefore, gentlemen of the jury, that the Defendant in this case cannot be convicted unless you believe beyond a reasonable doubt that he offered or promised a bribe with the requisite corrupt intent to gain for himself an advantage thereby.

I charge you further, gentlemen of the jury, that it is essential to the offense for which this Defendant is being tried that an offer or promise be made with the corrupt intent to influence the action or decision of the employees--that is, the tax agents in this case--of the United States in the discharge of their official duties.

I charge you, therefore, that the Defendant in this case cannot be convicted unless you believe beyond a reasonable doubt that he had a corrupt intent and with a corrupt intent made an offer and a promise to pay a bribe. I charge you that a bribe within the meaning of the law is something of value which is given or attempted to be given by the briber to one intended to be bribed to do some illegal act or to omit the doing of some legal act.

Let me charge you another principle of law before I forget it, and that is that when the facts in evidence--that is, as to what the man said, what the Defendant said--and all the reasonable deductions therefrom present two theories, one of guilt and the other consistent with innocence, the justice and humanity of the law compel the acceptance of the theory which is consistent with innocence.

Gentlemen of the jury, if you believe beyond every reasonable doubt that this Defendant did offer to these two Government agents a bribe with the intent to influence their action with respect to his tax returns which they were then investigating that would be favorable to him, then you ought to find him guilty.

If you believe, on the other hand, or if you have any reasonable doubt that he was engaging in idle irrelevant conversation, that he did not himself mean to make an offer, that he did not mean what he said to be an offer, or if you do not find or if you have a reasonable doubt that he did not intend for them to act upon the offer favorable to him, if you believe that the truth of this case is that these men would be paid some way, somehow, and sometime and some place $10,000 by someone else, the enemies of this man, if you call them such, or anyone else, and that the Defendant had no control over the other person, was not directing the payment by the other person, that they were doing it without his knowledge, acquiescence, or consent, then, of course, he would not be guilty.

As I said to begin with, there are two counts and, as inconsistent as it might seem to you, you can convict on one and acquit on the other. You can acquit on both. You can convict on both. But since there are two counts involved, it will be necessary for you gentlemen to pass on both counts in your verdict.

If you believe that the Defendant is guilty of both counts, the form of your verdict would be, we the jury find the Defendant guilty of Counts 1 and 2. If you believe he is not guilty of either count, the form of your verdict would be, we the jury find the Defendant not guilty of either of the two counts. If you believe he is guilty of one and not guilty of two or guilty of two and not guilty of one, let your verdict speak whatever you believe the truth of the case to be.

Gentlemen, we have no interest in this case, neither you nor I. We have the sole interest of doing our duty. If this man is guilty under the law and under the facts, he ought to be so adjudged. If he is innocent or if you have any doubt of his innocence, he ought to be acquitted.

Mr. Boole, defense attorney, brought an exception to the judge's attention, and as a result the judge added this for the jury:

THE COURT: Gentlemen of the jury, in this Court, as somewhat contradistinguished from the practice in the state court, counsel at the conclusion of the Judge's charge is required to call his attention to any inaccuracy, error, or omission which, in their judgment, the court committed during the charge, which I think is a very wise practice. That is what we have been discussing in the back.

My attention was called to the fact that I might have said or did say that the Defendant told these agents that he had leads and acquaintances who would pay them 10 or 20 thousand dollars. I didn't mean to say that. You recollect what the evidence was with respect to his acquaintances and the one- or two-years investigation much better than I, and it is not my job to know what it is or to pass upon it; but I did not intend to convey to you the definite impression that he made that statement because I don't think that he did. If I did make that, do not let that impress you at all.

Gentlemen of the jury, you will have the indictment out with you. Whatever your verdict may be, let it be written on the foot of the indictment here where it says "Verdict." Let it be dated and signed by one member of your body as foreman and returned into Court. You may retire now.

(Jury retired at 3:45 P.M.) (Jury returned at 4:35 P.M.)

<u>THE COURT</u>:   Mr. Foreman, has the jury reached a verdict?

<u>THE FOREMAN</u>:   We have, Your Honor.

<u>THE COURT</u>:   Deliver the verdict to the Marshal and he to the Clerk and he in turn to me for inspection, please. The verdict is in legal form and will be published by the Clerk.

<u>THE CLERK</u>:   Case No. 6926, United States v. Marion W. Stembridge. "We the jury find the Defendant guilty on both counts 1 and 2, this 27th day of April, 1953. Samuel J. McGehee, Foreman."

Sentencing was set for the next Monday, May 4. Stembridge decided to take action and bring justice to Milledgeville's court crowd on Saturday May 2.

APPENDIX 10

APPEAL OF ATTEMPT TO BRIBE IRS AGENTS

Personal comment: *Stembridge's attorney filed his appeal of the bribery conviction on Friday, April 30. Earlier that day, Stembridge began scouting for the campaign he planned for Saturday, May 2, 1953. Judge Conger had set Monday May 4 as the date to sentence Stembridge to federal prison.*

FILED at 4:30 P. M.
Apr 30 1953
Watty F. Doyle
Deputy Clerk, U. S. District Court

IN THE DISTRICT COURT OF THE UNITED STATES
FOR THE MIDDLE DISTRICT OF GEORGIA, MACON DIVISION
UNITED STATES
INDICTMENT NO. 6926

MARION W. STEMBRIDGE

The defendant moves the Court to grant him a new trial for the following reasons:

1. The Court erred in overruling and denying the defendant's motion to dismiss the indictment, which motion was properly presented in writing and urged prior to arraignment.
2. The Court erred in refusing to require the United States to furnish defendant with a bill of particulars or other information informing defendant as to the particular matters, things and questions mentioned and set out in defendant's timely written motion and request for a bill of particulars and for such information.
3. The Court erred in denying defendant's motion for judgment of acquittal and for direction of a verdict of not guilty made by defendant at the conclusion of the government's evidence.

4. The Court erred in denying defendant's motion for judgment of acquittal and for direction of a verdict of not guilty made by defendant at the conclusion of all of the evidence.

5. The verdict is contrary to the weight of the evidence.

6. The verdict is not supported by substantial evidence.

7. The evidence was insufficient to show and failed to show that the defendant committed any of the acts charged.

8. The Court erred in denying defendant's motion made in advance of the trial that the United States Attorney be instructed not to offer in the presence of the jury evidence showing or tending to show that neither the defendant nor his corporation, Stembridge & Company, had paid any income taxes since 1940 or 1941 or for any other period.

9. The Court erred in admitting testimony of the government witness, Julian R. Odom, that he had made an examination of the records of the Internal Revenue Office in Atlanta for the years 1940 through 1951 as to the tax returns of both the defendant and his corporation, Stembridge & Company, and that during that period of time neither the defendant nor said corporation had paid any income taxes, said testimony having been admitted over the objections of the defendant that it was immaterial, irrelevant, and calculated to prejudice the jury.

10. The defendant was substantially prejudiced and deprived of a fair trial by reason of the following circumstances: The attorney for the government stated in the presence of the jury: "We expect to show that he (defendant) has made financial statements showing his worth - - one place $300,000; I believe in another one $168,000, regular signed statements that he made - - to show why this witness would be investigating this man's income tax return." Said statement was highly prejudicial, and for that reason, should never have been made. It should not have been made for the further reason that the government had no financial statement - - "regular signed" or otherwise - - made by the defendant that he was worth either $300,000 or $168,000. At most the District Attorney had a signed statement showing that Stembridge & Company, the corporation, was worth $168,844.36, and that the defendant individually was worth $71, 739.24. As defendant's counsel was attempting to voice his objections and protests to this statement of the District Attorney, he was told by the Court, "Just one second. You sit down"… which, of course, he did.

11. The court erred in permitting the government witness, Julian R. Odom, to use for the purpose of refreshing his recollection as to his conversation with the defendant notes made by him, he testified, on the night of the day

of the conversations. The use of said notes was objected to by defendant upon the ground that the witness had testified under oath in detail as to what that conversation was on January 20, 1952, only fourteen days after the conversation, and a full court reporter's transcript of said testimony was then in court available to the witness for the purpose of refreshing his recollection and would constitute a more reliable and accurate reference source for the witness for the purpose of refreshing his recollection.

12. The Court erred in permitting the government witness, Julian R. Odom, to testify over the objection of defendant's counsel that he came back to Macon immediately after his conversation with the defendant and reported the incident immediately to his immediate supervisor, Mr. D. J. DeLorey.

13. The Court erred in permitting the government witness, Julian R. Odom, to testify over objection of the defendant's counsel that he reported: "The whole transaction - - the proposition that he made us and the fact that the machine was running and that it was recording." The defendant's counsel objected to the use of the word "proposition" as being a conclusion of the witness and the witness's interpretation of what the defendant had said, and contended that the witness should be required to testify as to the exact language of the parties.

14. The Court erred in refusing to permit the government witness, Julian R. Odom, to answer the following question propounded by the defendant's counsel: "And your understanding was that his enemies were going to pay that because of the fact that you two gentlemen annoyed him?"

15. The defendant was substantially prejudiced and deprived of a fair trial by reason of the following circumstances: After the government witness, Julian R. Odom, had heard the court rule while said witness was on the stand that the government could not show the making of financial statements by the defendant, and notwithstanding said witness's knowledge of said ruling, said witness on the next morning, testified: "It's (defendant's private bank) capitalized at $368,000, which is twice as big as any other bank there in Milledgeville. As a matter of fact, it's capitalized at more than all the other banks in Milledgeville are capitalized at." Said statement was made by said witness notwithstanding the fact that he did not know of his personal knowledge whether said private bank had any capital at all or not and notwithstanding the fact that he did not have any signed statement showing or purporting to show the capital of said private bank.

16. The Court erred in admitting testimony of the government witness, Yancy Edwards, that this defendant had not paid any income taxes for himself or

for the corporation, Stembridge & Company, during the years 1940 through 1951, said testimony having been admitted over the objection of the defendant that it was immaterial, irrelevant, and calculated to prejudice the jury.

17. The defendant was substantially prejudiced and deprived of a fair trial by reason of the following circumstances: After the court had once ruled that the District Attorney could not prove financial statements made by the defendant and after the government witness, Julian R. Odom, had with knowledge of said ruling testified that defendant's private bank was capitalized at $368,000 and was twice as big as any other bank in Milledgeville, Mr. Yancy Edwards, the next witness for the government, testified: "And of course Mr. Stembridge has a private bank which is not incorporated, and to my knowledge it's shown in the Southern Banker Directory that it has a capital of $368.000." Said testimony was ruled out by the Court, but this was the third time that the large figure, $368,000, had been injected into the case in the presence of the jury by the District Attorney and government witnesses, and defendant was irreparably prejudiced and deprived of a fair trial thereby.

18. The defendant was substantially prejudiced and deprived of a fair trial by reason of the following circumstances: After the court had once ruled that the District Attorney could not prove financial statements made by the defendant and after the government witness, Julian R. Odom, had with knowledge of said ruling testified that defendant's private bank was capitalized at $368,000 and was twice as big as any other bank in Milledgeville, and after the next government witness, Mr. Yancy Edwards, had testified in the presence of the jury that to his knowledge the private bank was shown in the Southern Banker Directory as having a capital of $368.000, which testimony was ruled out by the court, and after the District Attorney had elicited from the defendant testimony that the defendant had never made any kind of statement to said Southern Bankers Directory and had never given said Southern Bankers Directory any kind of information and had never even see one of the publications of said Southern Bankers Directory in his life, then the District Attorney asked the defendant this question: "And their listing of your bank the capitalization of $368,000 - - ."

The Court sustained the defendant's objection to said question, but this was the fourth time that   the District Attorney and the government witnesses had injected into the case in the presence of the jury the large figure $389,000, and the defendant was irreparably prejudiced and deprived of a fair trial thereby.

19. The Court erred in permitting the District Attorney to interrogate defendant with reference to whether or not he had made and submitted to the Citizens & Southern National bank, Macon, Georgia certain financial statements, said interrogation being objected to by defendant's counsel upon the ground that such interrogation was immaterial, irrelevant, and calculated to prejudice the jury. Said interrogation was highly prejudicial to the defendant especially in view of the fact that the Court had, over defendant's objection, permitted the district attorney to prove that neither the defendant nor his corporation, Stembridge & Company, had paid any income taxes for the years 1940 through 1951.

20. The Court erred in permitting the District Attorney to introduce into evidence a number of financial statements signed by defendant and submitted by him to the Citizens & Southern National bank, Macon, Georgia, seven of said statements relating to Stembridge & Company, the corporation, and five of said statements relating to defendant individually, over the objection of the defendant that said financial statements were immaterial, irrelevant, and calculated to prejudice the jury. Said statements were highly prejudicial to defendant, especially in view of the fact that the Court had, over objections of the defendant, permitted the District Attorney to prove that neither the defendant nor said corporation had paid any income taxes for the years 1940 through 1951.

21. The Court erred in refusing upon defendant's motion to rule out all testimony of government witness, Walter Chew, and the testimony of any and all other witnesses in reference to said financial statements and their contents, said motion being based upon the grounds that such testimony and said financial statements were immaterial, irrelevant, and calculated to prejudice the jury. Said testimony was highly prejudicial to defendant, particularly in view of the fact that the Court had permitted the District Attorney to prove that neither the defendant nor his corporation, Stembridge & Company, had paid any income taxes for the years 1940 through 1951.

22. The court erred in refusing to permit the defendant to introduce in evidence properly certified copy of the following judicial proceedings in the Superior Court of Johnson County, Georgia:
   a. Petition of defendant for writ of habeas corpus to be released from custody under a manslaughter conviction procured in the Superior Court of Baldwin County, Georgia, by the knowing use of perjured testimony.
   b. Motion to quash said petition.

  c. Order overruling said motion to quash.

  d. Answer to said petition.

  e. Order and judgment of the Superior Court of Johnson County, Georgia granting said petition for writ of habeas corpus and releasing defendant from custody, said order being a final order and unappealed from.

Said documentary evidence was highly relevant and material for that the government witnesses had repeatedly referred to "a personal matter", (page 4); "his personal troubles", (page 40); his being involved in court matters", (page 89); "his personal problems", (page 226), as having been used by defendant as a basis for request that his tax investigation be postponed. The references to his personal matters, personal troubles, personal problems and court matters had been so continuous and repeated that defendant found it necessary to tell the jury what the personal matter was, to-wit, conviction of manslaughter by fraud and by knowing use of perjury and framed testimony (page 132). Defendant felt also impelled to tell the jury what the personal troubles were because of the fact that both of our local newspapers in Macon, Georgia had been publishing immediately prior to and during the trial news articles which repeatedly referred to said manslaughter conviction.

  23, The defendant was substantially prejudiced and deprived of a fair trial by reason of the following circumstances: This case was assigned for trial at Macon, Georgia on April 21, 1953. The jury which tried the defendant came to court in Macon, Georgia on the said date and remained in attendance upon the Court from day to day until said case was called for trial and until the trial began on April 32, 1953. There are two newspapers published in Macon, Georgia, The Macon Telegraph and The Macon News. Articles concerning the defendant appeared in The Macon News on April 21, 1953, April 22, 1953, April 23, 1953, April 24, 1953, April 25, 1953 and April 27, 1953. Articles concerning the defendant appeared in The Macon Telegraph on April 21, 19153, April 22, 1953, April 23, 1953. April 24, 1953 and April 25, 1953. Each of said articles made reference to said manslaughter conviction except The Macon Telegraph articles of April 21st, April 23rd and April 25th, and except The Macon News article of April 25th. Copes of said articles are attached hereto and made a part of this ground of this motion, each article showing thereon in which paper it appeared and the date of its appearance.

  24 The Court erred in refusing to give the following charge to the jury as duly requested in writing by the defendant: "I charge you further that in each count of this indictment it is charged that the defendant did promise and offer a thing of value. I charge you, therefore, that before you can convict the defendant under either count of this indictment, it would be necessary

for you to believe beyond the reasonable doubt that he both promised and offered a thing of value as alleged in each count."

25 The defendant was substantially prejudiced and deprived of a fair trial by reason of the following circumstances: When the defendant was on the stand during the second day of the trial, Friday, April 24, 1953, his counsel asked him this question on direct: "I want to ask you one other thing. Did you ever say anything to Mr. Edwards or to Mr. Odom which you intended as an offer or a promise? You are charged, of course, with willfully and knowingly doing these things. Did you ever at any time say anything or do anything in the presence of or to Mr. Edwards or Mr. Odom which you intended to be an offer or a promise of a bribe or of anything else?" The District Attorney objected to that question, and the Court ruled, "Yes. Mr. Bootle, it would be for the jury to say, after the facts have been fully disclosed, what the defendant had in his mind. The objection is sustained." Thereupon, defendant's counsel stated: "Your Honor, yes sir, it would be a question for the jury, but certainly couldn't the defendant testify as to what he intended? Intent is a state of mind. He knows more about it. It is for the jury to pass upon it, but the question of intent like motive is a matter that is in the witness's or defendant's mind." The Court ruled further, "That is a question for the jury. The ruling stands."

26 On the same day, Friday, April 24th, the court recessed at 4:15 P. M. and reconvened on Monday morning, April 27th. On the morning of Monday, April 27th. On the morning of Monday, April 27th, defendant's counsel, outside the presence of the jury, state into the record what he expected to prove by defendant if the defendant had been or were permitted to answer the above quoted question, namely, that the defendant never said anything and never did anything at any time or place which he intended as an offer or a promise or a bribe or as an offer or a tender of anything of value or not of value to either Mr. Julian R. Odom or Mr. Yancy Edwards. Thereupon,

The Court ruled further: "The ruling heretofore is adhered to, predicated on the theory that the Government doesn't contend, as I understand, nor does the evidence disclose, as I regard, that any direct, unequivocal immediate offer was made, but that certain language was used, which I am leaving to the jury as to whether or not it constitutes an offer, and the interlinked question as to whether or not the language used likewise carried with it an intent to make an offer. If there was direct positive proof of an offer, I would sustain the objection; but the case being predicated on statements made the effect and meaning of which the jury must determine, the objection is overruled." The Court then immediately clarified the intent of its ruling and stated: "The Government's objection is sustained."

It was not then until after the government had completed its rebuttal testimony that the Court state to the jury: "Heretofore I have been of the opinion that probably what the defendant intended was a question solely for the jury, and I have not permitted the defendant to testify what he intended by these statements he made. In giving further consideration to that proposition, I have concluded that he ought to be entitled to state to this jury what his intentions were and his purposes were in making the statements he did to these two government agents. I am going to permit that to be done, if the defendant wishes to do so."

This last ruling of the Court was not made until shortly prior to the noon hour on Monday, April 27th. The defendant then availed himself of the opportunity afforded him by the last-mentioned ruling of the Court and resumed the stand and testified as his counsel had stated he would testify. Immediately after that testimony, both sides closed. A motion for judgment of acquittal was then made and argued, and then the trial recessed for the noon hour at 12:20 P. M.

So it is that this defendant was denied the privilege of testifying to one of the most vital issues in the case from the second day of the trial, Friday, April 24th, until shortly prior to the end of the trial and on Monday morning, April 27th, so that the jury were without the benefit of the defendant's testimony as to what his intentions were for the long period of Friday night, Saturday, Saturday night, Sunday, Sunday night, and until almost noon of Monday, April 27, 1953, and when defendant was belatedly permitted to testify as to his intentions, the jury, in all probability, must have thought that he was then being permitted to do so as a matter of grace and act as a matter of right, and because of the prior rulings on this crucial point in the presence of the jury, the defendant's testimony when it was finally permitted had become devitalized.

WHEREUPON, defendant prays that these his grounds for a new trial be inquired of by the Court and that a new trial be granted him.

(Signed) Grady Gillan, W. A. Bootle
Attorneys for Defendant.

Personal note: *The newspapers followed the case from before it went to trial and even picked up the typo from the U. S. Supreme Court and began to refer to the voluntary manslaughter conviction as **IN**voluntary.*

THE MACON NEWS,
Wednesday April 22, 1953
Front page

Judge Orders Stembridge Case to Trial

Judge A. G. Conger denied a motion to dismiss a charge that Marion W. Stembridge offered $10,000 bribes to two Bureau of Internal Revenue agents Tuesday and ordered the case to trial in U. S. District Court.

District Attorney Jack Gautier said the trial might begin Thursday morning in the court, but he said other court business already scheduled prevented it being called today.

Stembridge is accused of offering money to the two agents who were investigating his income tax returns if they would drop tax delinquency claims against him.

It still was not clear, meanwhile, whether any further steps will be taken toward forcing Stembridge to serve out a one-to-three-year prison sentence from Baldwin Superior Court where he was convicted in July, 1949 of **involuntary** manslaughter in the fatal shooting of a Negro woman.

Assistant Director J. B. Hatchett of the State Department of Corrections said Stembridge was assigned to the Johnson County work camp at Wrightsville on July 17, 1952 after two appeals in the case had been turned down, the second by both the Georgia Supreme Court and the United States Supreme Court.

Stembridge was freed on Sept. 6, 1952 by a writ of habeas corpus by Judge J. Roy Rowland of Dublin. Stembridge's attorney had filed a petition for the writ on July 18 and it was granted by the judge following a hearing on Aug. 27, 1952, according to the Associated Press.

The state attempted to appeal the decision, but Judge Rowland refused to sign the bill of exceptions, the AP said. Attorney General Eugene Cook refused to comment on the case until the federal court trial is completed, however.

Judge Rowland's decision reportedly was based on a claim that perjured evidence was used in the trial. Some legal sources said an appeal from the habeas corpus ruling would be practically impossible now, but they said Stembridge might be brought to trial again on the charge since he claimed in his habeas corpus petition that the original trial was fraudulent and a farce.

Ocmulgee Circuit Solicitor General George D. Lawrence of Eatonton said he was unwilling to comment now on whether he plans to prosecute Stembridge further on the charge which originally was murder. He said, however, he would have a statement after Stembridge's federal court trial is concluded.

THE MACON NEWS
Thursday, April 23, 1953, Front page

Trial Under Way for Stembridge

Marion W. Stembridge, Milledgeville banker and grocer, went on trial at 2 p.m. today on charges of attempting to bribe two Bureau of Internal Revenue agents investigating his income tax returns.

A jury was selected to try the case in U. S. District Court here just before the court recessed for lunch.

Stembridge is charged with offering $10,000 each to Special Agent Yancy Edwards and Revenue Agent Julian R. Odom when they approached him about income tax matters. The agents immediately reported the offer to their superiors, District Attorney Jack Gautier said.

The wealthy Milledgeville man served about six weeks in a state prison last summer on a conviction of involuntary manslaughter in Baldwin superior Court in the fatal shooting of Emma Johnekin, a Negro woman, in 1949.

The Georgia and U. S. Supreme Courts have turned down Stembridge's appeals in the case but Judge J. Roy Rowland freed him from prison on a writ of habeas corpus last September, saying the conviction was based on perjured testimony.

Ocmulgee Circuit Solicitor General George D. Lawrence has said he will not comment on whether he will press the murder charge against Stembridge in the case in a new trial until after the federal court trial is concluded.

THE MACON NEWS
Friday, April 24, 1953.

Milledgeville Business Man on Trial

U.S. TAX AGENT SAYS RECORDING MACHINE WAS ON DURING STEMBRIDGE 'PROPOSITION'

A federal tax agent testified in U. S. District Court today that a recording machine was in operation when Milledgeville businessman Marion W. Stembridge told him and another agent they could both be $10,000 "better off" if they followed his leads in checking his income tax returns.

Julian R. Odom, an Internal Revenue Bureau agent, said Stembridge, on trial in the court for offering bribes to the two agents, told them also that he knew bankers and influential persons and that "we could take trips together."

He said Stembridge made the "proposition" to him and Special Agent Yancy Edwards when they went to his office Jan. 6, 1953 to push an investigation of Stembridge's tax returns.

Judge A. B. Conger would not allow the witness to use the word "offer" to describe what Stembridge said to him, saying that was a conclusion which would have to be decided on by the jury. But he allowed use of the word "proposition."

Odom said under cross examination by Defense Attorney W. A. Bootle that he had discovered while he and Edwards were talking to Stembridge in the latter's office that a recording machine was "warm and humming" and apparently recording what was being said. He said he and Edwards discussed that and the conversation during lunch and returned to break off the investigation of Stembridge and return to Macon to report the whole situation to their superiors.

When the agents pressed Stembridge for further explanation of the statement that they could be "better off" by $10,000, asking if that meant the government would have a $20,000 tax liability at the end of their investigation, Odom said Stembridge told them, "No, the government would be left out. That would be yours."

Odom said he had begun investigation of Stembridge's personal returns and those of Stembridge and Company, Inc., which Stembridge owns, for 1949, in January 1951. He said Stembridge had not paid any tax for any of those years, although he ran a private bank, grocery store and brokerage business.

The agent said Stembridge repeatedly used "delaying tactics" to put off the investigation and that he refused to co-operate with the agents. He said Stembridge told him of enemies who would pay $10,000 to have him investigated and that he accused the federal agents of being in league with the "courthouse crowd" which he said was out to get him.

Asked about the size and importance of Stembridge's bank, known as Stembridge Banking Company, Odom said it is capitalized at $368,000, which is more than the capitalization of all other banks in Milledgeville. He said Stembridge owns the bank which is private and unincorporated.

Stembridge was convicted of **involuntary** manslaughter in Baldwin Superior Court in 1949 for the fatal shooting of Emma Johnekin, a Negro woman. After his appeals in the case were denied by the Georgia and U. S. Supreme courts, he reported to prison at Wrightsville but reportedly was released under bond when a habeas corpus petition was filed.

Judge J. Roy Rowland released Stembridge on a habeas corpus writ on Sept. 6, 1952 following his assignment to prison July 17, 1952. The judge refused to sign a bill of exceptions for an appeal by the state and state officials have not yet announced whether they will appeal or try Stembridge again on the original murder indictment.

Stembridge was indicted in Baldwin County last July for perjury and that case is scheduled for trial in July of this year. He is charged with falsely swearing in an affidavit filed with a mortgage and bill of sale.

Defense Attorney W. A. Bootle told the jury in an opening statement as the trail began Thursday afternoon that the defense will show the agents "for some reason became angry with Mr. Stembridge and misunderstood what he said."

APPENDIX 11

INDEX of STEMBRIDGE'S SECURITY DEEDS

Stembridge was the grantee in all of these transactions except those marked off. Unpaid debts meant he gained the land or property.

INSTRUMENT	MONTH	DAY	YEAR	HOUR	YEAR OF INSTRUMENT	YEAR OF RECORD	LOCATION	BOOK	PAGE
W.D.	Sept	7	1938	3:15PM	1938	1938	299 Acres in 115 Dist.	22	110
W.D.	Feb	13	1940	6:00PM	1939	1940	Lots 44 & 45 in Blk.B., Ennis Hts.Pl.Bk.OO,p562-	22	244
W.D.	"	13	1940	6:00PM	1940	1940	Lots 44 & 45 in Blk.B., Ennis Hts.Pl.Bk.OO,p562-	22	243
S.D.	Apr	4	1940	3:43PM	1940	1940	5 Acres in 115 Dist.	20	341
W.D.	Aug	17	1940	11:18AM	1940	1940	Lot 2 in City Block 159, on W/side N.Columbia St. See Plat in Bk.#21,p263	26	115-
S.D.	Sept	20	1940	5:00PM	1940	1940	Pt Lot 1,Sq.71 Columbia St/Pt.Lot 2,Sq.41,Wayne St/and 856 Acres,115Dist	26	160
Agreement	Oct	30	1941	10:07AM	1941	1941	Lot 2 in City Blk.159,W/ S.Columbia St.Fowler-sub	28	7
S.D.	Nov	10	1941	9:17AM	1941	1941	Lot on south side what's known as 600 W.Wall St.	27	127
W.D.	"	24	1941	3:25PM	1940	1941	Lots 41,42,43,Blk.B.Plat OO.p562-Ennis Heights	22	390
W.D.	Jan	24	1942	4:00PM	1939	1942	Lot 52x210ft.in Blk.168, E/side N.Clarke St.(¼A.)	22	401
Timber Deed	Mar	14	1944	7:10PM	1944	1944	and hardwood Certain pine timber/on 540 acres in 115 Dist.	29	102-
Trans. S/Deed	July	6	1945	4:48PM	1945	1945	900 acres in 318 Dist. See deed book 25,page 88	32	18
Timber Deed	Sept	6	1945	6:00PM	1945	1945	Certain timber growing on 900 acres in 318 Dist	32	69
W/Deed	Mar	18	1946	4:25PM	1946	1946	Lot on s/side W.Wall St. (Thomas St)w/s.r/wCGRyCo	30	439
S/Deed	June	27	1946	2:35PM	1946	1946	Part Lot 1 in Square 22, in city of Milledgeville	Mtg SS	606
do	July	3	1946	11:40AM	1946	1946	¼ acre,320 Dist.in Block 168,e/side N.Clarke St.	Mtg SS	607
do	Oct	5	1946	3:20PM	1946	1946	Lot 157½ft square,within interior of Square 82	Mtg SS	618

CONTINUED TO PAGE B/40

INDEX TO DEEDS AND REALTY MORTGAGES, BALDWIN COUNTY, GEORGIA

INDEX IN FRONT PORTION OF BOOK FOR ALPHABETICAL ARRANGEMENT AND PAGE REFERENCE TO NAMES IN THIS INDEX

	INSTRUMENT	DATE OF FILING				YEAR OF INSTRU-MENT	YEAR OF RECORD	LOCATION	BOOK	PAGE
		MONTH	DAY	YEAR	HOUR					
1	Trans. S/Deed	Dec	9	1946	12:25PM	1946	1946	Lot fronting 67 feet on Columbia--Street -- See deed book 23,p471-	33	154
	S/Deed	Jan	6	1947	3:40PM	1946	1947	½ acre in 321 District community of Harrisburg	Mtg SS	626
ps	do	Feb	27	1947	5:00PM	1947	1947	Lot 51x140ft on west/side N.Jefferson St	31	321
bridge	PLAT	Mar	19	1947	12:45PM	1935	1947	Survey and plat of lands on s/s W Wall St (Thomas St) w/s r/w of CofGaRyCo	33	289
	S/Deed	May	30	1947	6:30PM	1947	1947	Lot 105x210ft in 321 Dist in community Harrisburg	33	383-
	do	July	16	1947	6:00PM	1947	1947	Lot 50x80ft in 320 Dist., east/side Clarke St.,part Russell Bone sub-division	33	455
	do	"	23	1947	9:00AM	1947	1947	Lot in Block 127 on north/side Charlton St.	33	462-
	do	"	30	1947	9:00AM	1947	1947	Lot 17. See-plat,bk 4p132 (85x140ft) in Block 15	33	490-
	do	Sept	13	1947	9:00AM	1947	1947	Lot 8 of Latimer sub/plat bk 26 page 475 in 321Dist	33	546
	do	Oct	8	1947	9:00AM	1947	1947	Lot 12 of Garrard sub/in city Sq 174 pl,bk 29p73	33	574
idge for	do	"	31	1947	9:00AM	1947	1947	Lot 80x105ft in Mville west/side of Wilkinson St	35	12-
	Deed	Nov	8	1947	9:00AM	1947	1947	Pt Lot 1 in Sq 22 w/side an alley ¼ acre (32x70')	35	30
	S/Deed	"	26	1947	9:00AM	1947	1947	4¼ acres in 320 District in Mville w/s r/w CGRyCo	35	53
on	Deed of Gift	Feb	23	1948	10:07AM	1947	1948	3/4 of an acre in Block 99 w/side N Boundary st	35	188
	S/Deed	Mar	5	1948	3:32PM	1948	1948	Lot 80x105 feet on west/side Wilkinson st.	35	204-
	do	"	8	1948	9:00AM	1948	1948	Lot 50x110ft in 321 Dist in community Harrisburg	35	206
	Agree-ment	Apr	10	1948	11:45AM	1948	1948	Establishment of property lines located e/s Tattnall st/and s/s West Wall st	35	257-

CONTINUED TO PAGE C/40

IS	INSTRUMENT	DATE OF FILING				YEAR OF INSTRU-MENT	YEAR OF RECORD	LOCATION	BOOK	PAGE
		MONTH	DAY	YEAR	HOUR					
	S/Deed	June	15	1948	9:00AM	1948	1948	2 acres in 1714 District	35	371
	Lis Pendens	Sept	17	1948	9:40AM	1948	1948	22 acres in 318 District	Lis Pend-ens	Dkt 1
s	do	Nov	27	1948	11:00AM	1948	1948	Lot 51x140ft on west/side N Jefferson st 320 Dist.	Lis Pen-dens	#1p2
, al	S/Deed	Dec	29	1948	9:00AM	1948	1948	Lot in Square 173 on west/side N Wilkinson st	36	8-
nt	do	Mar	3	1949	1:04PM	1949	1949	1/8 of an acre in 321Dist community of Harrisburg	36	135-
	do	June	18	1949	9:00AM	1949	1949	Lot 5 of Ennis sub/plat, bk 36p211.In city Sq 158.	36	256-
								Also Lot 4 Block 24 &part Lots 6,7,8 and 9 Block A of Oconee Hts/pl,bk SSp8-	36	256-
rguson	W/Deed	Aug	12	1949	2:25PM	1949	1949	NE corner bet 1 Square 56 (Lot 5 see pl,bk 35p570) Washington--Wilkinson sts	36	323-
	S/Deed	Oct	31	1949	2:45PM	1949	1949	Lot 80x105 feet on west/side of Wilkinson st	36	430-

APPENDIX 12

ON THE SIDE
Jere N. Moore

The tragedy on last Saturday was shocking. People could not believe a madman had given Milledgeville a shock it would not find recovery from as sudden as the impact that it had happened.

Marion Stembridge leaves no act to be remembered by except the crime he so cunningly committed after premeditated planning in detail. Certainly his estate can be required to compensate this act that he, like the coward he was, ended in suicide, and therefore, was not required to account for on this earth.

Marion Ennis never knew who shot him, for he was assassinated, shot in the back, as he walked into his office. This entire episode so consumes my thinking, since I rushed to the office of Marion Ennis, it has been difficult to realign and make time normal.

Marion Ennis began the practice of law here and we immediately became friends. We saw in him an unselfish public servant, whose passion was to make this community better, lift its institutions above the level of secondary consideration, help make the life of all people more pleasant and healthful, to serve his generation well. How well he did this is evidenced by the many accomplishments that bear the product of his energy and thinking. Paved roads all over the county, new and improved bridges, the water system in Hardwick, the sewerage system that makes better living conditions for so many people, and many other improvements in which he had a hand and for which he gave many extra hours of tireless work to see them accomplished. He had entered into the Sesquicentennial Celebration with the same zeal and enthusiasm that characterized his attitude toward all things that he thought meant improvement, progress, success, and harmony for the community.

Only a short time ago I suggested to Marion that he advocate a plan whereby he could receive some remuneration for his many hours of work for improved conditions in the county, for his outside activities in the interest of the community than he was to his own law practice. Sims Garrett laughed and asked Marion when he was going to work for himself.

Marion was happiest when he was engaged in some activity that was going to bring about an improvement in the county which would mean better conditions. He stuck by his plan to give water and sewerage to Hardwick when others said it could not be done. His defeat by the people he was trying to help never caused any ill feeling by him, but renewed his determination to see that his plan met with final success.

His courage drew admiration from friend and foe, his legal ability demanded respect from court, jury and opponent, his loyalty to friends sometimes brought him opposition, his devotion to his family gained admiration, and his devotion to duty won the respect of everyone.

I saw Thomas Bivins grow up. His father was one of my friends, and I often saw this red-haired boy come by the county school superintendent's office. He finished school, attended college, served in the army and came back to Milledgeville with a wife before our acquaintance was renewed.

He had found his place here. He was teaching a Sunday School class of fine young men. He was the leader of a Scout troop, but his greatest passion and love after these groups and his home, were his birds. He always loved the song of birds, even as a little boy. Before law found his attention he studied Zoology and became one of the authorities on birds, and in knowing them he found in life a happier outlook and opportunity. I talked with him a few weeks ago about his birds, and he told me he had finally finished the houses and was expecting to make this a profitable venture in his oft-time hours. When the Sesquicentennial was over, we were going to take pictures and write a story about this new venture in our community.

Pete Bivins had a noble and generous heart. He believed in the right as he saw it. It was this desire to help those who had been mistreated and taken advantage of that brought the hatred of his assassin. Pete Bivins was too young to die as he did. He had great prospects and a bright future. He was a citizen we valued. His church appreciated him, the boys respected and admired him, and his birds loved him. What finer tribute could you pay any young man?

I wish this past week-end could be erased, but that is not the way. We must continue to strive to make things better and find in the lives of these two fine young men the inspiration to greater achievement.

A TRIBUTE TO THE LEADERS

Sims Garrett and his co-workers have done a magnificent job in staging this Sesquicentennial Celebration. There hasn't been anything like it since the coming of the Marquis de Lafayette.

The service Sunday evening gave the celebration a dignified and reverent approach to the observance for surely we were very grateful for the blessings that had been ours despite the horrible and untimely tragedy that had come on the eve of this Sesquicentennial celebration.

The week's observance shows convincingly what can be done when we work together and cooperate in a common effort. There have been many hours of planning, many moments of disappointment when people failed to respond, and many tired people who joined in the visits to the neighboring towns in their effort to make this week a complete success. To everyone, the heads of committees, their co-workers and the fellow who just joined in because he wanted to be a part, we are grateful for their generous support and assistance.

This Sesquicentennial Celebration continues through the week. There are programs of great and lasting importance. History is being written. The entire event must be preserved in a giant scrapbook that can be kept in the City Hall for future reference. We must include in this scrapbook the generous publicity of all the state papers, for the press has been most generous to us in this week-long program. It is fitting and we here and now express to the Georgia newspapers our appreciation for the generous use of space they have made available to us in giving notice and publicity to this week-long celebration.

APPENDIX 13
COURT RULING ON PROBATE

Opinion

18787

SUBMITTED NOVEMBER 8, 1954.

DECIDED JANUARY 10, 1955.

Probate of will. Before Judge Edwards. Baldwin Superior Court. August 27, 1954.

W. S. Edwards, George Jackson, Whitman Whitman, R. C. Whitman, Jr., for plaintiffs in error.

Milton F. Gardner, D. D. Veal, contra.

---

1. The administrator of the estate of Marion W. Stembridge was not a party to the probate proceedings in the court below, and is not an indispensable party in this court to the review of the judgment denying probate. *Continental Trust Co.* v. *Sabine Basket Co.*, 165 Ga. 591 (141 S.E. 664); *Hicks* v. *Atlanta Trust Co.*, 187 Ga. 314 (200 S.E. 301); *Cantrell* v. *Kaylor*, <u>203 Ga. 157</u> (<u>45 S.E.2d 646</u>). The motion of the administrator of the testator's estate to dismiss the writ of error because he was not made a party to the writ of error is denied.

2. The evidence of the subscribing witnesses was sufficient to make out a prima facie case of testamentary capacity upon the part of the testator to make a valid will; and where there was nothing in the evidence produced by the caveatrix which would have authorized a finding in her favor upon any of her contentions as contained in the caveat, the trial court should have granted the motion of the propounders to set aside the verdict and judgment in favor of the caveatrix and entered a judgment in accordance with the motion for a directed verdict. Accordingly, direction is given to enter a verdict and judgment in favor of the propounders.

SUBMITTED NOVEMBER 8, 1954 — DECIDED JANUARY 10, 1955.

Marion W. Stembridge executed a will on January 8, 1951, and died on May 2, 1953. His wife, Sara J. Stembridge, was his only heir at law. Mrs. Mildred Beman, Edward Beman, and Thelma Stembridge filed for probate in solemn form, in the Court of Ordinary of Baldwin County, the above will in which the testator named Mr. and Mrs. Beman as his executors, and in which he bequeathed one dollar to his wife, made provision for named employees, and left the residuum of his estate to his sister, Thelma Stembridge.

Mrs. Marion W. (Sara J.) Stembridge filed a caveat on the grounds that at the time the will was executed: (1) the deceased was not of sound and disposing mind and memory; (2) the testator was suffering from monomania or insane delusions toward the caveatrix, in that he believed she was trying to poison him or kill him with X-rays in order to get control of his money and property; (3) the testator suffered from monomania and thought his wife was trying to get his money, and his will was the result of and connected with his monomania; (4) the testator was laboring under a mistake of fact, in that he thought his wife did not love him and was against him, which was not true; and (5) that, after the execution of the will, the testator made material changes and alterations with the intention to revoke the same and did revoke the instrument.

To an adverse ruling in the court of ordinary the propounders appealed to Baldwin Superior Court. On the trial in the superior court, George M. Nottingham, a subscribing witness, testified in part for the propounders: He was a practicing attorney in Macon. The testator came to witness's office in January, 1951, and asked him to witness his will. He had seen the testator several times but never talked to him except once before, which was two or three years before the will was executed. All the subscribing witnesses were in the office. Testator signed the will and the three witnesses signed it. They were in the testator's presence and he was in their presence and they were in the presence of each other. The testator told the witnesses that the paper was his will. To the best of witness's ability the testator was of sound mind at the time. The will was a single sheet of paper and nothing was attached to it.

Mrs. Ethel M. Perdue, a subscribing witness, testified: She saw the testator sign the paper. All of the witnesses were in the room at the time they witnessed the will. They signed in the presence of each other and in the presence of the testator. At the time, the testator was apparently of sound mind.

Harry E. Nottingham, a subscribing witness, testified: He was an attorney in Macon and witnessed the signature of the testator. Each of the witnesses signed the paper in the presence of each other and in the presence of the testator. The testator requested all of them to witness his signature to his will. In witness's opinion the testator was of sound mind.

Following the testimony of the subscribing witnesses, the propounders introduced the will in evidence.

Dr. Edwin Allen, who operated Allen's Institution, testified for the caveatrix: In November, 1933, the testator was disturbed mentally and was treated two weeks in witness's institution. Testator had delusional ideas that people were trying to hurt him by putting poison in his food or medicine, and he involved his sister, Mrs. Leon Callaway, and the local doctor. At times the testator had hallucinations that people were shooting X-rays into his genital organs. He came to Allen's Institution voluntarily and was quiet and orderly for a while. Then he barricaded himself in his room and they had trouble getting his meals to him. Witness ate part of the food to demonstrate it was not poisoned, after which the testator ate. His condition improved and he got tranquil. He was in a panic state, which is more or less a temporary type of reaction. In November, 1942, the sheriff brought the testator, who had been placed in jail on a peace warrant and a lunacy warrant, to Allen's Institution and instructed witness to keep him until he called for him. Witness considered testator psychotic or suffering from mental illness. Money was important to him. He operated his business while he was a patient. The last time he was doing a brokerage business and he carried that on. He was not suffering from monomania about his money, but had delusional ideas on other subjects, particularly the idea that someone was trying to harm him. He was in a fear state. When his fears subsided to where he was fairly tranquil, he left the hospital. The last time witness saw the testator professionally was in 1942.

Mrs. Marion W. (Sara J.) Stembridge, the caveatrix, testified: She and the testator were married in August, 1947, and separated in July, 1949. In 1948 they were on a visit to her old home in South Georgia. Witness had not been back since her mother was buried in August, and asked testator to stop at the cemetery. He said he had to get back because he was losing important money. When questioned he became very angry, saying he was building a cathedral and if he built it strong they would not need friends, if you had money you had friends, money was your best friend. On their return home testator began to tell witness of Mrs. Callaway and Roger Stembridge trying to poison him so they could get his money, and that she was not to have anything to do with them; that witness was testator's protection and as long as he had a wife they could not get his property. Any associations witness had with testator's family upset him greatly. He admonished witness frequently not to have anything to do with Mrs. Callaway, Roger Stembridge, and Miss Stembridge. Shortly thereafter testator shot a negro woman, thus making it necessary for witness to be associated with his family. He was still very much upset and under the fears and delusions that they were against him and that witness expected to send him to prison so she could get his property. He left witness after the trial but she was in touch with him on January 7 and 8, 1951, and right along. He still persisted in the delusion that witness was a part of a conspiracy to get his money. Testator was upset about the trial and wanted witness to get out of the house. When testator did not get a new trial, he accused witness of interfering with his case and trying to send him to prison. He told her she would never get a penny of his money. Testator never ate with witness down town in Milledgeville. They went in a restaurant one time and ordered dinner, but he never touched it. At that time he ate everything that came in cans. He never drank any water or ate anything witness gave him. He did eat with her a time or two when they were first married. From time-to-time witness loaned testator about $17,000, some of which was paid back before and some after the separation, and $4,000 has not been repaid. From witness's contact with testator over the telephone on January 8, 1951, he was laboring under the delusion that she was trying to do him harm in his trial and in his business. From 1948 until testator's death in 1953, based on witness's contact with him over the telephone, his condition was progressively worse. Shortly after testator left witness, she found double rows of sheet lead between double rows of slats on the side of the bed where he slept, and found films between the mattress and spring underneath the pad. Witness did not give testator any reason to believe she was trying to take his money. She worked for him constantly in the business and did everything she could to help him. At the time the will was executed, the employees referred to therein were not working for the testator.

On cross-examination, the caveatrix testified she could not swear she talked to testator over the telephone January 6 or 7, or maybe the 8th. In January, 1951, testator was having witness's house painted, and was suffering with a delusion that a negro painter was stealing his paint. Witness called testator when the painter was going to quit, and testator accused her of interfering with the painter. The painting of the house was finished in the summer of 1951. After testator and witness had been separated about four years, witness filed suit for divorce, in which she sought to recover the $4,000 that had not been paid back to her. She was supporting herself and was in trouble and felt she was entitled to it.

W. S. Cox, a former bailiff, testified: About 1949 the testator was in the loan business and witness handled many papers for him in the justice of the peace court. On one occasion after the testator obtained a judgment against a negro, the latter reached an agreement with testator by paying part of the debt and executing new notes for the balance. When the negro defaulted on the new agreement, the testator took the fi. fa. off of the old judgment and demanded that witness levy it on the negro's property. Witness told him that he had made a new contract and his judgment was no good. Testator was upset and threatened to come into court and demand his money of witness. About January 7 or 8, 1951, witness did not remember the exact date, testator was having his house painted. Testator had the idea that the negroes were stealing his paint and wanted witness to put on old clothes and crawl under the house and watch to see if they stole any paint, which witness declined to do. Previously witness had had a violent dispute with testator about the fi. fa. On the question of the testator's mental condition in January, 1951, in witness's opinion, he was a hard man when it came to business affairs, who would not stop at anything if you crossed him up, and a man who thought he was right and you were wrong. Witness resigned the bailiff's office because he did not care to have any further trouble with testator. After the run in about the fi. fa., witness could not see any difference in testator's attitude. Testator always acted normally and was just as courteous and nice as could be and always paid his costs promptly without any argument.

C. S. Baldwin, Jr., Solicitor-General Emeritus, testified: In 1941 the testator brought samples of food and drink to witness's office and said his sister and her husband had been trying to poison him to get his money. Subsequently, upon being shown a report from the F. B. I., the testator had the appearance of thinking deeply, and then said: "Well, I will tell you what has happened. I have got enemies in the post office. . . Undoubtedly the samples" were switched in transit. About 1943, the testator brought more samples of food that he wanted witness to send off to be analyzed. He had been at Allen's Sanitarium and involved Dr. Allen. Testator mailed the specimens to J. Edgar Hoover. He did not have much to say when the report came back, but he then got the G. B. I. and a private detective and worked on that case for six months. After making reference to the trial in 1949, when the testator was accused of killing a negro woman, witness testified that in his opinion the testator had delusions of persecution, that people were trying to kill him, that his folks were trying to poison him, and that somebody substituted the samples in the mail. There was no doubt in witness's mind about testator being off. He was abnormal when it came to money matters. He could make money better than any of them. He would really go after it and he would get excited more over his money than anything else. From 1948 until testator's death he was under delusions of persecution and he was worse at the time of his death.

Paul Cox, a police officer, testified: In May, 1953, he was called to the Baldwin Hotel to unload some guns. He found five automatics and unloaded four. One was already unloaded. They were cocked or in position to fire. A refrigerator there had a padlock on it, and some of the bookcases had locks on them.

Robert J. Ashfield testified: He put a padlock on the refrigerator for testator, who said that the boys who ran the hotel were stealing his hair tonic. Witness declined to express an opinion as to whether testator's mind was sound or unsound on January 8, 1951.

G. D. Beck testified: He borrowed $6,000 from the testator on three trucks about 1949. Afterwards he thought he paid most of the money back. He paid testator so much a week and got a receipt from him. Testator claimed that witness still owed $4,400 and did not like it when he procured another finance company to take the loan up. When the matter was being closed, testator claimed witness owed him an additional 75 cents which he paid. Thereafter witness saw testator on the street once or twice a week, but he never spoke to witness, and on one occasion testator crossed the street when witness wanted to see him about a driver who owed testator some money. Witness traded at testator's store every week. Based on the transaction with reference to the loan on the trucks, in witness's opinion the testator was a little off, he was of unsound mind.

J. A. Gilmore, an attorney who was appointed administrator of the testator's estate before the will was offered, testified: He found five safes in testator's office, one of which he had not been able to open. The safe which was used by the testator was a heavy magnesium-steel screw-type safe, in which witness found, among other things, an automatic pistol, a series of notes, various keys, and papers including the will.

At the conclusion of the evidence, the trial court denied a motion by the propounders for the direction of a verdict, and the jury returned a verdict in favor of the caveatrix.

The propounders' motion for new trial, which was amended by adding five special grounds complaining that the trial court erred in the admission of evidence, was denied, and the exception is to that judgment and to the refusal to direct a verdict.

ALMAND, Justice.

Only the second headnote requires elaboration. "Where there is no conflict in the evidence, and that introduced, with all reasonable deductions or inferences therefrom, shall demand a particular verdict, the court may direct the jury to find for the party entitled thereto." Code § 110-104. The mere fact that there are conflicts in the testimony does not render the direction of a verdict in favor of a party erroneous, when it appears that the conflicts are immaterial, and that, giving to the opposite party the benefit of the most favorable view of the evidence as a whole and of all legitimate inferences therefrom, the verdict against him is demanded. *Skinner* v. *Braswell*, 126 Ga. 761 (2) (55 S.E. 914).

The evidence of the subscribing witnesses was sufficient to make out a prima facie case of testamentary capacity upon the part of the testator to make a valid will. The trial court, in a written opinion denying the motion for new trial, said: "Although the evidence was insufficient to overcome the testimony of the subscribing witnesses, as applied to ordinary cases of probate of wills, nevertheless, under the rules applicable to cases of this kind where the law requires close scrutiny of the will and refusal of probate upon the slightest evidence of aberration of intellect, the evidence was sufficient to raise an issue to be determined by the jury and to uphold their verdict refusing probate."

Code § 113-106, declaring that a testator may bequeath his entire estate to strangers, to the exclusion of his wife or children, but in such case the will should be closely scrutinized, is not applicable where, as here, the testator had no children, and approximately two years after separating from his wife, executed a will which provided: "I am informed that it will be necessary to give my legal wife a certain share of my estate and I am sorry that this is true. I am not able to avoid the thought that if she had brought to our marriage the love, the enthusiasm, and the willingness to work that I felt; our answer would have been different. After mature consideration, it is my unqualified belief that she married me for what she hoped to get out of the marriage in a financial way. I give and bequeath to my legal wife the minimum that the law requires. One dollar."

The wife having been bequeathed one dollar, it cannot be held that she was altogether excluded in the will of the testator, and in *Smith* v. *Davis*, <u>203 Ga. 175</u> (2) (<u>45 S.E.2d 609</u>), it was held: "The provisions of § 113-106 of the Code are applicable only when the wife, there being no child or children, is altogether excluded in the will of her husband." The present case is distinguishable by its facts from *Bowman* v. *Bowman*, <u>205 Ga. 796</u> (3) (<u>55 S.E.2d 298</u>), where the testator expressly excluded his wife from participating in his will.

It is well-settled law that a lunatic during a lucid interval may make a will. Code § 113-204. Even an incapacity to contract is not inconsistent with the capacity to make a will, as it takes a greater quantum or higher degree of mentality to make a contract than it does to make a will. Code § 113-202; *Wood* v. *Lane*, 102 Ga. 199, 201 (29 S.E. 180). The weak have the same rights as the strong-minded to dispose of their property by will, and anything less than a total absence of mind does not destroy that capacity. If the testator has sufficient intellect to enable him to have a rational desire as to the disposition of his property, this is sufficient. And the condition of the testator's mind at the time of the execution of the will determines whether he can make a valid will. *Griffin* v. *Barrett*, 183 Ga. 152, 164 (187 S.E. 828).

"As tending to illustrate the mental condition at that time evidence of such condition at other times may be received; but where it is sought to establish testamentary incapacity by such evidence, it does not controvert the positive testimony of the subscribing witnesses unless it would be proof of testamentary incapacity at the time the will was signed " *Fehn* v. *Shaw*, <u>199 Ga. 747, 754</u> (35 S.E.2d 253); *Anderson* v. *Anderson*, <u>210 Ga. 464, 472</u> (<u>80 S.E.2d 807</u>).

While there was much evidence in the present case tending to show that the testator was a highly eccentric person, the only medical expert testified: The last time he saw the testator professionally was in 1942. The testator operated his business while a patient. He was not suffering from monomania about his money but had delusional ideas on other subjects, particularly the idea that someone was trying to harm him. He was in a fear state which is more or less a temporary type of reaction.

The caveatrix testified: He had delusional ideas that members of his family were trying to poison him to get his money, but he left the residue of his estate to his sister Thelma. Caveatrix married the testator in August, 1947, and they separated in July, 1949, approximately a year and a half before the will was executed. A divorce suit caveatrix filed against the testator was pending at the time of his death. She admitted on cross-examination that she was not sure she talked with testator on the day the will was signed, and that she was not in Macon where the will was executed on that day.

The caveatrix assumed the burden of proving lack of testamentary capacity. The testimony of the subscribing witnesses, who gave their opinion as to the mental condition of the testator on the day the will was executed, that he did have mental capacity to execute the will, was not overcome by the non-expert witnesses testifying on behalf of the caveatrix, whose opinions were based upon facts from which no legal conclusion could be drawn that the testator did not have mental capacity to execute the will. All that their testimony amounted to was that the testator was highly eccentric and that he had delusional ideas that people were trying to harm him. The uncontroverted evidence showed that the testator not only conducted his brokerage business while a patient in Allen's Institution, but that he continued to conduct it until his death approximately two years after execution of the will.

Under section 2 of the amendment to the Rules of Practice and Procedure, adopted by this court on November 23, 1953 (Ga. L. 1953, Nov.-Dec. Sess., pp. 440, 444; Code, Ann. Supp., § 110-113), where a motion for a directed verdict has been denied, the party moving for a directed verdict may within 30 days after the reception of the verdict move to have the verdict and any judgment rendered thereon set aside and have judgment entered in accordance with his motion for a directed verdict. Where his motion is denied, the losing party "may take specific exception in the final bill of exceptions, and if the exception is sustained by the appellate court, direction shall be given that verdict be entered in accordance with the motion."

The evidence in the instant case being insufficient to authorize a verdict in favor of the caveatrix on any issue raised in the caveat, but demanding a verdict in favor of the propounders, the trial court should have granted the motion of the propounders to set aside the verdict and judgment in favor of the caveatrix and entered a judgment in accordance with the motion for a directed verdict. Direction is accordingly given: that, upon the return of the remittitur to the trial court, a verdict and judgment be entered in favor of the propounders.

The trial court having erred in not sustaining the propounders' motion to enter a judgment notwithstanding the verdict, the judgment denying the motion for a new trial was nugatory. Direction is given that the order overruling the motion for a new trial be set aside.

Judgment reversed with directions. All the Justices concur, except Candler, J., who dissents, and Mobley, J., who is disqualified.

INDEX

This index covers the main body of the book. An appendix is referenced when that individual is a major factor in the events. Logically it was not reasonable to index Marion Stembridge. Ladies who were single in the 1950s are indexed by their maiden names.

www.ingramcontent.com/pod-product-compliance
Lightning Source LLC
Chambersburg PA
CBHW080458110426
42742CB00017B/2932